Secondary Education
Reflective Reader

Secondary Education Reflective Reader

JONATHAN SAVAGE
and
MARTIN FAUTLEY

LearningMatters

First published in 2010 by Learning Matters Ltd.

British Library Cataloguing in Publication Data
A CIP record for this book is available from the British Library.

ISBN: 978 1 84445 473 0

Cover and text design by Code 5 Design Associates Ltd
Project management by Deer Park Productions, Tavistock, Devon
Typeset by Pantek Arts Ltd, Maidstone, Kent
Printed and bound in Great Britain by Bell & Bain Ltd, Glasgow

Learning Matters Ltd
33 Southernhay East
Exeter EX1 1NX
Tel: 01392 215560
Email: info@learningmatters.co.uk
www.learningmatters.co.uk

Contents

Theme 3: Your future teaching practice

The authors

Jonathan Savage is a Reader in Education at the Institute of Education, Manchester Metropolitan University. He has a number of research interests, including implementing new technologies in education, cross-curricular approaches to teaching and learning, creativity and assessment. He is Managing Director of UCan.tv, a not-for-profit company that produces engaging educational software and hardware including Sound2Picture (**www. sound2picture.net**) Sound2Game (**www.sound2game.co.uk**) and Hand2Hand (**www. hand2hand.co.uk**). Free moodle courses are available at **www.ucan.me.uk**

Martin Fautley is a Professor of Education at Birmingham City University. For many years he was a schoolteacher in the Midlands before undertaking doctoral research. His research interests encompass theoretical and practical issues concerning learning processes in schools and how teachers can help foster these, and the ways in which assessment, particularly assessment for learning, can be used as a means to raise standards. He has authored books and research papers on creativity and assessment.

Acknowledgements

Every effort has been made to trace the copyright holders and to obtain their permission for the use of copyright material. The publisher and author will gladly receive any information enabling them to rectify any error or omission in subsequent editions.

Chapter 1

Peshkin, A (1988) In search of subjectivity – one's own. *Educational Researcher*, 17: 7. Reproduced by permission of SAGE Publications: London, Los Angeles, New Delhi and Singapore.

Schön, D (1983) *The Reflective Practitioner*. Aldershot: Avebury. Reprinted by permission of Ashgate Publishing: Farnham.

Kompf, M, Boak, RT, Bond, WR and Dworet, D (1996) *Changing Research and Practice: Teachers' Professionalism, Identities and Knowledge*. London: Falmer Press. Reproduced by permission of Taylor and Francis Books: London.

Chapter 2

Bruner, J (1996) Folk Pedagogy, reprinted by permission of the publisher from *The Culture of Education*. Cambridge, MA: Harvard University Press. Copyright © 1996 by the President and Fellows of Harvard College.

Shulman, L (1986) Those who understand: knowledge growth in teaching. *Educational Researcher*, 15(2). Reproduced by permission of SAGE Publications: London, Los Angeles, New Delhi and Singapore.

Eisner, E (2002) *Arts and the Creation of Mind*. New Haven, Connecticut: Yale University Press. Reprinted by permission.

Chapter 3

Winch, C (2004) What do teachers need to know about teaching? A critical examination of the occupational knowledge of teachers. *British Journal of Educational Studies*, 52 (2), Routledge. **www.tandf.co.uk/journals/titles/00071005.asp**. Reproduced by permission of Taylor & Francis Group.

Brooks, V, Abbott, I and Bills, L (2004) *Preparing to teach in secondary schools: a student teacher's guide to professional issues in secondary education*. Buckingham: Open University Press. Reproduced by kind permission of Open University Press. All rights reserved.

Kutnick, P, Blatchford, P and Baines, E (2005) Grouping of pupils in secondary school classrooms: possible links between pedagogy and learning. *Social Psychology of Education*, 8:4. Reprinted by kind permission of Springer Science+Business Media.

Chapter 4

Harlen, W and James, M (1997) Assessment and learning: differences and relationships between formative and summative assessments. *Assessment in Education: Principles, Policy & Practice*, 4:3, Routledge. **www.tandf.co.uk/journals/titles/0969594X.asp**. Reproduced by permission of Taylor & Francis Group.

Black, P and Wiliam, D (1998) Assessment and classroom learning. *Assessment in Education: Principles, Policy & Practice,* 5:1, Routledge. **www.tandf.co.uk/journals/titles/0969594X.asp**. Reproduced by permission of Taylor & Francis Group.

QCDA (2008) *Assessing Pupils' Progress: Assessment at the Heart of Learning.* **www.qcda.gov.uk/libraryAssets/media/12707_Assessing_Pupils_Progress_leaflet_-_web.pdf**. Reprinted by permission of Qualifications and Curriculum Development Agency (QCDA).

Savage, J and Fautley, M (2008) *Assessment for Learning and Teaching in Secondary Education.* Exeter: Learning Matters. Reprinted by permission.

Chapter 5

Wertsch, J (1998) *Mind as Action.* New York: Oxford University Press. Reprinted by permission.

Anderson, T and Elloumi, F (2004) *The Theory and Practice of Online Learning,* Athabasca AB: Athabasca University. **http://cde.athabascau.ca/online_book**. Reprinted by permission.

Somekh, B (2007) *Pedagogy and Learning with ICT: Researching the art of innovation.* London: Routledge. Reproduced by permission of Taylor and Francis Books, London.

Chapter 6

DfES (2004) *A National Conversation about Personalised Learning.* **http://publications.teachernet.gov.uk/eOrderingDownload/DfES%200919%20200MIG186.pdf**. Sudbury: DfES. Copyright ©HMSO. Reproduced under the terms of the Crown Copyright PSI Licence C2010000141.

Burton, D (2007) Psycho-pedagogy and personalised learning. *Journal of Education for Teaching*, 33:1, Routledge. Reproduced by permission of Taylor & Francis Group.

DCSF (2008) *Personalised Learning: A Practical Guide.* London: DCSF. Copyright ©HMSO. Reproduced under the terms of the Crown Copyright PSI Licence C2010000141.

Chapter 7

QCDA (2004) *Creativity: Find it, Promote it!* **https://orderline.qcda.gov.uk/gempdf/1847211003.pdf**. Reprinted by permission of Qualifications and Curriculum Development Agency (QCDA).

NACCCE (1999) *All Our Futures: Creativity, Culture and Education.* Sudbury: DfES. **www.cypni.org.uk/downloads/alloutfutures.pdf**. Reproduced by permission.

Craft, A (2003) The limits to creativity in education: dilemmas for the educator. *British Journal of Educational Studies*, 51(2), Routledge. **www.tandf.co.uk/journals/titles/00071005.asp**. Reproduced by permission of Taylor & Francis Group.

Savage, J and Fautley, M (2007) *Creativity in Secondary Education.* Exeter: Learning Matters. Reprinted by permission.

Chapter 8

Jephcote, M and Davies, B (2007) School subjects, subject communities and curriculum change: the social construction of economics in the school curriculum. *Cambridge Journal of Education*, 37(2), Routledge. **http://www.tandf.co.uk/journals/titles/0305764X.asp**. Reproduced with permission of Taylor & Francis Group.

Page, M, Schagen, S, Fallus, K, Bron, J, de Coninck, C, Maes, B, Sleurs, W and van Woensel, C (2005) *Cross Curricular Themes in Secondary Education.* CIDREE. **www.cidree.be/uploads/documentenbank/4854365076a88c8ba93cbebe04fd9196.pdf**. Sint-Katelijne-Waver (Belgium): CIDREE. Reprinted by permission.

QCDA (2008) *Cross-Curriculum Dimensions: A Planning Guide for Schools.* **http://curriculum.qcda.gov.uk/uploads/Cross%20curriculum%20dimensions%20-%20a%20planning%20guide%20for%20schools%20publication_tcm8-14464.pdf**. Reprinted by permission of Qualifications and Curriculum Development Agency (QCDA).

Introduction

A personal note

Welcome to this reflective reader for secondary education. We trust that you will find it an exciting and helpful read. Before we get started on our first chapter, we would like to introduce ourselves and provide you with an overview of what is presented in the following pages.

Both of us work at universities involved in delivering initial teacher education courses of various types. Prior to this, we worked in high schools as teachers and heads of department. Although this was some time ago, we regularly visit schools for a range of purposes including helping our students with their teaching, conducting educational research projects or for other consultancy purposes. So, while we are not currently high school teachers, we do know that world extremely well. Also, and importantly for this book, we understand very well the process by which you become a teacher. We have travelled that road ourselves; we have walked alongside hundreds of other students and, on occasions, assisted their progress too!

For these reasons, we accepted the invitation from Learning Matters to write this book. We felt that we had something to offer potential readers who, most probably, will be starting (or are in the early stages of) their teaching careers.

Before we introduce the main structure and rationale underpinning the book, we would like to offer a few brief thoughts about why a reflective reader of this type is important for your development as a teacher.

Why a reflective reader? An ABC of critical reflective reading

Books like this are important for a number of reasons. We will articulate some of these below. In our courses of initial teacher education, we are committed to the notion that criticality and reflection are central to our work as teacher educators. By this, we mean that just doing things the way that they have always been done is not good enough. But just being critical or reflective in and of themselves is not going to get the job done. At worst, criticism can turn into self-serving, opinionated rhetoric; reflection can be conspired as individualistic navel-gazing. For these reasons, and many others, our thoughts and actions need to be challenged. Reading, listening and thinking about the ideas of others is one of the key ways in which this challenge can be brought to bear on our thoughts, words and actions. As teachers, the same will be true for you.

So, at the opening of this book we want to articulate the rationale, if needed – and in some senses we hope it is not – for studying the work of other educational writers, theorists and philosophers. There are three main points we want to make.

1. Associate and apply

Firstly, in the early stages of your teacher career we consider it important to associate your thinking with the considerable schools of thought that have analysed and dwelt on the huge themes of educational practice over the years. For this reason, we have included writings from some of the greatest educational thinkers of recent times. But association by itself is not enough. You will need to apply these ideas to your work. To this end, we have included a range of reflective and practical tasks, as well as points to consider. If you have time, we would urge you to incorporate these tasks within your work when convenient. All the tasks have been tried and tested on our students over the years. They work.

2. Be broad and balanced

Secondly, be broad and balanced in your range of reading. Try to avoid becoming overly dependent on one author and, importantly, on one 'type' of writing. For example, if you read only government reports on educational issues and policy, then you fall into the trap of ignoring the wider contextual and historical considerations that might have informed these political decisions. You will also be receiving only one 'message' on an issue. There will undoubtedly be others. Many government reports, although very interesting and potentially helpful, contain degrees of pragmatism that can be usefully challenged by developing a broader understanding of an educational issue.

Similarly, an overdependence on published educational research within journals may make it difficult to associate with ideas and apply them to your day-to-day work as a teacher. While the peer-reviewed structure of many educational journals means that the work published within them has at least been read and challenged by a number of other academics, it will be important to weigh up research findings alongside other sources and publications. Being balanced and testing ideas (from any source) is a key requirement before you consider making big changes to your teaching practice. For all these reasons we have sought to draw our key extracts from a range of sources (including all of the above). This moves us quickly along to our third, and final, point.

3. Challenge and connect

Just because something is in print, do not assume it is correct. This might be a bold thing to say in the introduction to our book, but it is true. It applies to everything that you will read in the course of your initial teacher education. You will need to challenge ideas and test them out. This testing process may involve you discussing ideas with tutors, colleagues at school or other students. It may involve you broadening your range of reading through considering other sources (for this reason, each chapter within this book has at least three extracts associated with it). But, and this is vitally important, your own thinking will also be challenged by the ideas that you encounter. As we will discuss briefly below, this will help you develop your skills of criticality and reflection. Connecting your engagement with ideas through the reading you undertake with your own emerging teaching practice will result in you become a more articulate, confident and skilful teacher.

So, for all these reasons we believe that a proactive engagement with the 'literature' of education is a vital component in your early teaching career. In fact, as we will consider in our final chapter, this is something that will sustain your motivation and engagement as a teacher throughout your whole career. Associating your thoughts with key educational thinkers and applying the ideas you discover to your own actions will broaden your perspective as a teacher; balancing these thoughts, challenging them and connecting them with your understanding and practice as a teacher will ensure that you remain critically alert and that your reflective practice is constantly being informed and developed. We trust that this reflective reader will prove itself faithful to these important principles. But we will have to let you be the judge of that.

The structure of this reflective reader

Our reflective reader is structured around three key themes:

- Theme 1: Starting your teaching: identity, subject and pedagogy

- Theme 2: Developing your teaching: some next steps

- Theme 3: Your future teaching practice.

Within each theme there are three chapters which explore its key elements. Obviously, these themes are somewhat artificial but they serve a purpose in organising our book. There will be many areas that overlap. But, in a general sense, they take their lead from the courses of initial teacher education that we have devised and developed over the years.

In terms of the choice of extracts throughout the book, we have tried to remain true to the themes (the 'ABC') that we discussed above. We have included a range of different types of readings from diverse sources. To this end, we hope that the book serves as an example of the type of approach, or discourse, for reading that will be helpful for you to develop in your career.

However, these choices are highly personal. Two other authors would have chosen very different themes and extracts. Many of the extracts that we have included here have been important in our journeys as teachers to this very day. Some have been chosen because they address important educational themes which will, we are sure, remain important over the next five to ten years. Either way, we are by no means wanting to claim that the extracts we have chosen are the only, or most important, pieces of reading that you could undertake on that chosen theme. However, we maintain that they all have a purpose and value for the key points we would like you to consider at this early stage of your teaching career.

Theme 1: Starting your teaching: identity, subject and pedagogy

Within this theme, we explore a range of fundamental issues that you will need to understand right at the beginning of your course of initial teacher education.

Chapter 1: Developing your teacher identity

You are not a blank slate. At the beginning of your teaching career, it is important to recognise that you bring with you a range of knowledge, skills and understanding which need to be translated or reinterpreted against the requirements of the twenty-first-century-classroom. This chapter will explore a range of readings which consider and challenge how one's sense of identify is formed within a new endeavour such as learning to teach. It will explore notions such as reflective practice and how this can underpin the development of a positive teaching identity.

Chapter 2: Teaching and learning

Building on Chapter 1, this chapter will explore how the development of an appropriate subject knowledge is a vital first step in establishing teaching and learning, but that this needs to be linked to ideas about how to teach your subject. It asks you to consider what the nature of knowledge is, both in your subject and in the wider school curriculum. It will also consider how you should plan for positive teaching and learning opportunities within a subject, including the constructive use of learning objectives and outcomes.

Chapter 3: Developing your classroom practice

The construction of an effective classroom pedagogy is central to all teaching. This chapter will help you explore the key elements of such a pedagogy, including how different teaching and learning strategies (e.g. formal didactic approaches versus informal, facilitative approaches) can be blended in relationship to your emerging teaching identity. Building on the importance of planning which was considered in Chapter 2, this chapter will also explore how you can implement positive behaviour for learning strategies through your planning and delivery.

Theme 2: Developing your teaching: some next steps

Within this theme, we explore three areas that will become increasingly important as you work through your course of initial teacher education.

Chapter 4: Embedding assessment for learning

Assessment for learning (or formative assessment) is the key way in which pupil development and understanding occur. Day-to-day assessment practices in the classroom are important but can often be difficult to recognise and implement in the early part of your teaching career. This chapter will consider how key principles of assessment for learning can be used to take learning forwards, as well as how summative assessment can be used to audit it appropriately. It will ask you to reflect on current thinking on assessment, and take into account recent governmental initiatives on assessment practice for teachers.

Chapter 5: Choosing and using technology for teaching and learning

Technology can be used in a variety of ways in the classroom. At a fundamental level, pieces of technology are 'tools' that you, and your pupils, can exploit to initiate, reinforce and extend their learning. This chapter will consider how the use of technology impacts on the processes of teaching and learning from the teacher's and the learner's perspective. This would include how technology influences approaches to learning, communication, collaboration and presentation within and beyond the classroom.

Chapter 6: Personalisation and personalised learning

Recent curriculum reforms have emphasised the centrality of the pupil at the heart of the teaching and learning process. They have also urged teachers to consider the wider social contexts within which pupils live and learn. Approaches to personalisation, including those identified within government reports such as *Every Child Matters*, have enshrined this concept in statute. This chapter will consider a range of readings that explore issues such as ethnicity, gender, class and special educational needs. It will promote inclusivity as a key aspect of personalisation within the classroom.

Theme 3: Your future teaching practice

Our final theme explores ideas that we hope will enrich your teaching throughout your career. Our final chapter is a call to continue the approaches we have exemplified throughout this reflective reader during the remainder of your career.

Chapter 7: Creativity as a way of teaching and learning

Creativity is a contested term but is prioritised as a key concept within the majority of subjects in the National Curriculum. This chapter will explore a well-established three-pronged approach to how creativity relates to teaching and learning. The common conceptions that beginner teachers hold in relation to creative teaching, teaching for creativity and creative learning will be challenged through a selection of key texts. These will allow you to develop your understandings of the appropriate terminologies for creativity which you can then use in your own planning.

Chapter 8: Enriching collaborations

Cross-curricular approaches to teaching and learning are an important part of recent government reforms at Key Stages 3–5. This chapter will consider the powerful nature of change that can result when teachers allow cross-curricular thinking to inspire the content of the curriculum, the design of the curriculum and, perhaps most importantly, their pedagogy through skilful practice.

Chapter 9: Moving onwards

This chapter will draw together the range of themes considered in the above. It will set out a series of ideas for the further development of the beginner teacher's knowledge, skills and understanding throughout the early part of their teaching career. Key texts here will explore how the momentum and desire to maintain this development can be achieved. In particular, the role of intrinsic motivation and its importance in continuing professional development will be highlighted.

Chapter 1
Developing your teacher identity

Introduction

Good teaching cannot be reduced to technique; good teaching comes from the identity and integrity of the teacher.

(Palmer, 2009)

The process of learning to teach is an exciting one. It contains challenges of various types – intellectual, practical, physical and emotional. It will be unlike anything else you have ever done. But there will be important things that you have done in your life that you can draw on to help you become a teacher. While this may be true in a practical sense (i.e. you may have been able to establish and maintain good, professional relationships with young people through helping out at a local youth club), it is also true in a psychological sense. The person that you are today has been formed through a mixture of your genetic disposition and your life experiences, relationships and activities. These have shaped your personality, your speech, body language and ways of thinking and acting. Teaching is a new type of mental and physical activity. But 'you' are going to do it. Every part of you will be challenged by it and, if you are doing it properly, it will be demanding. So, we hope that you are prepared.

Developing your sense of identity as a teacher is the theme for this opening chapter. As authors and academics involved in delivering courses of initial teacher education, we have made this a deliberate choice. We firmly believe that as you seek to develop a broader understanding of where you have come from as a person, relate and apply this to your new, emerging role as a teacher, and complete the reflective cycle by reflecting on the teaching you are undertaking, the chances of you becoming a skilful and effective teacher will be increased. The extracts that we have chosen to assist us in this process all identify different areas related to identity, teaching and reflection that will help you begin to get to grips with developing your teacher identity.

Let's start at the very beginning ...

Palmer's article (2009) is a useful exposition of this chapter's key theme. Good teaching is firmly based in the identity of the teacher. But what does that really mean? How can I begin to understand my 'identity' and use that knowledge to help ensure that my teaching is really built upon a firm foundation?

Our dictionary gives a range of definitions for the term 'identity'. These include the following.

1. The collective aspect of the set of characteristics by which a thing is definitively recognisable or known.

2. The set of behavioural or personal characteristics by which an individual is recognisable as a member of a group.

3. The quality or condition of being the same as something else.

4. The distinct personality of an individual regarded as a persisting entity; individuality.

There is a number of important, basic points to note here. Firstly, identity is about something being *known* or *recognised*. For our discussion, it is what makes you the person you are (physically, emotionally, intellectually, spiritually, etc.). It may also be elements or characteristics that other people can recognise in you. Secondly, identity is often linked to a relationship. An object's identity may be related to or distinct from another object within a particular group. The particular aspects of your identity are best understood when one contextualises them in different ways (e.g. your actions in a particular context could be seen as being representative or demonstrative of a specific element of your identity, which can be perceived by others and, therefore, mark you out as a particular individual). This is particularly important when you seek to develop a new identity for a new type of activity (e.g. teaching). The contextualisation of aspects of your 'pre-teaching' identity within the new activity of teaching that you are undertaking will be an important aspect of your reflective practice in the process of your early initial teacher education.

REFLECTIVE EXERCISE

Think back through your own education to this point. Which teachers stand out in your memory? What was it about them or their work that made them memorable? Were there any aspects of these teachers' identities that helped you recall them?

Alan Peshkin was a Professor of Education at the University of Illinois, Campaign and, in the final years of his career, at Stanford University. His research focused heavily on the nature of communities and schools. His work is highly regarded in numerous ways. His case studies serve as models for the conduct of qualitative inquiry in educational research. They were always thorough and respectful in their dealings with sensitive issues (e.g. race (Peshkin, 1991) and religious fundamentalism (Peshkin, 1986)). Peshkin's analyses always attended carefully to issues of subjectivity and identity, and how these should be interpreted in educational contexts. It is this aspect of his work that we will draw on for our first extract.

Identity, subjectivity and the individual

We cannot rid ourselves of our subjectivity, nor should we wish to; but we ought, perhaps, to pay it very much more attention

(Cheater, 1987, page 172)

Before reading the first extract there are a few preliminary points to be made. Firstly, in Peshkin's terms, subjectivity is an irremovable part of our identity. He uses a metaphor to describe it. It is like a *garment that cannot be removed* (Peshkin, 1988, page 17) but which needs to be acknowledged, understood and interrogated. Secondly, Peshkin is writing primarily about his experiences as an educational researcher. However, as we will see in our discussion following the extract, our argument is that the process of examining one's subjectivity is as valuable for the teacher as for the researcher. Finally, the process that Peshkin describes in the extract leads to the discovery of a number of subjective 'Is. In the later part of Peshkin's article, these are described in considerable detail. Here is the opening of the article.

EXTRACT ONE

Peshkin, A (1988) In search of subjectivity – one's own. **Educational Researcher, *17: 7*. London, Los Angeles, New Delhi and Singapore: Sage, pp. 17–18.**

A dictionary definition (Webster's Third New International) notes subjectivity as 'the quality of an investigator that affects the results of observational investigation.' This 'quality' affects the results of all, not just observational, investigation. It is an amalgam of the persuasions that stem from the circumstances of one's class, statuses, and values interacting with the particulars of one's object of investigation. Our persuasions vary in time and in intensity.

Though social scientists claim in general that subjectivity is invariably present in their research, they are not necessarily conscious of it. When their subjectivity remains unconscious, they insinuate rather than knowingly clarify their personal stakes. If, in the spirit of confession, researchers acknowledge their subjectivity, they may benefit their souls, but they do not thereby attend to their subjectivity in a meaningful way. This paper will demonstrate how and why researchers should be meaningfully attentive to their own subjectivity.

I hold the view that subjectivity operates during the entire research process (Peshkin, 1982b). The point I argue here is that researchers, notwithstanding their use of quantitative or qualitative methods, their research problem, or their reputation for personal integrity, should systematically identify their subjectivity throughout the course of their research. When researchers observe themselves in the focused way that I propose, they learn about the particular subset of personal qualities that contact with their research phenomenon has released. These qualities have the capacity to filter, skew, shape, block, transform, construe, and misconstrue what transpires from the outset of a research project to its culmination in a written statement. If researchers are informed about the qualities that have emerged during their research, they can at least disclose to their readers where self and subject became joined. They can at best be enabled to write unshackled from orientations that they did not realize were intervening in their research process.

Awareness of subjectivity

Subjectivity is not a badge of honor, something earned like a merit badge and paraded around on special occasions for all to see. Whatever the substance of one's persuasions at a given point, one's subjectivity is like a garment that cannot be removed. It is insistently present in both the research and nonresearch aspects of our life. As conventional wisdom (see Freilich, 1970, p.568; Reinharz, 1979, p.141; Stein, 1971, p.143), this view of subjectivity takes its place among other usually unexamined maxims of research, such as 'rapport is good,' 'random samples are wonderful,' and 'informants can mislead.' By remaining conventional wisdom, our subjectivity lies inert, unexamined when it counts, that is, beyond our control while actively engaged in the research process.

I became acutely aware of my own subjectivity in the course of writing God's Choice: The Total World of a Fundamentalist Christian School and Community *(Peshkin, 1986). The research I did for this book continued the studies I have conducted since 1972 on the community- school relationship in different environmental settings. Long interested in the concept of community, I looked at the nature of community in the fundamentalist Christian setting of Bethany Baptist Academy. I had previously done so in rural Illinois (Peshkin, 1978, 1982a) and, most recently, in multiethnic 'Riverview', California, the locus of my pursuit of subjectivity in this paper. But as regards my awareness of subjectivity at Bethany, I began writing Chapter 1 of* God's Choice, *no more and no less alert on my subjectivity than most of us ordinarily are, when I confronted it in a way that I never had before.*

What I realized was this: Mansfield, the village site of previous research, was no more nurturant as a community than was the community I studied at Bethany. Moreover, Mansfield High School contributed no more to promoting a sense of community than did Bethany Baptist Academy. Yet I found that I was not addressing community and school at Bethany in the strong, positive terms I had easily found to describe Mansfield. Struck by this differential generosity (explained in Peshkin, 1985), I knew that 'I had indeed discovered my subjectivity at work, caught red handed with my values at the very end of my pen' (Peshkin, 1985, p. 277).

Having stumbled upon my own subjectivity in this way, I drew two conclusions. First, I decided that subjectivity can be seen as virtuous, for it is the basis of researchers' making a distinctive contribution, one that results from the unique configuration of their personal qualities joined to the data they have collected (Peshkin, 1985, pp. 276–278). Second, I decided that in subsequent studies I would actively seek out my subjectivity. I did not want to happen upon it accidentally as I was writing up the data. I wanted to be aware of it in process, mindful of its enabling and disabling potential while the data were still coming in, not after the fact. Here are the results of what I did.

Subjective Is uncovered

Throughout 11 months of fieldwork in Riverview High School, a multiethnic school of 1,600 students, I pursued my subjectivity. How did I know when my subjectivity was engaged? I looked for the warm and the cool spots, the emergence of positive and nega- tive feelings, the experiences I wanted more of or wanted to avoid, and when I felt moved to act in roles beyond those necessary to fulfill my research needs. In short, I felt that to identify my subjectivity, I had to monitor myself to sense how I was feeling. When I felt that my feelings were aroused, and, thus, that my subjectivity had been evoked, I wrote a note on a 5" × 8" card, the researcher's friend. Perhaps equally (or more) useful, Smith (1980) kept a diary to document her 'feelings and reactions': She wrote, for example, about 'spinning into the realm of the irrational' (p.8) and 'a weight on my chest and a tightening of my throat' (p.9). I preferred to record my sensations as I was experiencing them, a matter of personal taste, as is so much of fieldwork procedure.

The results of my subjectivity audit are contained in the following list (a) the Ethnic Maintenance I; (b) the Community-Maintenance I; (c) the E-Pluribus-Unum I; (d) the Justice Seeking I; (e) the Pedagogical-Meliorist I; and (f) the Nonresearch Human I.[5] These discretely characterized Is are, in fact, aspects of the whole that constitutes me. They are no more truly discrete than the organs of my body are independent of each other. These I's comprise a subset that emerged under the particular circumstances of Riverview High School. In another school, a different subset would possibly emerge, even containing I's that do not overlap with those I learned about at Riverview. That I's may change from place to place I call 'situational subjectivity'. By this concept I suggest that though we bring all of ourselves – our full complement of subjective Is – to each new research site, a site and its particular conditions will elicit only a subset of our Is.

In this paper, Peshkin argues that coming to know and understand your subjectivity is a vital prerequisite for the educational researcher. Our argument below will apply this principle to the emerging identity of the teacher. Subjectivity that lies inert and unexamined will affect the results of the researcher's observation and analysis of educational events and interactions; it will skew their thinking about important issues related to the teaching and learning that they are researching. Our argument here is that issues relating to subjectivity will affect the work of the teacher as much as, if not more than, the educational researcher. Teachers are a vital, one might say integral, part of the educational process. The way that they think, feel and act implicates that process in fundamental ways. Peshkin comments that personal qualities have the capacity to *filter, skew, shape, block, transform, construe and misconstrue* (1988, page 17) the activities related to educational research. If all these are possible from the perspective of an outsider looking in to a particular educational community or classroom (a typical representation of how some researchers work), how much more would they be factors affecting the work of participants within these scenes?

To help with this, Peshkin outlines a process that he went through to help himself understand his subjectivity a little more deeply. This was an active and deliberate process on his part.

It did not happen accidentally. Towards the end of the extract, he comments that *he wanted to be aware of it [his subjectivity] in process, mindful of its enabling and disabling potential while the data were still coming in, not after the fact* (Peshkin 1988, page 18). The practical process that Peshkin employed saw him examining his feelings about particular situations that he found himself in while watching educational events unfold at Riverview High School. He tried to identify occasions when he felt a compulsion to move beyond his remit as a researcher and questioned why this was; he monitored his feelings and wrote notes on small A6 cards which documented these feelings, sensations and reactions. This 'subjectivity audit' unveiled what Peshkin describes as six subjective Is. These Is are explored in more detail throughout the rest of his paper. Here, we will provide a short summary for each of them (Figure 1).

Figure 1 An analysis of Peshkin's Is

Peshkin's Is	Foundation	Key quote
Ethnic maintenance I	Pre-Riverview in his own religious background and beliefs	*This is, of course, my Jewish I, the one that approves of my own retention of ethnicity. (p.18)*
Community-maintenance I	Discovered through a sense of a place and its history	*I felt this one in various places, perhaps nowhere more strongly than at Mario's Snack Shop ... where an important sense of community was perpetuated every day. (pp.18–19)*
E-Pluribus-Unum I	All the before, in-between, and after-class times at Riverview High School	*The visual impression of the school captivated me from the first time I went there to the last. I had never seen such diversity; indeed, it did not exist to the same degree anywhere else in the community. I saw students together in a way that I found wonderful. (p.19)*
Justice-seeking I	Through observation of Riverview's denigration and inherent racism of neighbouring communities	*Riverview's denigration distressed me ... Although feelings of distress helped focus my enquiry – a positive outcome – they could make me defensive in a way that would not facilitate my analysis and understanding. (p.19)*
Pedagogical-meliorist I	Reflection on teaching from the back of a classroom	*This emerged from seeking ordinary-to-poor instruction given to youngsters who would suffer, I imagined, as a consequence of that instruction. (p.19)*
Non-research human I	The warmth of people's reception and welcoming in their community (including that felt by his wider family)	*This softens one's judgement; its by product is affection, which tends to reduce the distance between self and subjects that scholars presume is necessary to learning and write about a person, place or institution. (p.20)*

The final sentence of our extract from Peshkin's work emphasises what is becoming a common theme in the opening of this chapter. The subjectivities that he has uncovered and explored within his identity are labelled as 'situational'. They are context-dependent. In other words, we cannot dissect ourselves and cut off aspects of our subjectivities at will. They are an integral part of our identity. But particular sets of circumstances, a location or activity will bring aspects of subjectivity to the fore. Mapping these reactions and feelings will be an important aspect of your work as you begin your teaching career.

REFLECTIVE EXERCISE

Following Peshkin's example, start a process of reflection that begins to uncover some of your own subjective Is. Like Peshkin, these may be related to aspects of your beliefs or values about education or life in general; they might be linked to key personal, family or professional relationships; they might be in response to experiences that you have within a specific place (a new school or university) or when undertaking a new activity (i.e. beginning teaching). You may uncover them in other situations. This is a highly personal exercise.

Specifically, consider the following.

1. *Chart your own feelings, reactions and thoughts about the activities that you are undertaking during your initial teacher education. Look out for strong responses that you feel in relation to new ideas that you discuss with tutors or colleagues, your reading, your classroom work, the planning processes you are undertaking or while compiling your evaluations. Keep a list of these as part of a teaching file. Do this for at least a couple of weeks.*

2. *Spend some time reviewing your list. Look for patterns or commonalities within your responses (e.g. issues to do with my pedagogy, strong feelings of injustice, etc.). Group together any responses that you notice have similarities in some way.*

3. *Give each group of similarities a name or label or some sort. This could be specific term or a short phrase. These terms become your subjective Is.*

4. *Finally, and most importantly, having got to this point, commit to regularly reviewing your work in light of your subjective Is. Look out for them as you go about your teaching. Try to ascertain to what extent they shape your actions either positively or negatively.*

Our discussion to this point has centred on issues related to your identity (as a human being, first of all, and, secondly, contextualising these within your work as a beginning teacher). It has used a specific device (the subjective I), drawn from the work of an experienced academic and educational researcher, to help you examine in more detail aspects of your own identity that will impinge directly on the development of your teaching identity. The purposes of doing this are not to help you tame your subjectivity and overcome it. That is impossible. Rather, it is to help you recognise what is there and, in some sense, manage its influence on your work. In Peshkin's words:

A further point of this paper is not the absurd one of saying, 'Here I am, holier than thou and released from my subjectivity because I have owned up, whereas you, being unrepentant, remain afflicted.' The point is this: By monitoring myself, I can create an illuminating, empowering personal statement that attunes me to where self and subject are intertwined. I do not thereby exorcise my subjectivity. I do, rather, enable myself to manage it.

(Peshkin 1988, page 20)

Identity and schools

This kind of individual, reflective thinking may seem a little divorced from reality for some readers. In the hurly-burly of school life is there really time for this type of reflective practice? Our answer would be, not surprisingly, yes there is (or at least one should aim to make time for it to happen). It is an essential type of activity for all teachers to undertake. This is especially true during moments of transition (e.g. when you are coming into teaching, when you are moving between jobs or taking on a new role). This is because new sets of circumstances challenge our identity in all kinds of different ways. The processes we have discussed above are a simple way of keeping things in check, of managing our subjectivity and its impact, and ensuring that it we can be explicit about its affect on our work as a teacher.

Our second excerpt, drawn from the work of one of the most famous writers on reflective practice, examines the impact of bureaucratic systems on the nature of reflective practice of the type we are suggesting teachers would benefit from undertaking more regularly.

This extract comes from Schön's final chapter of his famous book, and deals with the implications of a reflective practice approach within particular professional contexts. One of these is education. In the passage running up to our extract, Schön asks us to imagine a school. This school is characterised by a range of features (some of which you may recognise):

- A school is built around a theory of knowledge which dictates that it is the teachers' job to teach and students' to learn. Knowledge is imparted by teachers in 'measurable doses', with students digesting these chunks and teachers planning for students' progressive development.

- It is orderly, in terms of space and time. It has self-contained classrooms and a regular timetable through which knowledge bases (subjects) are partitioned and delivered.

- It is controlled by systems of sanctions and rewards for students, with expectations for individual students set and checked regularly.

- It is controlled by systems of sanction and rewards for staff, with management structures ensuring standards are maintained.

- It is characterised by objectivity, with quantitative measures of proficiency and progress preferred to qualitative or narrative accounts of learning and teaching.

Within what Schön calls this 'educational bureaucracy', he asks us to consider what happens when teachers being to think like reflective practitioners. As you read through the extract, jot down the characteristics of a reflective practitioner that Schön identifies.

EXTRACT TWO

Schön, D (1983) **The Reflective Practitioner.** *Aldershot: Avebury, pp. 332–336.*

What happens in such an educational bureaucracy when a teacher begins to think and act not as technical expert but as reflective practitioner? Her reflection in action poses a potential threat to the dynamically conservative system in which she lives.

She tries to listen to her students. She asks herself, for example, How is he thinking about this? What is the meaning of his confusion? What is it that he already knows how to

---

do? But if she really listens to a student, she entertains ideas for action that transcend the lesson plan. She may wish, for example, to concentrate for a time on the nature of a student's error or confusion. Why does he write, '36 + 36 = 312'? As she begins to understand how he thinks about the task, she may invent new questions, new activities for the student to try, and new ways of helping him learn addition. The lesson plan must be put aside then, or else it must become a rough ground plan for action, a skeleton around which the teacher develops variations according to her on-the-spot understanding of the problems of particular students. Curriculum becomes an inventory of themes of understanding and skill to be addressed rather than a set of materials to be learned. Different students present different phenomena for understanding and action. Each student makes up a universe of one, whose potentials, problems, and pace of work must be appreciated as the teacher reflects-in-action on the design of her work.

The freedom to reflect, invent, and differentiate would disrupt the institutional order of space and time. If the teacher must somehow manage the work of thirty students in a classroom, how can she really listen to any one of them? If she is held rigorously accountable to a sequence of hour-long periods in which specified units of subject matter are to be covered, then she cannot follow the logic of her reflection-in-action. Classes must be small or readily divisible into smaller units, and each teacher must be free to introduce variations in the institutional schedule.

The teacher's isolation in her classroom works against reflection-in-action. She needs to communicate her private puzzles and insights, to test them against the views of her peers.

She must expand the scope of her interest in students. What they know how to do in the world outside the school becomes deeply interesting to her, for it suggests the intuitive competences on which she can build.

A reflective teacher needs a kind of educational technology, which does more than extend her capacity to administer drill and practice, Most interesting to her is an educational technology which helps students to become aware of their own intuitive understandings, to fall into cognitive confusions and explore new directions of understanding and action.

Accountability, evaluation, and supervision would acquire new meanings. There would be a shift from the search for centrally administered, objective measures of student progress, toward independent, qualitative judgments and narrative accounts of experience and performance in learning and teaching. Supervision would concern itself less with monitoring the teacher's coverage of curriculum content than with assessment and support of the teacher's reflection-in-action.

As teachers attempted to become reflective practitioners, they would feel constrained by and would push against the rule-governed system of the school, and in doing so they would be pushing against the theory of knowledge which underlies the school. Not only would they struggle against the rigid order of lesson plans, schedules, isolated classrooms, and objective measures of performance; they would also question and criticize the fundamental idea of the school as a place for the progressive transmission of measured doses of privileged knowledge.

In fact, the participants in the Teachers' Project had a variety of kinds of experiences as they attempted to live out in their classrooms the new understandings and attitudes they were acquiring. Their schools were in varying degrees approximations to the stereotyped picture I have just drawn. A few teachers had a great deal of discretionary freedom, and were able to make their classrooms into enclaves of nontraditional teaching. Some were frustrated by the traditional patterns and expectations built into the institutional routines of the school. A few felt that the new approach to teaching was 'too good for that school.'

What is clear is that, in a real world school which tried to encourage reflective teaching (as in the reflective contract between professional and client), conflicts and dilemmas would surface which are absent, hidden, or of minor importance in an ordinary school. In order to engage the learning capacities and difficulties of particular students, a school would have to manage student/teacher ratios much smaller than twenty five to one. In the face of resource constraints, how would appropriate differentiations of curriculum and teaching attention be determined? Where teachers were encouraged to reflect-in-action, the meaning of 'good teaching' and 'a good classroom' would become topics of urgent institutional concern. Such questions could no longer be dismissed by reference to objective measures of performance. Indeed, a major question would hinge on the relationship between such measures and the qualitative judgments of individual teachers. Principals would have to ask, in framing their own roles, whether to 'let a thousand flowers bloom' or to advocate their own standards of excellence. If they chose the former, in the name of the teacher's freedom of action or in the spirit of participatory democracy, would the school fall into the kind of permissiveness and intellectual sloppiness which characterized some of the alternative schools of the 1960s? And if principals chose the latter course, what would happen to the teacher's freedom to reflect-in-action? In a school supportive of reflective teaching, a supervisor would advocate his own standards of educational quality while at the same time inquiring into teachers' understandings, confronting what he sees as poor teaching while at the same time inviting teachers to confront his own behavior. Yet in the Model I worlds of most schools, it is far more likely that supervisors would oscillate between centralized control and 'a thousand flowers.'

In a school supportive of reflective teaching, teachers would challenge the prevailing knowledge structure. Their on-the-spot experiments would affect not only the routines of teaching practice but the central values and principles of the institution. Conflicts and dilemmas would surface and move to center stage. In the organizational learning system with which we are most familiar, conflicts and dilemmas tend to be suppressed or to result in polarization and political warfare. An institution congenial to reflective practice would require a learning system within which individuals could surface conflicts and dilemmas and subject them to productive public inquiry, a learning system conducive to the continual criticism and restructuring of organizational principles and values.

Is the model of teaching that Schön envisages something that you aspire to achieving? In reviewing your list of attributes for the reflective practitioner, we hope that there are elements here that reflect your desire to be a successful teacher. Here is our list.

The teacher who wants to be a reflective practitioner:

- listens to their students and really seeks to understand them as unique individuals, tailoring their instruction, speech and learning resources to respond to their specific requirements;

- thinks beyond their lesson plan in seeking to respond to individual students' needs and requirements;

- uses the curriculum as an inventory of themes to be understood rather than a set of materials to be learnt;

- expands their knowledge of the students to encompass their learning and interests outside of the classroom;

- uses technology in a way to empower students to undertake their own learning rather than to reinforce old-fashioned, teacher-centric pedagogies;

- prioritises independent, qualitative, narrative accounts of learning over blunt, accountability-driven assessment frameworks that depersonalise the student and their achievements;

- challenges set theories of knowledge and its organisation within the school systems of timetables and classrooms, seeking to make links in imaginative ways across and in between subject boundaries.

Schön acknowledges that there are many stereotypes on both sides of his argument (Schön, 1983, page 334). We are sure you have been able to spot them. But this does not undermine his argument. The bureaucratic model of schooling he outlines imposes significant restraints on the work of the aspiring reflective teacher. Their sense of identity, formed from their wider life experiences, impacts and responds to this bureaucracy in different ways. As with the process of defining one's subjective Is, it is important for teachers to be aware of the potential conflicts that can emerge and for them to be able to manage these effectively.

REFLECTIVE EXERCISE

Reflect for a few minutes on the school where you work, or where you are undertaking a teaching placement. Can you identify any bureaucratic elements that impinge on your work as a teacher there? Thinking about Schön's call for reflective practitioners, how can you respond positively to these elements? How can you use them to mitigate some of the more bureaucratic elements of educational institutions in some way by changing, perhaps subtly, elements within your teaching practice?

Schön's final comment is aimed at those with responsibility for leadership and management in our schools. To what extent are they promoting an environment where teaching of this type can not only occur but also be facilitated? This would be the topic of another book.

But the teachers of today will be the senior managers and head teachers of tomorrow. Why not start as you mean to go on? Maintain this philosophy and approach throughout your teaching career. It will reward you and your students immensely.

Identity and teaching

So, how do you perceive your own sense of identity? How is it changing and developing as you engage with the process of learning to teach? Have you been able to identify individual elements or subjectivities within your identity and trace their impact on your work? Have you been able to analyse the school context in which you work, isolating bureaucratic elements and seeking to respond in a positive and reflective manner?

The final part of this opening chapter seeks to challenge your notion of what exactly a teaching identity might be. It does this by considering a metaphor and applying this to the act of teaching.

Elliot Eisner is a Professor of Education and Art at the University of Stanford. He has made an invaluable contribution to the world of art and education in various ways, not least through his expositions on the artistry of teaching. Artistry, Eisner argues, has much to teach the world of education:

> *Artistry, therefore, can serve as a regulative ideal for education, a vision that adumbrates what really matters in schools. To conceive of students as artists who do their art in science, in the arts, or the humanities, is, after all, both a daunting and a profound aspiration. It may be that by shifting the paradigm of education reform and teaching from one modelled after the clock-like character of the assembly line into one that is closer to the studio or innovative science laboratory might provide us with a vision that better suits the capacities and the futures of the students we teach. It is in this sense, I believe, that the field of education has much to learn from the arts about the practice of education. It is time to embrace a new model for improving our schools.*

> (Eisner, 2004)

In the following extract, Eisner questions whether teaching is an art. As the extract unfolds, keep track of the five key points that he makes in response to this question.

EXTRACT THREE

Kompf, M, Boak, RT, Bond, WR and Dworet, D (eds) (1996) **Changing Research and Practice: Teachers', Professionalism, Identities and Knowledge.** *London: Falmer Press, pp. 17–19.*

Is teaching an art? The answer seems to me to be, 'It can be'. Teaching like most other human activities can be artless or artful. We prefer the later to the former But the question of utility remains. What is the value of regarding teaching as an art? What does it buy us? The last section of my remarks addresses this question.

I shall have five points to make about the utility of reorganising artistry in teaching. First recognizing artistry in teaching provides us with a way of thinking about teaching – a

---

metaphorical field – through which to see and reflect upon features of teaching that we might not have seen or thought about before. When teaching is conceived of as the practice of an art we are more likely to seek out its artistic features, we are more likely to pay attention to form in teaching, to consider style, tempo, the way a lesson crescendos in a teaching episode, to look for expressivity in the performance of both teachers and students. Art and artistry, if we follow Lakoff and Johnson, are metaphorical concepts embedded in a metaphorical field. This field brackets our perceptions, it defines the world in particular ways. The absence of artistry in our conception of teaching leads to its absence in our discussions and research on teaching and keeps a potential window closed. When that window is closed we cannot secure the vision that the presence of the concept not only permits, but invites. Thus, the first benefit we receive from regarding teaching as an art is a fresh view of what teaching entails.

A second benefit from recognising artistry in teaching is padoxical. On the one hand the very presence in our consciousness of the artistic aspects of teaching makes it possible to develop theory that in principle can account for its presence and its effects. A theory of artistry in teaching is intended to do what theory does – explain and when possible pre-dict and control. On the other hand our recognition of the presence of artistry in teaching is also very likely to increase our awareness of the limitations of theory. Artistry, if it's anything, is ideographic. Theory is nomothetic. It traffics in regularity. Theory idealizes. The consequences of recognizing artistry in teaching is to arrive at a paradoxical point in which both the lure of theory construction and an awareness of its limitations operate at the same time. I do not regard this state of affairs as disastrous; in intellectual life it comes with the territory.

A third benefit from recognizing artistry in teaching is that it invites the use of forms of feedback to teachers that are normally given to those in the arts. The feedback I speak of is in the form of the critique. Critiques in the arts are intended to increase awareness of the qualities of a work of art. The aim of criticism, wrote Dewey, 'is the re-education of the perception of the work of art.' This re-education begins with the critic's refined perception which is then transformed and rendered publicly to help others see what has transpired in the course of teaching. This critical rendering exploits the capacities of lan-guage in all its forms – poetic, literacy, figurative, literal – to reveal and interpret what the critic has seen. Artistry here too comes into play in the rendering of the work.

For teachers such feedback goes well beyond reports written on the basis of commando raids into their classrooms, tallies calculated from check-off sheets, or decontextualized admonitions about the features of good teaching or about 'what works'. It is more than logs provide and much more than factual descriptions can reveal. Criticism itself is a demanding art that depends upon a highly differentiated sensibility in some domain and a thorough understanding of the context in which the work is created. I have described this approach to assessment in detail in my book The Enlightened Eye. *It is truly sad that we have created schools and sustained professional norms that discourage the provision of constructive edu-cational criticism; all of us could benefit from sensitive observation and interpretation of our teaching. The recognition of artistry in teaching might help us overcome the isolating char-acter of schools and mechanistic approaches to the study of teaching.*

A fourth potential consequence of viewing teaching as an art is that it may increase our readiness to accept differences in the ways in which teachers teach and in the destinations toward which individual teachers wish to travel. Both bureaucracies and technologies have a tendency to standardize processes and outcomes: Goals 2000 is an encomium to the standardization of aims just as the assembly line pays homage to routine as essential to its successful operation. Artistry courts surprise. It welcomes initiative. It celebrates imagination. The values related to artistry may be just the sort we need to reduce the attrition rate among teachers; we lose about half of the incoming cohort five years after they start their careers. Artistry acknowledged and prized might encourage teachers to make their professional lives interesting by thinking of themselves as being engaged – when they are at their best – in the practice of an art.

A fifth potentially productive outcome is related to the fourth, namely the creation of a professional ambience that has less tolerance for over-simplified solutions to educational problems. The 'solutions' I speak of are old ideas like teacher-proof curricula, or five steps to effective teaching, or incentive or choice programs that see the answer to educational problems located in competition among schools. The theory seems to be: if capitalism is good for our economy, it must be good for our children's schools.

Artistry does not reduce complexity, it has a tendency to increase complexity by recognizing subtlety and emphasizing individuality. It does not search for the one best method. It puts a premium on productive idiosyncrasy. It is a crucial compliment to getting it down to a science. In the vernacular, 'getting it down to a science', means, ideally, getting it down to errorless procedure. A procedure becomes errorless when there are no surprises. When there are no surprises, there is no problem. When there is no problem, there is neither challenge nor growth. Artistry in teaching as a pervasive concept goes beyond routine, invites risk, courts challenge, and fosters growth.

Let me bring my remarks to a close by returning to the question that serves as the title of my paper. The question that I asked at the start of this paper was: 'Is the art of teaching a metaphor?' Insofar as metaphor resides at the core of our thinking, insofar as it lives at the root of our conceptual life, sure it is. How could it not be? But what if we turn the question around and ask, 'Is teaching an art?' The answer to that question depends on what the teaching is that we are considering. Teaching can be an art when teachers are artists, that is, when their teaching is artful. Teaching is artful when it has some of the characteristics I described earlier.

Did you spot the five key points that Eisner discusses? These are summarised and discussed briefly below.

Firstly, Eisner suggests that recognising artistry as teaching gives us a way of seeking out its particular artistic elements and using these to help to think, and talk, about teaching in different ways. Eisner gives us some examples. The idea of a teacher as a performer might conjure up images in your mind of an actor or musician delivering a performance of some type. It is worth pausing to consider this in a bit more detail. What makes for a convincing dramatic or musical performance? What are the features that might make it compelling or engaging? How does the performer present or shape the music or words in an expressive way to communicate their thoughts or emotions at particular moments? All of these questions could be applied and developed to help you consider aspects of your own work as a teacher.

Eisner's second point is a paradox. The identification and presence of artistic elements within teaching might lead one to want to develop a theory that, in principle, can account for these elements and ensure their logical progression and development. This could lead to a predictive or controlling model of artistic development for teaching. The paradox occurs when one considers that the recognition of artistry in teaching moves, quickly, into an awareness that theories themselves are limiting and idealistic. They often leave out more than they encompass and do not allow for individual differences or promote the subtleties that artistic practices exhibit. Artists cross boundaries, explore new territory and care little for rules and regulations. These are there to be broken.

Applying and developing metaphors is a helpful activity for any process of creative thought. But they can be stretched too far. This second point needs careful handling because the value we place on artistry is itself contextualised within our own identities and life experiences (it is probably also enculturated within a broader social and political context). We would suggest that you do not try to be too mechanical or rigid in your thinking about an artistic 'theory' for teaching. This is likely to stifle the very benefits of the approach you are trying to develop. Rather, take and apply the big themes in the way that Eisner has done in this extract.

Thirdly, he talks about the specific aspects of feedback that teachers receive about their work. He draws on the ideas behind artistic criticism which aims, in Dewey's terms, towards a *re-education of the perception of the work of art*. Eisner's application of his teaching-as-artistry metaphor urges us to rediscover a form of educational criticism, characterised by sensitive observations and interpretations of our teaching which reflect the particular context of our work.

Fourthly, viewing teaching as artistry will allow us to become more tolerant of how other teachers teach. Again, we note here Eisner's aversion to bureaucracies and standardisation of processes of teacher development. For us, this is one of the most exciting parts of Eisner's chapter. Substitute the word 'teaching' for 'artistry' in the following paragraph drawn from the extract:

> *Artistry courts surprise. It welcomes initiative. It celebrates imagination. … Artistry acknowledged and prized might encourage teachers to make their professional lives interesting by thinking of themselves as being engaged in the practice of an art.*

> (Eisner 1996, page 18)

The types of questions that we can draw from these sentences about our own teaching are very challenging.

- How often does my teaching surprise my students? Does it ever surprise me?

- How does my teaching celebrate the imaginative and respond positively to new initiatives or approaches?

- How much time do I spend seeking out the experimental and new approaches that might help me conceive of what I do as a teacher in terms of being an artist?

- Do I respond appropriately when my pupils show these attributes in their work?

- To what extent do I value uniformity in my teaching approach? Am I prepared to allow for the differences in pupils' learning that might occur if I loosen the reigns of a structured and systematic (mechanistic) approach to the development of my teaching?

Finally, conceiving of teaching as artistry will lead, Eisner believes, to the creation of a profession where there is less tolerance for simplified (perhaps we might say 'top-down') solutions to educational problems. Rather, the notion of teaching as an art will lead to a greater degree of complexity because it emphasises the individual identity of the teacher and prioritises the subtleties that they will exhibit through their artistic teaching practice. In this sense, one size does not fit all. In Eisner's terms, it *invites risk, courts challenge, and fosters growth* (ibid).

Eisner's work is a challenge to all teachers. For those of us who have been teaching for longer it will be harder to break free from old, restricting habits and pedagogies. For those readers starting out at the beginning of their teaching careers, we would urge you to consider the key messages of this chapter very carefully. Start as you mean to go on. Use Peshkin's work to help provide yourself with a greater understanding of your identity and how it applies to your work as a teacher. Respond positively to Schön's call for reflective practitioners. Although schools can be very bureaucratic places, there is room for individuality, talent and flair. Eisner's concept of teaching as artistry can empower you to break out of mechanistic models of teaching, pinned down by external curriculum requirements or approaches, and allow you to develop your pedagogy in such a way that celebrates life in its fullness and inspires your pupils to do the same.

POINTS TO CONSIDER

- *What type of teacher do I want to be? How can the work of these three writers help me establish key foundations for the early part of my career?*

- *What practical processes can I employ to ensure that I really do start as I mean to go on?*

- *As teaching can be quite a lonely activity, can I identify two or three other friends or colleagues whom I can work with and support as I seek to develop these ideas in the context of my own teaching?*

C H A P T E R   S U M M A R Y

This chapter considers issues related to identity and education. It explores how the development of a positive teacher 'identity' is the basis for effective teaching and learning. Through the use of a reflective tool drawn from the work of an experienced educator, it asks you to consider your own identity and how this shapes your decisions as a teacher. The chapter goes on to consider the bureaucratic nature of institutions such as schools and how these can be explored constructively by the creative and reflective teacher. Finally, the concept of teaching as 'artistry' is introduced. Metaphorical approaches to the act of teaching are helpful in extending and applying our thinking about what teaching is, what teachers do and, importantly, how teaching is centred on a relationship between a teacher and a student.

REFERENCES

Cheater, AP (1987) The Anthropologist as Citizen: The diffracted self, in Jackson, A (ed) *Anthropologist at Home*. London: Tavistock.

Eisner, E (1996) Is 'The Art of Teaching' a Metaphor?, in Kompf, M, Bond, WR, Dworet, D and Boak, RT (1996) *Changing Research and Practice: Teachers' professionalism, identities and knowledge*. London: Falmer Press.

Eisner, EW (2004) Artistry in teaching. **www.culturalcommons.org/eisner.htm** [accessed 2/2/10].

Palmer, P (2009) **www.newhorizons.org/strategies/character/palmer.htm** [accessed 2/2/10].

Peshkin, A (1986) *God's Choice: Total World of a Fundamentalist Christian School*. Chicago: University of Chicago Press.

Peshkin, A (1988) In search of subjectivity – one's own. *Educational Researcher* 17(7): 17–22.

Peshkin, A (1991) *The Color of Strangers, the Color of Friends: The play of ethnicity in school and community*. Chicago: University of Chicago Press.

Schön, D (1983) *The Reflective Practitioner: How Professionals Think in Action*. New York: Basic Books.

Chapter 2
Teaching and learning

Introduction

REFLECTIVE EXERCISE

What is teaching? How does it relate to learning?

Think about what it is that you do as a teacher. How do you teach a topic in your subject, and what does this entail? How do the learners learn, what are they engaged in, and how does this manifest itself in your classroom?

Teaching and learning are complicated constructs. What you wrote in response to the reflective task above will be determined by many factors, including what subject you teach, what your personal philosophy of education is, along with many other factors. In this chapter we consider some of these issues, and ask you to reflect on your personal philosophies of teaching and learning which we discussed in Chapter 1, and what this means for the pupils you teach.

Our first extract is drawn from the writings of Jerome Bruner. Bruner is an American psychologist and a key figure in cognitive approaches to education. He has researched and written about the ways in which people learn, and the role of society and culture in this. The extract we are using is from his 1996 book, *The Culture of Education*.

As you read through the extract, ask yourself the following questions.

- What does Bruner say about teaching?

- What is a folk pedagogy?

- What is knowledge?

- Where is knowledge?

EXTRACT ONE

Bruner, J (1996) Folk Pedagogy, in The Culture of Education. Cambridge, MA: Harvard University Press, pp. 44–53.

Thoughtful people have been forever troubled by the enigma of applying theoretical knowledge to practical problems. Applying psychological theory to educational practice is no exception to the rule, not much less puzzling than applying science to medicine. Aristotle comments (rather touchingly) in the Nichomachean Ethics *(Book V, 1137a): 'It is an easy matter to know the effects of honey, wine, hellebore, cautery, and cutting. But to know how, for whom, and when we should apply these as remedies is no less an undertaking than being a physician.' Even with scientific advances, the physician's problem is not much easier today than it was in the times of hellebore and cautery: 'how, for whom, and when' still loom as problems. The challenge is always to situate our knowledge in the living context that poses the 'presenting problem,' to borrow a bit of medical jargon. And that living context, where education is concerned, is the schoolroom – the schoolroom situated in a broader culture.*

That is where, at least in advanced cultures, teachers and pupils come together to effect that crucial but mysterious interchange that we so glibly call 'education.' Obvious though it may seem, we would do better to concentrate in what follows on 'learning and teaching in the setting of school' rather than, as psychologists sometimes do, generalising from learning in a rat maze, from the nonsense-syllable learning of sophomores incarcerated in a laboratory cubicle, or from the performance of an AI computer simulation at Carnegie-Mellon. Keep before you a busy classroom of nine-year-olds, say, with a hard-working teacher, and ask what kind of theoretical knowledge would help them. A genetic theory that assures them that people differ? Well, perhaps, but not much. Do you work harder with the not-so-bright or ignore them? What about an associationist theory that tells you that nonsense syllables are associated with each other through frequency, recency, contiguity, and similarity effects? Would you want to design a curriculum on knowledge about how nonsense syllables are learned? Well, perhaps a little – where things are a little-nonsense like anyway, such as the names of elements in the periodic table: cerium, lithium, gold, lead ...

There is one 'presenting problem' that is always with us in dealing with teaching and learning, one that is so pervasive, so constant, so much part of the fabric of living, that we often fail to notice it, fail even to discover it – much as in the proverb 'the fish will be the last to discover water.' It is the issue of how human beings achieve a meeting of

EXTRACT ONE *continued*

minds, expressed by teachers usually as 'how do I reach the children?' or by children as 'what's she trying to get at?' This is the classic problem of Other Minds, as it was origi-nally called in philosophy, and its relevance to education has mostly been overlooked until very recently. In the last decade it has become a topic of passionate interest and intense research among psychologists, particularly those interested in development. It is what this chapter is about – the application of this new work to the process of education.

To a degree almost entirely overlooked by anti-subjective behaviorists in the past, our interactions with others are deeply affected by our everyday intuitive theories about how other minds work. These theories, rarely made explicit, are omnipresent but have only recently been subjected to intense study. Such lay theories are now referred to profes-sionally by the rather condescending name of 'folk psychology'. Folk psychologies reflect certain 'wired-in' human tendencies (like seeing people normally as operating under their own control), but they also reflect some deeply ingrained cultural beliefs about 'the mind.' Not only is folk psychology preoccupied with how the mind works here and now, it is also equipped with notions about how the child's mind learns and even what makes it grow. Just as we are steered in ordinary interaction by our folk psychology, so we are steered in the activity of helping children learn about the world by notions of folk ped-agogy. Watch any mother, any teacher, even any babysitter with a child and you'll be struck by how much of what they do is steered by notions of 'what children's minds are like and how to help them learn,' even though they may not be able to verbalize their pedagogical principles.

From this work on folk psychology and folk pedagogy has grown a new, perhaps even a revolutionary insight. It is this: in theorizing about the practice of education in the class-room (or any other setting, for that matter), you had better take into account the folk theories that those engaged in teaching and learning already have. For any innovations that you, as a 'proper' pedagogical theorist, may wish to introduce will have to compete with, replace, or otherwise modify the folk theories that already guide both teachers and pupils. For example, if you as a pedagogical theorist are convinced that the best learn-ing occurs when the teacher helps lead the pupil to discover generalizations on her own, you are likely to run into an established cultural belief that a teacher is an authority who is supposed to tell the child what the general case is, while the child should be occupy-ing herself with memorizing the particulars. And if you study how most classrooms are conducted, you will often find that most of the teacher's questions to pupils are about particulars that can be answered in a few words or even by 'yes' or 'no.' So your introduc-tion of an innovation in teaching will necessarily involve changing the folk psychological and folk pedagogical theories of teachers – and, to a surprising extent, of pupils as well.

Teaching, in a word, is inevitably based on notions about the nature of the learner's mind. Beliefs and assumptions about teaching, whether in a school or in any other context, are a direct reflection of the beliefs and assumptions the teacher holds about the learner. (Later, we will consider the other side of this coin: how learning is affected by the child's notion of the teacher's mind-set, as when girls come to believe that teachers expect them not to come up with unconventional answers.) Of course, like most deep truths, this one is already well known. Teachers have always tried to adjust their teaching to the backgrounds, abilities, styles and interests of the children they teach. This is important, but it is not quite what we are after. Our purpose, rather, is to explore more general ways in which learners' minds are conventionally thought about, and the pedagogic practices that follow from these ways of thinking about mind. Nor will we stop there, for we also want to offer some reflections on 'consciousness raising' in this setting: what can be accomplished by getting teachers (and students) to think explicitly *about their folk psychological assumptions, in order to bring them out of the shadows of tacit knowledge.*

One way of presenting the general matter of folk psychology and folk pedagogy most starkly is by contrasting our own human species with non-human primates. In our species, children show an astonishingly strong 'predisposition to culture'; they are sensitive to and eager to adopt the folkways they see around them. They show a striking interest in the activity of their parents and peers and with no prompting at all try to imitate what they observe. As for adults, as Kruger and Tomasello insist, there is a uniquely human 'pedagogic disposition' to exploit this tendency, for adults to demonstrate correct performance for the benefit of the learner. One finds these matching tendencies in different forms in all human societies. But note that these imitative and demonstrational dispositions seem scarcely to exist at all in our nearest primate kin, the chimpanzees. Not only do adult chimpanzees not 'teach' their young by demonstrating correct performance, the young for their part seem not to imitate the actions of adults either, at least if we use a sufficiently stringent definition of imitation. If by imitation one means the ability to observe not just the goal achieved but also the means to that achievement, there is little evidence of imitation in chimpanzees raised in the wild and, even more conspicuously, little attempt at teaching. It is very revealing, however, that when a young chimpanzee is raised 'as if' he were a human child, and exposed to the ways of humans, he begins to show more imitative dispositions. The evidence on 'demonstrations' dispositions in adult chimpanzees is much less clear, but such dispositions may also be there in a rudimentary form.

Tomasello, Ratner, and Kruger have suggested that because non-human primates do not naturally attribute beliefs and knowledge to others, they probably do not recognize their presence in themselves. We humans show, tell, or teach someone something only because we first recognize that they don't know, or that what they believe is false. The failure of non human primates to ascribe ignorance or false beliefs to their young may, therefore, explain the absence of pedagogic efforts, for it is only when these states are recognized that we try to correct the deficiency by demonstration, explanation, or discussion. Even the most humanly 'enculturated' chimpanzees show little, if any, of the attribution that leads to instructional activity.

Research on lesser primates shows the same picture. On the basis of their observations of the behavior of vervet monkeys in the wild, Cheney and Seyfarth were led to conclude: 'While monkeys may use abstract concepts and have motives, beliefs, and desires, they ... seem unable to attribute mental states to others: they lack a 'theory of mind.' Work on other species of monkeys reveals similar findings. The general point is clear: assumptions about the mind of the learner underlie attempts at teaching. No ascription of ignorance, no effort to teach.

EXTRACT ONE *continued*

But to say only that human beings understand other minds and try to teach the incompetent is to overlook the varied ways in which teaching occurs in different cultures. The variety is stunning. We need to know much more about this diversity if we are to appreciate the relation between folk psychology and folk pedagogy in different cultural settings.

Understanding this relationship becomes particularly urgent in addressing issues of educational reform. For once we recognize that a teacher's conception of a learner shapes the instruction he or she employs, then equipping teachers (or parents) with the best available theory of the child's mind becomes crucial. And in the process of doing that, we also need to provide teachers with some insight about their own folk theories that guide their teaching.

Folk pedagogies, for example, reflect a variety of assumptions about children: they may be seen as willful and needing correction; as innocent and to be protected from a vulgar society; as needing skills to be developed only through practice; as empty vessels to be filled with knowledge that only adults can provide; as egocentric and in need of socialization. Folk beliefs of this kind, whether expressed by laypeople or by 'experts,' badly want some 'deconstructing' if their implications are to be appreciated. For whether these views are 'right' or not, their impact on teaching activities can be enormous.

A culturally oriented cognitive psychology does not dismiss folk psychology as mere superstition, something only for the anthropological connoisseur of quaint folkways. I have long argued that explaining what children do *is not enough; the new agenda is to determine what they* think *they are doing and what their reasons are for doing it. Like new work on children's theories of mind, a cultural approach emphasizes that the child only gradually comes to appreciate that she is acting not directly on 'the world' but on beliefs she holds about that world. This crucial shift from naive realism to an understanding of the role of beliefs, occurring in the early school years, is probably never complete. But once it starts, there is often a corresponding shift in what teachers can do to help children. With the shift, for example, children can take on more responsibilities for their own learning and thinking. They can begin to 'think about their thinking' as well as about 'the world.' It is not surprising, then, that achievement testers have become increasingly concerned not just with what children* know *but with how they think they came by their knowledge. It is as Howard Gardner puts it in* The Unschooled Mind: *'We must place ourselves inside the heads of our students and try to understand as far as possible the sources and strengths of their conceptions'.*

Stated boldly, the emerging thesis is that educational practices in classrooms are premised on a set of folk beliefs about learners' minds, some of which may have worked advertently toward or inadvertently against the child's own welfare. They need to be made explicit and to be reexamined. Different approaches to learning and different forms of instruction – from imitation, to instruction, to discovery, to collaboration – reflect differing beliefs and assumptions about the learner – from actor, to knower, to private experiencer, to collaborative thinker. What higher primates lack and humans continue to evolve is a set of beliefs about the mind. These beliefs, in turn, alter beliefs about the sources and communicability of thought and action. Advances in how we go about understanding children's minds are, then, a prerequisite to any improvement in pedagogy.

Obviously, all this involves much more than learners' minds. Young learners are people in families and communities, struggling to reconcile their desires, beliefs, and goals with the world around them. Our concern may be principally cognitive, relating to the acquisition and uses of knowledge, but we do not mean to restrict our focus to the so-called 'rational' mind. Egan reminds us that 'Apollo without Dionysus may indeed be a well informed, good citizen, but he's a dull fellow. He may even be "cultured," in the sense one often gets from traditionalist writings in education. … But without Dionysus he will never make and remake a culture.' Although our discussion of folk psychology and folk pedagogy has emphasized 'teaching and learning' in the conventional sense, we could as easily have emphasized other aspects of the human spirit, ones equally important for educational practice, like folk conceptions of desire, intention, meaning, or even 'mastery.' But even the notion of 'knowledge' is not as peacefully Apollonian as all that.

Consider for example the issue of what knowledge is, where it comes from, how we come by it. These are also matters that have deep cultural roots. To begin with, take the distinction between knowing something concretely and in particular and knowing it as an exemplar of some general rule. Arithmetic addition and multiplication provide a stunning example. Somebody, say, has just learned a concrete arithmetic fact. What does it mean to grasp a 'fact' of multiplication, and how does that differ from the idea that multiplication is simply repeated addition, something you already 'know'? Well, for one thing, it means that you can derive the unknown from the known. That is a pretty heady notion about knowledge, one that might even delight the action-minded Dionysus.

In some much deeper sense, grasping something abstractly is a start toward appreciating that seemingly complicated knowledge can often be derivationally reduced to simpler forms of knowledge that you already possess. The Ellery Queen mystery stories used to include a note inserted on a crucial page in the text telling the reader that he or she now had all the knowledge necessary to solve the crime. Suppose one announced in class after the children had learned multiplication that they now had enough knowledge to understand something called 'logarithms,' special kinds of numbers that simply bore the names '1,' '2,' '3,' '4,' and '5,' and that they ought to be able to figure out what these logarithm names 'mean' from three examples, each example being a series that bore those names. The first series is 2, 4, 8, 16, 32; the second series 3, 9, 27, 81, 243, and the third series 1, 10, 100, 1,000, 10,000, 100,000. The numbers in each series correspond to the logarithmic names 1, 2, 3, 4, and 5. But how can 8 be called '3,' and so too 27 and 1,000? Not only do children 'discover' (or invent) the idea of an exponent or power, but they also discover/invent the idea of exponents to some base; that 2 to the third power is 8, that 3 to the third power is 27, and that 10 to the third power is 1,000. Once children (say around age ten) have gone through that experience, their conception of mathematical knowledge as 'derivational' will be forever altered; they will grasp that once you know addition and know that addition can be repeated different numbers of times to make multiplication, you already know what logarithms are. All you need to determine is the 'base.'

Or if that is too 'mathematical,' you can try getting children to act out Little Red Riding Hood, first as a class drama with everybody having a part, then by actors chosen to represent the main characters to an audience, and finally as a story to be told or read by a storyteller to a group. How do they differ? The moment some child informs you that in the first instance there are only actors and no audience, but in the second there are both, the class will be off and running into a discussion of 'drama' to match Victor Turner for excitement. As with the previous example, you will have led children to recognize that they know far more than they thought they ever knew, but that they have to 'think about it' to know what they know. And that, after all, was what the Renaissance and the Age of Reason were all about! But to teach and learn that way means that you have adopted a new theory of mind.

Or take the issue of where you get knowledge, an equally profound matter. Children usually begin by assuming that the teacher has the knowledge and passes it on to the class. Under appropriate conditions, they soon learn that others in the class might have knowledge too, and that it can be shared. (Of course they know this from the start, but only about such matters as where things are to be found.) In this second phase, knowledge exists in the group – but inertly in the group. What about group discussion as a way of creating knowledge rather than merely finding who has what knowledge? And there is even one step beyond that, one of the most profound aspects of human knowledge. If nobody in the group 'knows' the answer, where do you go to 'find things out'? This is the leap into culture as a warehouse, a toolhouse, or whatever. There are things known by each individual (more than each realizes); more still is known by the group or is discoverable by discussion within the group; and much more still is stored somewhere else – in the 'culture,' say, in the heads of more knowledgeable people, in directories, books, maps, and so forth. Virtually by definition, nobody in a culture knows all there is to know about it. So what do we do when we get stuck? And what are the problems we run into in getting the knowledge we need? Start answering that question and you are on the high road toward understanding what a culture is. In no time at all, some kid will begin to recognize that knowledge is power, or that it is a form of wealth, or that it is a safety net.

So let us consider more closely, then, some alternative conceptions about the minds of learners commonly held by educational theorists, teachers, and ultimately by children themselves. For these are what may determine the educational practices that take place in classrooms in different cultural contexts.

Knowledge, skills and pedagogy

Some of what Bruner writes about here takes us back to the questions with which we opened the chapter. Let us start with Bruner's assertion that *children usually begin by assuming that the teacher has the knowledge and passes it on to the class* (Bruner, 1996, page 52). Is this what you thought about teaching? Is it what you still think? This could be considered to be one of the folk views of pedagogy to which Bruner was referring. This is an important point, and is one we need you to really get to grips with. Bruner helps with this by observing that folk pedagogies make a number of assumptions about children.

1. They are wilful and need correction.

2. They are innocent and need protecting from a vulgar society.

3. They need skills to be developed only through practice.

4. They are empty vessels to be filled with knowledge.

5. They are egocentric and in need of socialisation.

These can be divided into two groups: one group is concerned with social aspects, the other with learning *per se*. Into the first group items 1,2 and 5 can be placed, and into the second group items 3 and 4. Let us consider item 4 first.

The folk pedagogy assumption that children are like empty vessels which need to be filled with knowledge is a commonly-held one. We also know that it is quite regularly held by beginning teachers too, and that they tend to:

> ...*think of teaching as a simple and straightforward activity that results in learning. Teachers teach; students learn. Teaching is telling. Learning is listening to what the teacher says and giving it back more or less intact.*
> (Feiman-Nemser et al., 1987, page 3)

The consequence of this assumption is a simple transmissional view of knowledge, and is one which is becoming increasingly unrecognisable in schools for the twenty-first century. Teaching is much more than telling.

Thinking about the complexities of teaching and learning in this way makes us consider the place of knowledge in this. Many views of learning often encompass aspects of knowledge. Indeed, a folk view of this might be stated as being 'learners learn, and what they learn is knowledge'. But this raises another question which will be central to our discussion: what is knowledge? Bruner asks this question by requesting us to consider *the issue of what knowledge is, where it comes from, and how we come by it* (Bruner, 1996, page 50). He uses the example of addition, and how multiplication can be thought of as repeated addition, and that understanding this means *you can derive the unknown from the known. This is a pretty heady notion about knowledge* (page 51). Bruner also asks questions concerning the mind. He observes that folk psychology has a view as *what children's minds are like and how to help them to learn* (Bruner, 1996, page 47). This is a key matter for you to consider as a beginning teacher.

REFLECTIVE EXERCISE

Think of something you know. What is it? How does it manifest itself? How did you learn it?

What you thought about here is significant. Let us assume that one reader thought that they know that the capital of France is Paris. They know it, because someone at school when they were very young taught it to them – in primary school, maybe. This could be one of those pieces of knowledge which they cannot recall how they first knew it. But since being told this fact at primary school, this piece of knowledge has become overlaid with others: the school trip when they were 14 where they first sampled a glass of wine; a romantic trip with a partner; a long weekend on a Eurostar special offer; the smell of fresh bread from a baker in the Marais district; and so on. All knowledge, all acquired differently.

Another reader may have thought 'I know how to play the piano'. This was achieved by years of lessons with Mrs Scroggins (who smelled of fish), by hours of practice on Grandma's old piano, of examinations in drafty village halls, of school concerts playing three minutes of Mozart to rapturous parental applause. Again, all knowledge.

But to know Paris is the capital of France is different from knowing how to play the piano. As a teacher you can tell someone that Paris is the French capital in a few seconds, you do not need to go there to do it. You cannot 'tell' someone how to play the piano, they actually have to have a go for themselves.

In pedagogic terms, this discussion links to thinking about what learning is. As Bruner observes, *if you ... are convinced that the best learning occurs when the teacher helps lead the pupil to discover generalisations on their own, then you are likely to run into an established cultural belief that the teacher is an authority who is supposed to tell the child what the general case is* (Bruner, 1996, page 46). This cultural belief is, commonly, not that of education professionals, but of the 'folk pedagogy' of the laity.

Let us take a key example of this, which Bruner tackles in a few sentences: *if you study how most classrooms are conducted, you will often find that most of the teacher's questions to pupils are about particulars that can be answered in a few words or even by 'yes' and 'no'* (page 46). Questioning is a key theme in education, and we know that the sorts of questioning that Bruner is referring to does commonly take place, and that much teacher questioning involves low-level engagement, mainly recall (Black and Wiliam, 1998). We know too that:

> Questioning lies at the heart of learning and teaching. Research over many decades has shown that some teachers and practitioners ask too many closed and unproductive questions. Learning is enhanced when we ask fewer but better questions, and seek better answers...

> (DfES, 2004, page 61)

This is all well known, but to develop your questioning skills you will need to be encouraged by your mentors to avoid asking short-answer, recall-based questions, to allow wait-time, and to involve all the pupils, not just those itching to be fastest to put their hands up. This involves changing a series of folk views of questioning, including, possibly, your own, and that of the pupils. In Bruner's terms, what we are doing here is getting you to *think explicitly about [your] folk psychological assumptions in order to bring them out of the shadows of tacit knowledge* (page 47). And that is a key part of teacher training. A lot of teacher knowledge is tacit, and undertaking training to be a teacher involves unpicking these elements, and in making the invisible visible.

The third item on Bruner's list concerned skills, and how folk pedagogy assumes that skills are things which can be developed through practice. Skills vary from subject to subject to subject in the secondary school, and it will be worth thinking about the skills which are involved in the learning of your subject. They may be like the piano-playing example above, where repeated practice is needed; they could be sporting, where training is involved; or they could be cognitive skills, such as those involved in mental arithmetic.

The need for skills changes over time. The skills needed to find out things from the internet are different from the skills required to find information in a library. The pupils we are

REFLECTIVE EXERCISE

Think of a skill involved in your subject. Who teaches it? How is it learned? What is it needed for?

teaching now will need skills we do not even know about for their future lives. This brings us back to another question from the beginning of this section, 'Where is knowledge?'. This may seem like an odd question, but it is important in the way we think about teaching and learning. Let us turn to investigating it now.

Answers to all of these questions lead to different views on the location of knowledge.

REFLECTIVE EXERCISE

When a football team plays, where is the knowledge?

When a rock band performs, where is the knowledge?

When you look something up on the internet, where is the knowledge?

Let us think about what this means from a classroom perspective. Bruner asks *what about class discussion as a way of creating knowledge…?* (page 52). This takes us into the area of the social construction of knowledge, and Bruner is a key figure in the field of social constructivism. In this way of thinking, knowledge arises from the interactions between people. It is not a case that one person 'owns' the knowledge and passes it on to others, but that new knowledge comes from the social interactions between the participants. One of Bruner's key contributions with regard to this is the notion of *scaffolding* (Wood et al., 1976). Scaffolding is where the teacher guides the pupils through the learning process by providing appropriate levels of support, and gradually withdrawing this support as the learners grow in confidence. As Bruner observes, if you do this as a teacher, you will have *adopted a new theory of mind*. This is quite important. Working in groups is, in Bruner's terms, about the creation of knowledge. Working in this way facilitates learning for the pupils in your classes. It is not about them talking about the knowledge they have 'received' from you, but about them being co-creators of new knowledge. Notice that this can be new knowledge for the pupils, but it might not be new knowledge for humanity. By doing this the pupils have become active agents in the creation of their own new forms of knowledge, they are not simply passive recipients of what is being handed to them. They are not the empty vessels we referred to earlier. The current curriculum emphasis on creativity springs from this type of thinking. We will be considering this further in Chapter 7.

The 'where is knowledge' question that we asked has further implications for the way we think about learning. Sfard (1998) writes of two metaphors for learning, the acquisition metaphor and the participation metaphor. In the acquisition metaphor, the focus of attention is on acquiring knowledge. This, as Sfard observes, *brings to mind the activity of accumulating material goods* (Sfard, 1998, page 5). So knowledge becomes like a commodity, and can be owned:

Since the time of Piaget and Vygotsky, the growth of knowledge in the process of learning has been analysed in terms of concept development. Concepts are to be understood as basic units of knowledge that can be accumulated, gradually refined, and combined to form ever richer cognitive structures.

(Sfard, 1998, page 5)

The participation metaphor, on the other hand, involves moving from acquiring, to taking part, *the permanence of having gives way to the constant flux of doing* (Sfard, 1998, page 6). This marks a significant change in the ways we can think about learning and knowledge. In your subjects there are likely to be aspects of knowledge which are acquired, and those which are participatory.

REFLECTIVE EXERCISE

Think about knowledge in your subject. What knowledge do the pupils need to acquire? How will they do this? What is your role in it?

What participatory knowledge is there in your subject? How do you foster this? What opportunities do you give for participation?

In asking you to challenge your own thinking about pedagogy, we are building on Bruner's notion that *beliefs and assumptions about teaching are a direct reflection of the beliefs and assumptions the teacher holds about the learner*. What you think about yourself, your identity as a teacher and a representative of a particular subject culture will all come into play here. These elements, all discussed in Chapter 1, exert a strong influence on your pedagogical decision-making processes and will determine how you act in the classroom context. In order to challenge these things, you need to think very hard about what teaching and learning in your subject might, or should, involve. These leads us helpfully on to our next extract.

What should teachers know about teaching and learning?

Lee Shulman is an American educational psychologist who has made a considerable contribution to the literature on teaching and pedagogy. One of his key contributions to the field has been the notion of pedagogic content knowledge, which this article delineates.

POINTS TO CONSIDER

What sorts of knowledge does Shulman propose that teachers need?

How are these types of knowledge acquired?

What do you understand by the term 'pedagogical content knowledge'?

Shulman, L (1986) Those who understand: knowledge growth in teaching. Educational Researcher, *15(2): 9–10.*

A perspective on teacher knowledge

As we have begun to probe the complexities of teacher understanding and transmission of content knowledge, the need for a more coherent theoretical framework has become rapidly apparent. What are the domains and categories of content knowledge in the minds of teachers? How, for example, are content knowledge and general pedagogical knowledge related? In which forms are the domains and categories of knowledge represented in the minds of teachers? What are promising ways of enhancing acquisition and development of such knowledge? Because I see these as among the central questions for disciplined inquiry into teacher education, I will now turn to a discussion of some ways of thinking about one particular domain content knowledge in teaching and some of the categories within it.

How might we think about the knowledge that grows in the minds of teachers, with special emphasis on content? I suggest we distinguish among three categories of content knowledge: (a) subject matter content knowledge, (b) pedagogical content knowledge, and (c) curricular knowledge.

Content Knowledge. This refers to the amount and organization of knowledge per se in the mind of the teacher. We already have a number of ways to represent content knowledge: Bloom's cognitive taxonomy, Gagné's varieties of learning, Schwab's distinction between substantive and syntactic structures of knowledge, and Peters' notions that parallel Schwab's.

In the different subject matter areas, the ways of discussing the content structure of knowledge differ. To think properly about content knowledge requires going beyond knowledge of the facts or concepts of a domain. It requires understanding the structures of the subject matter in the manner defined by such scholars as Joseph Schwab. (See his collected essays, 1978.)

For Schwab, the structures of a subject include both the substantive and the syntactic structures. The substantive structures are the variety of ways in which the basic concepts and principles of the discipline are organized to incorporate its facts. The syntactic structure of a discipline is the set of ways in which truth or falsehood, validity or invalidity, are established. When there exist competing claims regarding a given phenomenon, the syntax of a discipline provides the rules for determining which claim has greater warrant. A syntax is like a grammar. It is the set of rules for determining what is legitimate to say in a disciplinary domain and what 'breaks' the rules.

Teachers must not only be capable of defining for students the accepted truths in a domain. They must also be able to explain why a particular proposition is deemed warranted, why it is worth knowing, and how it relates to other propositions, both within the discipline and without, both in theory and in practice.

Thus, the biology teacher must understand that there are a variety of ways of organizing the discipline. Depending on the preferred color of one's BSCS text, biology may be formulated as (a) a science of molecules from which one aggregates up to the rest of the field, explaining living phenomena in terms of the principles of their constituent parts; (b) a science of ecological systems from which one disaggregates down to the smaller units, explaining the activities of individual units by virtue of the larger systems of which they are a part; or (c) a science of biological organisms, those most familiar of analytic units, from whose familiar structures, functions, and interactions one weaves a theory of adaptation. The well-prepared biology teacher will recognize these and alternative forms of organization and the pedagogical grounds for selecting one under some circumstances and others under different circumstances.

The same teacher will also understand the syntax of biology. When competing claims are offered regarding the same biological phenomenon, how has the controversy been adjudicated? How might similar controversies be adjudicated in our own day?

We expect that the subject matter content understanding of the teacher be at least equal to that of his or her lay colleague, the mere subject matter major. The teacher need not only understand that something *is so; the teacher must further understand* why *it is so, on what grounds its warrant can be asserted, and under what circumstances our belief in its justification can be weakened and even denied. Moreover, we expect the teacher to understand why a given topic is particularly central to a discipline whereas another may be somewhat peripheral. This will be important in subsequent pedagogical judgments regarding relative curricular emphasis.*

Pedagogical Content Knowledge. A second kind of content knowledge is pedagogical knowledge, which goes beyond knowledge of subject matter per se to the dimension of subject matter knowledge for teaching. I still speak of content knowledge here, but of the particular form of content knowledge that embodies the aspects of content most germane to its teachability.

Within the category of pedagogical content knowledge I include, for the most regularly taught topics in one's subject area, the most useful forms of representation of those ideas, the most powerful analogies, illustrations, examples, explanations, and demonstrations – in a word, the ways of representing and formulating the subject that make it comprehensible to others. Since there are no single most powerful forms of representation, the teacher must have at hand a veritable armamentarium of alternative forms of representation, some of which derive from research whereas others originate in the wisdom of practice.

Pedagogical content knowledge also includes an understanding of what makes the learning of specific topics easy or difficult: the conceptions and preconceptions that students of different ages and backgrounds bring with them to the learning of those most frequently taught topics and lessons. If those preconceptions are misconceptions, which they so often are, teachers need knowledge of the strategies most likely to be fruitful in reorganizing the understanding of learners, because those learners are unlikely to appear before them as blank slates.

Here, research on teaching and on learning coincide most closely. The study of student misconceptions and their influence on subsequent learning has been among the most fertile topics for cognitive research. We are gathering an ever-growing body of knowl-edge about the misconceptions of students and about the instructional conditions necessary to overcome and transform those initial conceptions. Such research-based knowledge, an important component of the pedagogical understanding of subject matter, should be included at the heart of our definition of needed pedagogical knowledge.

Curricular Knowledge. If we are regularly remiss in not teaching pedagogical knowledge to our students in teacher education programs, we are even more delinquent with respect to the third category of content knowledge, curricular knowledge. The curriculum is repre-sented by the full range of programs designed for the teaching of particular subjects and topics at a given level, the variety of instructional materials available in relation to those pro-grams, and the set of characteristics that serve as both the indications and contraindications for the use of particular curriculum or program materials in particular circumstances.

The curriculum and its associated materials are the materia medica of pedagogy, the phar-macopeia from which the teacher draws those tools of teaching that present or exemplify particular content and remediate or evaluate the adequacy of student accomplishments. We expect the mature physician to understand the full range of treatments available to ameliorate a given disorder, as well as the range of alternatives for particular circum-stances of sensitivity, cost, interaction with other interventions, convenience, safety, or comfort. Similarly, we ought to expect that the mature teacher possesses such under-standings about the curricular alternatives available for instruction.

How many individuals whom we prepare for teaching biology, for example, understand well the materials for that instruction, the alternative texts, software, programs, visual materials, single-concept films, laboratory demonstrations, or 'invitations to enquiry'? Would we trust a physician who did not really understand the alternative ways of dealing with categories of infectious disease, but who knew only one way?

In addition to the knowledge of alternative curriculum materials for a given subject or topic within a grade, there are two additional aspects of curricular knowledge. I would expect a professional teacher to be familiar with the curriculum materials under study by his or her students in other subjects they are studying at the same time.

This lateral curriculum knowledge (appropriate in particular to the work of junior and senior high school teachers) underlies the teacher's ability to relate the content of a given course or lesson to topics or issues being discussed simultaneously in other classes. The vertical equivalent of that curriculum knowledge is familiarity with the topics and issues that have been and will be taught in the same subject area during the preceding and later years in school, and the materials that embody them.

We know that having a good subject knowledge base is important for a teacher, but is that all that is required? Shulman thinks not, and proposes thinking about knowledge in terms of teaching and learning under three headings.

- Content knowledge: this is about what the subject domain is, and the sorts of knowl-edge it contains.

- Pedagogical content knowledge: this concerns the way in which the subject is taught.

- Curricular knowledge: this is concerned with the full range of the curriculum.

Content knowledge

The subject matter for each subject in the secondary school curriculum is delineated by the National Curriculum, and by the examination specification for whichever courses the school has chosen. Within these strictures, there is some flexibility as to what can be taught and learned, particularly at Key Stage 3. We will return to this point when we think about curricular knowledge.

You will all be experts in your subjects, and will know about what Shulman, drawing on the work of Schwab, refers to as substantive and syntactic structures. Shulman observes that this area includes knowing *why a particular proposition is warranted, why it is worth knowing, and how it relates to other propositions.* Pupils will often ask you, 'Why are we doing this?' While this can be a red herring at times, it is useful for you to know the answer, and better still if you can answer it succinctly.

REFLECTIVE EXERCISE

Recall a topic you have taught, or seen taught recently. Consider the following questions.

Why were the pupils learning it?

Why were they learning it this *way?*

What other ways of learning it might there be?

In the section on teaching biology, Shulman discusses ways in which knowledge within the subject can be organised. For non-biology teachers, the important point from this section is to think about what is valued knowledge in your subject, and whether or not it is contested knowledge. This also involves picking out from the whole range of possibilities that which the pupils need to know to progress. The whole field may be complex; it is the job of the teacher to reduce it to bite-size chunks so that learners can understand. To do this, Shulman observes, you will *need not only to understand* that *something is so; the teacher must further understand* why *it is so. Moreover, we expect the teacher to understand why a given topic is particularly central to a discipline whereas another may be somewhat peripheral.* We will return to this in our consideration of curricular knowledge below.

But content knowledge alone is not enough; the teacher also needs what Shulman refers to as pedagogical content knowledge.

Pedagogical content knowledge

Pedagogical content knowledge is the key notion which Shulman propounds. This is concerned with *the subject matter for teaching*. We saw above that you will know what the subject content of what you are teaching should involve. Indeed, a common scenario for beginning teachers is to commence their school experience by working on a sub-component of a particular topic. The subject mentor will tell the trainee what the topic to be covered is, share with them the unit of work, and then the trainee will begin to prepare their own lesson plans from this. It is at this point that pedagogical content knowledge comes into operation. What you will be doing here is to develop your knowledge of

> *... the most useful forms of representation of those ideas, the most powerful analogies, illustrations, examples, explanations, and demonstrations – in a word, the ways of representing and formulating the subject that make it comprehensible to others.*

(Shulman, 1994, page 9)

Shulman goes on to observe that *there are no single most powerful forms of representation*, and so what you, the trainee, need to do is to find out for yourself ways that work for *your* teaching of the topic. Here, there is scope for professional discussion with subject mentors and with other teachers. You need to work out what are the most appropriate ways for you to engage with developing your pedagogical content knowledge. Other teachers will tell you what works for them, but this does not mean it will automatically work for you. As we will go on to consider in Chapter 8, being creative about your pedagogical content knowledge is a key to motivating and inspiring pupils to learn.

Pedagogical content knowledge also involves knowing about what *makes the learning of specific topics easy or difficult*. An important part of this will be the role of pupils' prior knowledge about a subject or topic. What the pupils know already, and what they can do already, are significant pieces of information for you to know before you begin to teach your topic. It is also helpful to know about likely misconceptions, and so you will need to know *strategies most likely to be fruitful in reorganising the understanding of learners*. Again, this is where experienced mentors can help you, but it is not always possible to be forewarned of all such eventualities. You may well be teaching the same topic to two parallel classes, and find that while 9Z have grasped the topic quite readily, some individuals in 9Y are really struggling with it. Developing your pedagogical content knowledge will help you deal with these learning disjunctures as they unfold in realtime in your classes.

As a beginning teacher, you will have many opportunities to develop this type of knowledge. You should try out as many different approaches as possible within your early teaching practices. This is a time for experimentation, trial and, on occasions, error. We are hoping that you will not be relying solely on a 'chalk and talk' approach. Pedagogical content knowledge will help you as you reflect on what seem to be good ways to facilitate your pupils' learning. The important factor of pedagogical content knowledge is that it should make a difference to learning, and it is learning which we want you to foster in your classes.

Intra-subject curricular knowledge

The final area Shulman discusses is curricular knowledge. This is quite a complex area to understand. Shulman discusses a number of aspects of curricular knowledge, including what we can call intra-subject curricular knowledge, and inter-subject curricular knowledge.

Intra-subject curricular knowledge is probably the point of entry for you when you begin to get to grips with teaching your subject. In the first instance you will be reliant on your placement school for much of this information. Referring back to the scenario we explored in our discussions of pedagogical content knowledge, you are likely to be told what topic the subject mentor wants you to teach. In some subjects you will also be told what (Shulman refers to as) the 'instructional materials' for that particular topic are. In other words, this school uses this chapter in this book to teach this topic. You will normally fit into this and continue. But in some subject areas this is not the case. While textbooks are common in, say, mathematics, they are less so in art. Here there may be no texts. The instructional materials could be examples of artists' work, or poems in English, or recordings in music. The teachers themselves can also provide the materials; in PE, for example, it is common for the teacher to demonstrate skill acquisition directly to the learners. As you move to becoming a more experienced teacher, both while you undertake your school placements and beyond your NQT time, Shulman suggests that you need to be developing *understandings about the curricular alternatives for instruction*. In other words, what other materials there are, how else might you teach the topic, and what is the range of possible alternative approaches.

Still within the realm of intra-subject curricular knowledge, it is also appropriate for you to be thinking about why this topic is included in the curriculum. Shulman refers to this as a *set of characteristics that serve as both the indications and contraindications for the use of particular curriculum or programme materials in particular circumstances*. The time for teaching in schools in limited. At Key Stage 3 there is often some leeway within the programme of study as to what topics can be included. The National Curriculum is designed to offer schools the potential to tailor it to meet local circumstances. As the QCDA observes, this will allow:

> ... *more opportunities for schools to adapt the National Curriculum to make the most of their local environment, resources and circumstances to better meet all young people's needs, aptitudes and interests.*

> (QCDA, 2009, page 4)

What this means in the context of this discussion is that the content of the taught curriculum is not necessarily predetermined. Later on in your career you are likely to be involved in decisions relating to the content of the curriculum at different key stages. You will need to decide what should be included and why. You will need to defend these decisions to senior managers and outside agencies. Remember that in order to teach one thing, you will not have time to teach something else. Getting an approach balance of topics and activities within a subject across a key stage is a skilful decision-making process. The following task asks you to consider some of these key skills with an appropriate mentor.

REFLECTIVE EXERCISE

Focusing on Key Stage 3, ask your mentors why they have included the topics they have in their curriculum planning. Try to find out if there are topics they would like to include but do not have time for. Would you make the same decisions? Are there things you think ought to be included? To what extent have decisions been made by reference to external factors (e.g. National Curriculum documentation)?

Inter-subject curricular knowledge

Inter-subject curricular knowledge is much harder for you to get to grips while you are in the early days of your teaching placements. You may well have done a pupil trail, where you follow a pupil through a day of their timetable in school, as part of your induction to the school. This can be very revealing in terms of the ways pupils experience their schooling. In inter-subject curricular knowledge you will be thinking about how topics in your subject join up with others across the school. Some schools have undertaken a curriculum mapping process, often at key stage 3, to see how topics feature through a range of different subjects. This is a useful way of approaching the joined-up formulation of the key stage experience for pupils. Schools who have undertaken this exercise have found that the results have been revealing. Take, for example, the common Key Stage 3 topic of slavery. This might seem to belong to history, but also has links with:

- geography: the effect of people migrating;
- sociology: the responses of society;
- citizenship: how it affects us today;
- religious education: the moral implications;
- English: stories and poems of the experience;
- art: drawing, pictures, sculptures both about and reflecting the topic;
- music: the origins and songs of the blues;
- and probably a lot more besides.

If all these topics were introduced without careful thought, there are numerous examples of potential repetition. By looking at where the topic is taught in the curriculum map, and adjusting the Key Stage 3 map accordingly, it becomes possible to give coherence across the whole school. We will be considering this issue in more detail in Chapter 8, where we examine notions of cross-curricularity and collaborative approaches to teaching and learning.

REFLECTIVE EXERCISE

Find out if your school has undertaken a curriculum mapping exercise of the type described above. If so:

What was found out?

What actions were taken?

If they have not, then try asking around different subject areas to find out where there might be points of commonality between subjects, A topic like 'measurement', for example, could figure in multiple locations.

Eisner: what education can learn from the arts

In Chapter 1 we drew on the work of Elliot Eisner and introduced the concept of 'teaching as artistry'. We saw how Eisner's application of this metaphor had five main consequences for the development of our teaching. You were urged to apply this metaphor to your own work at this early stage of your career.

Here, we will return to Eisner's more recent work and see how it impacts on some more specific issues related to teaching and learning.

Some of you reading this book will be teachers of arts subjects, others will not. This does not matter at this point. What Eisner has to say in the following extract from *What Education Can Learn From the Arts* is concerned with thinking about teaching and learning more generally.

As you read this extract, think about the following questions in relation to your own specialist teaching area.

POINTS TO CONSIDER

In my subject, where is there more than one answer to a question?

Where is there more than one way to arrive at the answer?

What do we do about this?

How do we differentiate between content and form in my subject?

Is there a role for imagination in my subject?

If so, what is it?

EXTRACT THREE

Eisner, E (2002) Arts and the Creation of Mind. *New Haven, Connecticut: Yale University Press, pp. 196–198.*

Promoting a love affair between the student and his or her work is one of our schools' most important aims

To suggest that education has something to be learned from the arts is to turn topsy-turvy the more typical view that the arts are basically sources of relief, ornamental activities intended to play second fiddle to the core educational subjects. Yet those interested in enhancing the processes of education, both in and out of schools, have much to learn from the arts. Put simply, the arts can serve as a model for teaching the subjects we usually think of as academic.

This chapter describes what art's lessons might be for education in general and indicates why they are important lessons for those who teach and shape educational policy.

One lesson the arts teach is that there can be more than one answer to a question and more than one solution to a problem; variability of outcome is okay. So much of current schooling is predicated on the assumption that success in teaching means getting a class to converge on the single correct answer that exists in the curriculum guide, or in the textbook, or in the teacher's head. The aim of teaching is to get everyone to the same destination and, in our culture, at about the same point in time.

For some of what we teach, but certainly not everything, single correct answers to an array of questions may be a legitimate way to think about some aspects of student performance in a field.

For example, most teachers are not particularly interested in what might be referred to as 'creative spelling.' We want students, and we should want students, to put letters in the right order in the words that they spell, and if a class is given the same set of words to spell, success in teaching spelling means that all children will spell words in exactly the same way. Children need to learn cultural conventions. Spelling is one of them.

Spelling is not alone in this desideratum. Arithmetic is also taught in this manner, though it need not be. Typically, students are taught how to prove the correctness of their arithmetic solutions: if they add, they can subtract to prove their answer; if they subtract, they can add. If they divide, they can multiply; and if they multiply, they can divide. Children in the process are learning the lessons of certainty.

In contrast, the arts teach children that their personal signature is important and that answers to questions and solutions to problems need not be identical. There is, in the arts, more than one interpretation to a musical score, more than one way to describe a painting or a sculpture, more than one appropriate form for a dance performance, more than one meaning for a poetic rendering of a person or a situation. In the arts diversity and variability are made central. This is one lesson that education can learn from the arts.

Another lesson that education can learn from the arts is that the way something is formed matters. We tend in our culture to differentiate between content and form. What is said, for example, is believed to constitute content. How it is said is believed to constitute form. It's all very tidy.

However, what is said cannot be neatly separated from how something is said. Form and content interpenetrate. The way in which something is spoken shapes its meaning; form becomes content. Actors have learned this lesson well. So, too, have poets, painters, and musicians. How a historical episode is described creates a spin that influences readers' views of the episode being rendered. The interpenetration of content and form is a fundamental insight that the arts reveal. That revelation is not limited to the arts; it can be manifest in any activity humans undertake.

What would attention to the relationship of form and content mean in the teaching of mathematics? How would it play out in the social studies? What would it mean in any of the sciences? Addressing such issues, when one digs deep enough, brings us into epistemological considerations. Attention to such matters would help students understand the sources of our experience, how the ways in which a form is crafted affects our experience and, therefore, how we relate to what we pay attention to.

In the arts and humanities, the implications of the content-form relationship are rather transparent. The 'shape' of a poem matters. So, too, does the form-content relationship matter in all the other arts. But what does the form-content relationship mean in fields not usually regarded as belonging to the arts or the humanities? This question is not an easy one to answer, but it is one that ought to be on the intellectual agenda of those who design curricula and teach students. In fact, it may very well be that the impact of form-content relationships on the student's experience influences his or her inclination to pursue the ideas represented in a particular field of study.

Another lesson that the arts can teach education is the importance of imagination and, as intimated earlier, of refining and using the sensibilities. In the arts, imagination is given license to fly. In many – perhaps most – academic fields, reality, so to speak, imposes its factual face. Little time and attention are given to matters of imagination. Yet inventive scholarship depends upon imagination, not to mention the delights that imaginative processes make possible. In schools we tend to emphasize facticity, correctness, linearity, concreteness. We tend to underestimate and underplay those imaginative processes that are so characteristic of the cognitive life of preschool and even primary-school children. We often fail to nurture a human capacity that is absolutely central to our cultural development.

This reading opens up some of the greatest differences between subject areas. For some subjects, the personal response is central to the domain; for others the 'lessons of certainty' are more important. One of Eisner's points relates directly to the homogeneity of responses: *the aim of teaching is to get everyone to the same destination.* Mixed-ability teaching, and its merits and problems, are hot topics in education.

What are your views about the issue of mixed-ability groups?

Is your subject best taught in mixed-ability groupings, or in streamed or set classes?

Does everyone agree?

What about other subjects? Try asking teachers of, say, mathematics, English, art, PE. Do you get different answers?

What do your subject and professional mentors think? Do they agree?

Eisner challenges us to think about how we arrive at answers to these questions and, in particular, how the responses of individual teachers can vary – within and across subjects. He uses the example of arithmetic, often thought of as an area where certainty is important. But even here, this emphasis on certainty can be mediated or mitigated by a slightly different pedagogical approach. For example, at some schools the mathematics teachers now do not mark some Key Stage 3 work with the typical ticks and crosses. Instead, at the end they will write 'You got six out of ten of these sums right'. The pupil's task is to find out which were right and which were wrong. This re-engages the pupil in their work and could also enable them to work jointly to see how others arrived at their answers. In this example, the personal response, although maintaining the centrality of right answers, is mediated through the understanding of the individual pupils and their collaborative work.

On a different level, it encourages the pupils to revisit their work, and not simply think that they can, or can not,do the homework task.

Eisner notes differences between form and content. He observes that *the interpenetration of content and form is a fundamental insight that the arts reveal*. This can be seen in different ways across many topics in schools. For example, if in a science lesson the results of writing up an experiment are deemed to constitute worthwhile scientific knowledge, what does this say about those pupils who have understood, but are lacklustre in their enthusiasm for writing up? The form of the knowledge need not take precedence over its content. Eisner's approach in this extract is to try to connect the learner to the learning. Ways in which these connections can be achieved will vary between subjects, but we are aware that for some pupils we will need to intervene and make these types of connections for them within their learning.

Eisner writes of the role of imagination, and this is a key area which we shall revisit in Chapter 7 when we consider the role creativity can play in teaching and learning. But it is important to think about how this affects the way you teach and the ways that pupils learn.

Conclusion

This chapter has looked at teaching and learning, and asked you to think about a range of topics. We hope that you will have moved away from the 'empty vessels' view (if you ever held it), and have thought about the complexities of learning which the classes you teach will manifest. Bruner challenges us to think about views of mind and knowledge, and to question what our views of teaching, learning and pedagogy are based upon. Shulman introduces us to the complex notion of pedagogical content knowledge, and of how teachers need to think not about what topics we will teach, and why they are important, but also about what tools we need to bring to the teaching process. Finally, Eisner has helped us think about the role of the learner in constructing and participating in the creation of knowledge, and how the learner needs to be engaged and active in this process.

These are complex themes, and ones which you will doubtless revisit many times over your teaching career. Pedagogy is not straightforward. There is not usually an 'only do it this way' solution to educational problems. It is probably best to be wary of anyone who says there is. Trainee teachers often say, 'Tell me what to do, and I'll do it'. Hopefully the readings in this chapter will have challenged this simplistic perspective of learning to teach. There is a metacognitive dimension to this. You are a learner in this process, the 'self' which Eisner implies in his writing, and so you need to be thinking about the ways in which you can use your imagination to develop appropriate teaching and learning strategies for the classes you are teaching now, and the ones you will be teaching in the future.

C   H   A   P   T   E   R   S   U   M   M   A   R   Y

In this chapter we have discussed the nature of teaching and learning, and thought about the impact that the one has on the other. We have discussed knowledge, and considered how there is knowledge attached to subjects, as well as to the important notion of pedagogic content knowledge. The notion of curriculum has been discussed, and we have thought about how this manifests itself in schools. Finally we have considered the very nature of teaching itself, and asked what it is that is going on during teaching and learning encounters.

REFERENCES

Black, P and Wiliam, D (1998) Assessment and classroom learning. *Assessment in Education*, 5(1): 68.

Bruner, J (1996) *The Culture of Education*. Cambridge, MA: Harvard University Press.

DfES (2004) *Excellence and Enjoyment: Creating a learning Culture – Conditions for Learning*. London: DfES.

Eisner, E (2002) What education can learn from the arts. In *Arts and the Creation of Mind*, chapter 8. New Haven: Yale University Press.

Feiman-Nemser, S, Williamson McDiarmid, G, Melnick, SL and Parker, M (1987) *Changing beginning teachers' conceptions: a description of an introductory teacher education course*. Paper presented at the annual meeting of the American Educational Research Association, Washington, DC, 20–24 April.

QCDA (2009) *The 11–19 curriculum – From implementation to development*. London: QCDA.

Sfard, A (1998) On two metaphors for learning and the dangers of choosing just one. *Educational Researcher*, 27(2): 4–13.

Shulman, L (1994) Those who Understand: Knowledge growth in Teaching. *Educational Researcher*, 15(2): 4–14.

Wood, D, Bruner, J and Ross, G (1976) The role of tutoring in problem solving. *Journal of Child Psychology and Psychiatry*, 17: 89–100.

Chapter 3
Developing your classroom practice

CHAPTER OBJECTIVES

By the end of this chapter you should have:
- examined notions of teachers' professional knowledge and how this affects the process of learning to become a teacher;
- explored models of positive behaviour management within the classroom and its various associated components from theoretic and practical perspectives;
- considered how group work can be organised and used within your classroom;
- developed a firm grasp of the interlinking nature of educational theory and practice in your work as a trainee teacher.

Q Standards: Q7, Q8, Q9, Q10, Q25, Q29.

In the previous chapter we considered teaching and learning, and what various commentators have said with regard to these important topics. We now turn to a consideration of what it is that you will be doing in the classroom, both from theoretical and practice perspectives. The way in which you will enact the processes of teaching and learning involves the combination of a number of factors. These include:

- the way you think pupils learn;

- the way you think learning should be organised;

- the way you think your pupils respond;

- how you organise your teaching;

- how you structure your teaching;

- how you organise your classroom;

- how you organise the pupils within your classroom;

- your views on interpersonal relationships;

- your views on discipline;

- your values within your subject;

- your values within school;

- your teaching style;

- your mentor's teaching style;

- the way the school expects you to organise things;

- the National Curriculum and examination specifications.

We will investigate a number of these areas in this chapter. Let us begin by thinking about what it is that you need to know to be a teacher. We looked at Shulman's notion of pedagogic content knowledge in the last chapter, so we will begin this one by branching out somewhat from this idea. The first extract we shall be looking at is by Christopher Winch. Christopher Winch is an academic and writer on education matters, with a particular interest in the philosophy of education and the nature of professional expertise. The extract we will be investigating is from his 2004 publication *What do Teachers Need To Know about Teaching? A critical examination of the occupational knowledge of teachers* (Winch, 2004).

As you read the extract, think about the following questions.

- What does it mean to be professional?

- What do I know that makes me a teacher?

- Are there things I do not know that I think I should know?

- What does society think of the role of the teacher?

- How does one become a teacher?

EXTRACT ONE

Winch, C (2004) What do teachers need to know about teaching? A critical examination of the occupational knowledge of teachers. **British Journal of Educational Studies,** *52 (2): 185–187.*

How do teachers fit into these definitions of professionalism?

There is no coherent definition of professionalism that can decisively distinguish some occupations from others on the grounds of knowledge, skill or ethical commitment. Professions are those occupational groups that have succeeded in getting themselves called 'professions' by dint of political action as much as by any intrinsic features of their occupational knowledge. But this leaves us with a problem – what is the most useful categorisation of the teacher?

Why do teachers not fit comfortably into conventional definitions of the professions?

1 There are no well-established forms of applied theoretical, as opposed to practical knowledge associated with successful pedagogy

If there is no distinctive theoretical pedagogic knowledge, one important epistemic claim to professionalism, based on the first criterion, fails, Teachers do have a body of subject knowledge (which is not the same as knowledge of what should be taught,

---

which, arguably, is part of the normative theory of teaching), which grows less distinctive as society becomes better educated. Teachers in secondary and higher education have specialised subject knowledge which, because of the application, ability and time that it takes to acquire, puts them in a distinctive position relative to teachers of younger children. However, there is no concomitant growth of specialised pedagogic knowledge alongside the growth of specialist subject knowledge. Arguably, the contrary is the case: the complicated nature of learning and class management with young children makes the practical pedagogic task at that age much more demanding to acquire. I do not wish to argue that there could be no applied theoretical pedagogical knowledge, but rather that at present no universally recognised such body of knowledge exists.

2 There are no distinct ethical elements to the work of teachers

It is sometimes claimed that being a moral exemplar is the most important role that a teacher has (Carr, 2000). This claim puts teachers on a par, for example, with church functionaries. In this sense, teaching is a vocation whether or not it is a profession (Carr, 2003, ch. 3). How far one should take being a moral exemplar as a defining characteristic of teaching is questionable. One of the aims of education is arguably the development of practical moral knowledge, but it is difficult to maintain that this is the sole aim since all occupations have a moral dimension, which includes development of the virtues associated with that profession. These include technical virtues associated with the successful practice of technique and occupational virtues associated with the standing of an occupation within society (Winch, 2002). These are not virtues specific to occupations, but virtues that are exercised within these occupations acquire a particular texture within that occupational context. For example, both soldiering and teaching require courage, but it is a different variant of courage in each case. In fact, school teaching, since it is not a preparation of young people for any particular occupation or way of life, arguably lacks the operational occupational context that gives practical moral education its immediacy and purpose (Kerschensteiner, 1968).

3 Teaching tends to have relatively weakly developed forms of occupational closure and defence of its interests.

This is partly due to the sheer weight of numbers of teachers, but is also due to the often transitory nature of their careers. Women, in particular, because of family responsibilities, often move in and out of the teaching workforce, often on a temporary or casual basis (Gallie et al., 1998). In addition, the different outlooks on their work and different interests that different categories of teachers have, mean that it is very difficult for them to form self-governing bodies like guilds to regulate their affairs with other sectors of society and the state. As already pointed out, the state usually takes a very active role in regulating the supply and conduct of teachers, although in the UK it is increasingly the case that occupational organisations such as the General Teaching Council, which has significant teacher representation and, indeed, the teaching unions, are playing a more active role in these matters.

Even if we could satisfactorily define professions epistemically, ethically, politically or through a combination of these criteria, it is far from clear that at the present time, teaching would convincingly qualify on any of these grounds.

There are a lot of complex issues in this article. Winch begins with this provocative statement, *There is no consensus on what kind of occupation teaching is.* We know that teaching involves a wide variety of activities, and that being a teacher is complex. What decisions do you make during the course of your teaching day? Winch puts it like this:

> *There are, one might say, some educational decisions that properly belong to teachers and others that belong to society or the state. To say that teachers are competent to make their own judgements does not answer the question about the proper scope of those judgements. Do they concern pedagogy, assessment, the curriculum or the aims of education?*

> (Winch, 2004, page 180)

There are clear divisions here between the everyday decisions you will be making in the classroom and the bigger-issue questions of the role of education and what its aims should be.

REFLECTIVE EXERCISE

Do you ever step back and ask yourself these 'big picture' questions? One day, we hope, you will be in a senior position in a school. You may need to then. What do you think about them now?

The answers you give to these questions will be governed and informed by a number of factors, many of which will be based on your own context and personal understanding (or 'subjectivity' as we discussed in Chapter 1). As Winch observes, over the past 30 years the situation in the United Kingdom has changed very significantly. Some older teachers look back wistfully to a time when the only legal requirements of schools were to take registers and teach religious education. This is definitely not the case for you. The nature of what it is to be a professional is the framework Winch uses for starting a discussion concerning these issues. Let us consider some aspects of this too.

Teachers and their professional knowledge

Our discussions of Shulman's notion of pedagogical content knowledge (Shulman, 1986) in the previous chapter fell very much into the category of teacher professional knowledge. You will be, or have been, undertaking a course of professional training in order to become a teacher. This includes working towards and obtaining qualified teacher status, and this involves you in the process of practising teaching. There is no other way. One thing that you will quickly find out is that which Winch refers to when he asks *whether teachers' knowledge is systematic on the one hand and whether it is true on the other, i.e. whether it really is knowledge rather than opinion* (page 181). Pedagogy is sometimes referred to as the art and science of teaching, and herein is the problem. There is no simple 'do *x*, and *y* will happen' causality in teaching. Neither is it consistent. Your mentor may visibly succeed at *x*, but you do not. Another teacher may say to you, 'Do it this way, it always works for me', you try it, and it fails. Teaching style or pedagogy can be a matter of personality. As Winch later observes, *it is, therefore, difficult to maintain 'professional knowledge' as a distinct category with sharp boundaries.*

Winch's notion of 'functional competence' relates closely to the competency statements within the Q Standards. These are agreed national standards which you need to pass in order to enter the profession, but, as you have probably realised, that does not mean the end of your engagement with learning to teach. A good way of looking at gaining QTS is that you are ready to begin to teach, not that you have already mastered it all.

The notion of there being a moral dimension to teaching is one which is hard to argue. We know about the important aspects of safeguarding, but there are deeper implications too. You will be expected to act in a moral way. Some would argue that there is no such thing as an 'off-duty teacher'. How you behave out of school matters, as does how you act when in school. But it also means how you conduct discussions with pupils. Society expects its teachers to act in a moral fashion, and you will be aware of many of the issues concerning this.

In the section on professional closure, Winch argues that *teaching in the United Kingdom has only some of the characteristics of a profession, the main omissions being the absence of full self-regulation, full state recognition and, in some cases, the lack of degree-level entry qualifications* (page 185). The history of teaching in this country is bound up in the early days with the teaching practices of the public schools, where the tradition was to go to such a school, then on to Oxford or Cambridge for a degree, then back to a public school to teach, with no training in pedagogy in between. Today, there is still no statutory regulation relating to teachers working within independent schools. Indeed, there is a whole area of political opinion which states teachers do not need QTS, or much training. You will probably hear sentiments like these in social circles outside schools.

While Winch does not cite Shulman directly, nonetheless the notion of pedagogic content knowledge can be detected in a number of places; for example, *Teachers do have a body of subject knowledge (which is not the same as knowledge of what should be taught ...).* He also acknowledges that *at present no universally recognised such body of knowledge exists* (page 186). This, allied to the downplaying of learning theory in day-to-day teaching, and the fact that some established teachers tend to put on a show of being anti-theoretical, means that there is a problem with establishing such a body of knowledge. Winch concludes this extract by observing the issues associated with teachers forming self-governing bodies, and this is certainly the case.

What we can take from Winch's arguments are that the notion of professionalism is itself a challenged construct, and that within this teaching has a complex series of knowledge sets with which practitioners need to come to grips.

Positive approaches to behaviour management

It is to one of the knowledge sets which is normally of major concern to both beginning and established teachers that we now turn. This is the issue of behaviour management. As Bill Rogers, one of the gurus of behaviour management notes:

Effective behaviour management is essential to the smooth running of a school and in the creation of an environment where everyone's rights and responsibilities are addressed. A balance between fundamental rights and responsibilities is at the heart of behaviour management and discipline issues in schools.

(Rogers 2007, page 5)

This can be a hard balancing act for beginning and new teachers. The extract that we will be reading for this section of the chapter is by Jo Crozier. Jo is a noted academic and author, who has researched the experience of disaffected pupils. She has also investigated gender issues with relation to school disaffection. The extract we shall be using is entitled 'Positive Approaches to Supporting Pupil Behaviour', and comes from the 2007 publication *Preparing to Teach in Secondary Schools: A student teacher's guide to professional issues in secondary education* (Brooks et al., 2007).

POINTS TO CONSIDER

As you read the extract, think about the following questions.

What learning theories are discussed?

How do they match with what you think about learning?

How do the techniques described compare with what you have seen in schools?

Does your school have a coherent approach to behaviour management?

If so, what is it?

What new approaches are suggested here that you could try in your own teaching?

EXTRACT TWO

Brooks, V, Abbott, I and Bills, L (2004) *Preparing to teach in secondary schools: a student teacher's guide to professional issues in secondary education.* Buckingham: Open University Press, pp. 144–146.

A for Antecedent; B for Behaviour; C for Consequences.

Changing behaviour may involve changing the antecedents (e.g. reorganizing seating arrangements), observing precisely the frequency and context of the behaviour and looking at what reinforces it. To increase the incidence of good behaviour, the teacher needs to notice and respond to this, while unwanted behaviours should be dealt with by use of sanctions but not rewarded by lots of attention.

Many schools have adopted whole school approaches such as Assertive Discipline or Discipline for Learning as a main method of behaviour management. These programmes seek to enable teachers to respond schematically to behaviours with a clear tariff of responses. Within the classroom a discipline plan allows for clear rules that are taught to the pupils, positive recognition of pupils for following the rules, and a system of consequences for not following the rules. Much effective behaviour change has been achieved by these approaches – not least because they are accompanied by training of all the staff and support staff, the development of a coherent policy and consistency in application of the approach.

There are some concerns that arise with this approach – do the pupils internalize the better behaviour or is it bound to the context? For some it works well. Better behaviour enables better learning, so it is possible that the passing of time, the better educational achievement and consequent improvement in self-esteem will enable some pupils to pass through difficult periods. Others, especially some who are having a difficult time outside school, may need approaches that give them more space to look at feelings.

Cognitive approaches

A further set of theories attaches more importance to the child's experience and to understanding its impact on behaviour. Cognitivists believe that young people's perceptions, their understanding of a situation, their emotional state, the stage of their development and the context all impact on their behaviour. Interventions are targeted at helping them think through irrational, distorted or impulsive responses. Pupils with behavioural problems may not have the cognitive skills they need for appropriate interactions with their peers or with teachers and other staff. Problem-solving training and social learning approaches can help pupils develop new behaviours.

How people feel about themselves determines their self-esteem. Self-esteem plays a significant part in the ability of pupils to be effective learners and pupils with low self-esteem are vulnerable to failure and to criticism. A young person with high self-esteem can take risks in their learning and in their relationships. Low self-esteem means playing very safe and avoiding trying out new things. There are ways in which teachers can help protect and develop the self-esteem of vulnerable pupils.

Supporting self-esteem:

- Learn names and use them;
- Use praise – specific and personal;
- Reprimand the behaviour, not the person;
- Repair the relationship;
- Apologise if you are wrong;
- Look after your own self-esteem;
- Develop sensitive practices – for example, let pupils choose whether they read aloud;
- Don't show pupils up by making comparisons and/or mocking them.

Figure 3.1 Supporting self-esteem

The ecosystemic model is based on systems theory, which sees the school as part of interconnected systems, each part influenced by change in the other parts. Porter (2000) characterizes this as one of the 'democratic' theories. These look at young people and teachers as equal actors in the teaching and learning enterprise and as each having rights to have their needs met, albeit in different roles. Relationships lie at the heart of these theories, and the emotional needs of participants in learning are included in the framework. Central to the ecosystemic model is the idea that different people have different understandings of the same events and that any event may be subject to various interpretations. Some interpretations are more useful to enabling progress than others.

EXTRACT TWO *continued*

To change the situation, we need to look at where it is stuck and seek ways of under-standing it that will encourage change. Teacher and pupils can get locked in a negative cycle: this theory would encourage the teacher to look at the situation from the pupils' perspective and seek ways to cooperate with them. The assumption is that there are dif-ferent interpretations of a situation, each equally valid, and the behaviour of teachers and pupils draws on those interpretations. The technique for thinking about a problem from a different perspective is called 'reframing' and requires the teacher to think of alterna-tive explanations for the behaviour and ways in which they might respond differently. Teachers who took part in research by Tyler and Jones (2002) found that, in spite of initial resistance and scepticism, there was an improvement in dealing with entrenched problem behaviours and that they were more relaxed and so were their classes.

The extract begins with a very useful theoretical discussion of causality and response in terms of pupils' behaviour. As Crozier notes, *theories link to different stances about the social world and human behaviour and you will be able to make links between your own belief systems and some of these ideas.* We have already noted how established teachers can be antagonistic towards educational theory, but it is a tenet of this book that the development of theoretically-informed teachers is fundamental to developing a robust pedagogy, so to have a chance to do this in relation to the key matter of behaviour management is both important and worthwhile.

Crozier discusses three theoretical approaches, behavioural, cognitive, and ecosystemic. There is a number of school behaviour-management systems which are based upon the notion of behavioural approaches. The ABC formulation (antecedent, behaviour, consequences) is to be found in varying shades in many schools. The essence of many of these approaches is often found in a formula, what Crozier refers to as a schematic, which both pupils and teachers are aware of. These have 'consequences' as an integral part of the formula, and pupils will know that the level of consequence will be proportional to the level of behavioural issue. As Crozier observes, *much effective behaviour change has been achieved by these approaches – not least because they are accompanied by training of all the staff and support staff, the development of a coherent policy and consistency in application of the approach.* This last matter is a key one. Schools where behaviour management has been addressed as an issue tend to have found that consistency is key. Teachers are trained in what are appropriate responses, and act accordingly. This can be an issue for you if you are new to the school, for example on a placement, but careful discussion with your mentors should enable you to work out how you can fit into the system. Where these systems are in place it is important that you do slot in appropriately. You need to find out what is the scale of consequence you should be adopting. The section later in the extract on whole-school policy is germane to this. As the generals of trench warfare knew, the big guns can fire only once; you do not want to escalate hostilities to their maximum for a first, small infringement.

In the cognitive approach, the very notion of the term used in the last paragraph, *hostilities,* will be seen as suspect. This is because cognitive approaches see the importance as lying in the area of the student's perceptions. We know that, as Crozier observes, *self-esteem plays a significant part in the ability of pupils to be effective learners and pupils with low self-esteem are vulnerable to failure and to criticism*. Low self-esteem is a problem. All of these are good and sensible suggestions, but let us pick up on one in particular, *reprimand the behaviour, not the person*. This is an important piece of advice to follow. It is the behaviour which is the issue, the person doing the behaviour needs to understand that. Cognitive approaches emphasise understanding, and this involves separating the action from the actor. This can take some time to develop, but it is worth doing. Teaching is based on relationships, and you need to establish positive ones, which takes us to the next model.

The ecosystemic model places the emotions of the individuals concerned as an integral part of a behavioural approach. As Crozier notes, *relationships lie at the heart of these theories, and the emotional needs of participants in learning are included in the framework*. One of the issues with behaviour management is that, as Crozier points out, *teacher and pupils can get locked in a negative cycle*. Getting out of these negative cycles involves 'reframing' and thinking this through from the perspective of the student. Crozier's observation that *teachers who took part in research ... found that, in spite of initial resistance and scepticism, there was an improvement in dealing with entrenched problem behaviours and that they were more relaxed and so were their classes* is interesting and noteworthy. You will meet teachers who tell you that behaviour management is solely a matter of developing a forceful personality. This is not the case. Some teachers may have been at the school a long time and with this longevity comes an improvement in discipline anyway, in many cases. For some teachers, this will be a novel way of addressing behaviour management, but is worthwhile nonetheless.

So, in summary, *behavioural approaches seek for pupils to comply with external controls, while cognitive approaches (often combined with behaviourism) seek to internalise compliance and control over emotions. Systems theory looks for co-operation and integrity in the interactions in school.*

REFLECTIVE EXERCISE

Which of these theoretical approaches most closely matches your own view? Which does not?

Would you be able to enact the latter in your pedagogy?

Crozier also offers a useful piece of advice: *practice based on theories that assume the teacher is a calm and objective judge of the situation and plays a neutral role in any conflict do not invite an emphasis on self-awareness and self-evaluation. Effective teachers are often able to reflect on where their own behaviours have contributed to a conflict situation and this awareness is itself a useful contribution to positive teacher–pupil relationships based on mutual respect.* This matters to you as a beginning teacher. You will be expected to write evaluations and reflections on your teaching and learning activities, and thinking back to how you handled your role in behaviour-management situations will be an important one.

> **REFLECTIVE EXERCISE**
>
> *Next time you are reviewing your progress with your mentors, see if you can critique your own responses to behaviour management incidents before your mentors do. To what extent do your mentors agree with you?*

Crozier goes on to explore a number of other themes related to the themes of behaviour management. We will briefly consider each of these below.

Developing appropriate expectations

We discuss at a number of points in this book how having high, but appropriate, expectations is an important part of your development as a teacher and an important feature of positive relationships with your pupils. In this extract Crozier links these ideas to behaviour management. Later on in the extract, it is noted that *work pitched at too low a level will bore pupils and at too high a level will make some defensive and anxious. Both may lead to disruptive behaviour*. This is why your expectations need to be appropriate. While careful planning can not sort out all behavioural issues, it allows you the opportunity to have strategies and activities ready for all the pupils in your class. There is a useful section on planning later in the extract.

Self-fulfilling prophecies

An important part of your development as a new teacher will be interacting with other, more experienced, teachers. You need to spend time in the staffroom. But you need to be aware of acting on what other teachers say. Just because one student is a problem for some teachers does not mean that that student will be a problem for you. Some pupils hit it off with some teachers, and do not with others. There is no simple formula for this. Maybe you teach PE, and they just like football; maybe you teach art, and they like the respite from writing; maybe you teach English, and they like reading. Or maybe they just like you. Treat staffroom gossip carefully and do not be too quick to act upon it. Crozier provides a nice example of Jaz and the self-fulfilling prophecy. Try to make sure you do not fall into this trap.

Positive relationships

If you are a young beginning teacher, it might be that the pupils are nearer your age than you are to your mentors. Do not let this affect your judgement. For most school pupils, all teachers are well over 35 anyway. What you will find tricky to start with is the way established teachers move from the jocular friendliness of the staffroom to the formal register of the corridor. They can do this at the opening and closing of the staffroom door. It is a technique you need to develop. While we fully concur with Crozier's philosophy that *warmth and genuine engagement with pupils is an important quality and a valuable tool*, we also recognise that establishing positive relationships with pupils can be challenging to put into place at the start of your career.

Rewards and sanctions

'Catch them being good' is well-worn but good advice. Too often you will be caught with the consequences of negative behaviour, and will find yourself sucked into petty squabbles. Part of your training is to learn how to deal with these. Make a point of being positive during your lessons as often as possible.

REFLECTIVE EXERCISE

If you are on a paired teaching placement, ask your teaching partner to keep a tally chart of negative and positive comments you make. If not, ask your mentor to make this a focus of a lesson observation. Just counting how many times you use each can be very revealing.

The use of praise might need some rehearsal before you feel comfortable, and you may well want to develop strategies which differentiate how you treat Year 7 children compared with those in the sixth form but, however it is delivered, praise is vitally important in developing your pupils' self-esteem and confidence in themselves and in relationship to you as their teacher.

There are many pieces of good and useful advice in this extract, and you will want to try them out in the context of your own teaching. Do not forget Crozier's exhortation at the end, *good teachers are constantly reflecting on their own practice and seeking ways to develop new approaches that fit with their value system and suit their personal style. It is tempting, and easy, to blame the pupils when a lesson goes wrong*. We want you to be reflecting constantly on what you do, on causes and effects, and on what you can and will do differently next time. There are often no right answers. What you will find out with experience is that there are more answers upon which to draw.

Establishing group work within your classroom

One of the aspects of the organisation of teaching and learning which is likely to figure in most pedagogical encounters is that of group work. Our next extract looks at this important aspect of your everyday work in the classroom. The principal author of this extract is Peter Kutnick, a significant contributor to the field of the study of social development of children, and of the promoting of academic achievement within classrooms. He has undertaken some important research into the use of within-class groups, and it is from one of these studies that this next extract (*The Grouping of Pupils in Secondary School Classrooms: Possible links between pedagogy and learning*), is taken (Kutnick et al., 2005).

POINTS TO CONSIDER

As you read this, think about these questions.

What does this reading tell you about pupil groupings?

How do you group pupils in your teaching?

What strategies for other forms of grouping have you observed elsewhere?

EXTRACT THREE

Kutnick, P, Blatchford, P and Baines, E (2005) Grouping of pupils in secondary school classrooms: possible links between pedagogy and learning. Social Psychology of Education, 8(4): 366–370.

Discussion

This study drew from a range of literature and provided data from a classroom mapping survey of pupil grouping in secondary school classrooms. The literature concerned the social pedagogy of classroom groups and how pupil groupings may affect classroom learning with particular reference to the control of knowledge and learning practices. Classroom maps of pupil seating and working practices from 250 Year 7 and 10 classes showed a range of social pedagogic relationships between classroom actors (pupils and teachers) and the tasks/interactions in which they participated. This discussion considers three main themes that arise from the results: expressions of pedagogy in the classroom, social pedagogic contexts of grouping and the role of the teacher in controlling classroom knowledge.

Pedagogy in the classroom: Few previous studies have identified or explored tasks assigned, patterns of interaction and the placement of the teacher in the promotion of classroom learning in secondary schools. In line with the limited number of studies that exist, this research has confirmed that: lessons tend to be presented in three phases – introduction, extensions and application of learning task, revision work undertaken (similar to Ball, 1981); and lesson phase has implications for pupil grouping size and teacher intention for the use of groupings (Kutnick et al., 2002). Further, we found that classroom tasks were dominated by application and extension of pupils' existing knowledge. There was comparatively little evidence of the introduction and consideration of new cognitive knowledge and skills or practice tasks taking place in classrooms. Unlike studies of primary school classrooms (Bennett et al., 1984; Kutnick et al., 2002) which are dominated by practice tasks, secondary classrooms spend proportionally more time extending pupil knowledge. Also, classroom maps showed that secondary school pupils were seated in a range of grouping sizes but positioned mainly in rows; whereas previous primary school studies found children mainly seated around tables (Galton et al., 1999; Hastings & Chantry, 2002). The mapped seating patterns related to curriculum area, but did not relate with consistency to the work patterns of pupil groupings. Over 50% of the tasks assigned by teachers required pupils to work alone for most secondary school learning tasks (similar to findings in primary schools by Galton et al., 1999; Pollard et al., 2000). Teachers allowed pupils to converse with other pupils sitting in close proximity. In less than 5% of groupings, pupils sat as individuals. And, while there were diverse learning tasks assigned in secondary school classrooms, there was little evidence of consistent planning for the grouping by size, composition, or ability. Planning for purposeful interaction within classroom groups did not appear to exist.

Social pedagogy: identification of the seating, task and interactions found in secondary school classes allows consideration of the social contexts likely to promote or hinder classroom learning and achievement. ... there were only a few examples of classroom relationships between group size and learning task that replicated those found in the experimental literature and likely to promote learning; where, for example, Kutnick's (1994; drawing on such studies as Damon & Phelps, 1989; Slavin, 1990b; Kulik & Kulik, 1992) review of group size and learning tasks found that cognitive enhancement (new knowledge and skills) was most likely to be promoted in dyads, application/extension tasks in small groups and practice in individual groupings. Classroom-based findings in this study showed that: new cognitive knowledge was most likely to take place in whole class grouping; application/extension was likely to take place in a mixture of dyads, small groups and whole class; and practice took place in a mixture of individual, dyad and whole class groupings. There was some indication that pupils' within-class seating may not promote classroom learning, for example: (I) while 20% of classroom tasks concern new (cognitive) knowledge, 57% of these tasks took place in whole class settings where the teacher dominated proceedings ... ; and (2) practice and revision tasks (19% of assigned tasks) were least likely to take place in an individual setting as pupils were rarely seated as individuals (with the possible exception of mathematics). Teachers showed little differentiation in their use of pupil grouping for diverse learning tasks – often relying on the whole class for the presentation, application and practice of curriculum knowledge.

Within pupils' seating groups, there was a strong likelihood of working with a partner (within a dyad) even though pupils often sat in larger groupings. Depending on task, these partners can either promote or inhibit learning – as identified in the following: (1) Whereas dyads are often used for cognitive enhancement, if assigned a practice task dyads can force partners 'off task' (Jackson et al., 2001). Dyads in this study were predominantly assigned practice tasks. (2) If classroom tasks required discussion (new and applied knowledge), then partners will need good communication and support skills to carry on a dialogue (Light & Littleton, 1994; Webb et al., 1997). Teachers in this study rarely provided support or training for group working skills. (3) it may be left to the power of friendship to provide the necessary circumstances for communication and support, allowing enhancement of cognitive activity (Zajac & Hartup, 1997). Within the 'working' dyads found in classes, friendship was the predominant explanation for various pupils being seated together. It may be naïve, though, to expect that friends will productively work together in class. Rarely were pupils asked to undertake the new knowledge tasks that Hartup identified for friends. Friendships identified on the maps were often stereotypical – legitimating gendered, ability and other preferences. Sitting/working with a friend may disrupt practice tasks. Gendered, school-based activities of friendship may not promote equivalent school-learning for girls and boys. As previously identified, activities within gendered friendships in secondary schools tend to include schools and learning issues among girls and exclude school/learning issues among boys (Rudduck et al., 1996) and there is evidence of differentiated cognitive-based interaction among boy and girl friendship pairs (Kutnick & Kington, 2005). (4) Same ability grouping may also inhibit classroom learning, particularly when classroom tasks involve some form of cognitive discussion. Same ability groupings have been found to disadvantage certain pupils. Webb (1989) noted that low ability groupings rarely have the range of cognitive perspectives that will allow discussions to develop and that high ability groupings rarely share information. And Kutnick et al. (2002) found in primary schools that low attaining (predominantly male) groups were much less likely to receive teacher attention than high attaining (predominantly female) groups. Classroom maps in this study found that pupils sat/worked in predominantly homogeneous ability groupings and we would expect similarly differentiated cognitive activity and teacher involvement with high and low attaining groups.

EXTRACT THREE *continued*

(5) Stereotypical friendship pairings may also be at the root of within-class polarisation; whereby group social identification is established by similarity of gender and ability, and confirmed by enforcing dissimilarity from other groupings (Tajfel, 1981). Certainly in relation to same sex groupings, Myhill (2002) has associated gendered classroom behaviours with achievement results – differentiating levels of under-achievement in boys from levels of over-achievement in girls. Without efforts (or training) to overcome within-class stereotyped differences, polarisation and differentiation (Hargreaves, 1967; Lacey, 1974) as well as differentiated social capital (Putnam, 2000) may be shown to have its roots within the seating and working practices characteristic of classrooms.

The role of the teacher and 'control' of classroom knowledge: *Pedagogic and social pedagogic evidence in this study showed that the teacher was central to setting learning tasks, patterns of interaction and composition of the groupings. When teachers structured the composition of groupings in their classrooms, they allowed friendship choice to dominate. Even when teachers did not actively structure grouping, they appeared to legitimise stereotypical friendship preferences voiced by pupils. This friendship choice has been aligned with studies of polarisation and differentiated social (relational) capital. Teachers rarely introduced practices that supported or encouraged a collaborative group working context even if group seating characterised their classrooms.*

Teachers were often found working with or circulating nearby when (cognitive-based) learning tasks were being undertaken in the classroom … ; they were present in approximately 85% of the learning tasks identified. Moreover, teachers had a very high presence when new cognitive knowledge was introduced (directly involved in 41% of these tasks and circulating in a further 37% of the tasks). One implication of such a high level of teacher presence during cognitive tasks is that teachers were central for the presentation (and control) of knowledge; a concept that has been critically challenged in the literature over the last thirty years (from Young, 1971). Teachers' high level of presence with regard to cognitive tasks may represent an involvement in the asymmetric 'zone of proximal development' – scaffolding for novice learners. This ZPD exemplifies an aspect of the social relational nature of learning (from inter- to intra-personal) in one-to-one exchanges where experts 'instruct' novices; but it would be difficult to establish and maintain this relationship within classrooms of 25+ pupils (all requiring scaffolding). Even if we move away from the concept of the teacher working with individual pupils for scaffolding and towards teachers working with pupil dyads, the teacher can only interact with one pairing at a time. Evidence from other studies (Dahllof, 1971; Younger et al., 1999; Kutnick et al., 2002) further suggests that the focus of teacher attention is most likely to be placed on higher performing pupils. Other pairings will have to work autonomously from the teacher (Baines et al., 2003) – although very few groupings were found to be assigned work in this manner. From a different perspective, high levels of teacher presence during cognitive tasks appear to militate against pupils mutually developing new knowledge with their peers. This alternative, mutual-based practice is highly endorsed by cognitive researchers such as Damon and Phelps (1989) and co-operative/collaborative education researchers such as Slavin (1990b) and Mercer (2000); yet, there was little evidence for this practice found in the study.

EXTRACT THREE continued

Teachers also showed a strong presence during the application of existing knowledge and practice tasks. We may speculate that such a constant teacher presence is intended to support learning, but teacher presence is also likely to distract pupils from developing their own understanding and ownership of knowledge (Galton et al., 1999). One explanation for this high level of teacher presence is offered by Mahony and Hextall (2001), who cite the constant pressure placed upon schools and teachers for increasingly high levels of examination performance ('performativity'); this may necessitate teacher presence to mediate and ensure that pupils are constantly focused on assigned (national curriculum oriented) tasks; controlling pupil behaviour as well as learning opportunities.

In conclusion, this exploration of the social pedagogic context of pupil grouping in secondary school classrooms identifies predominant features of seating and working in classrooms and raises questions concerning the likelihood of pupil groupings promoting or hindering classroom learning. Pupils are always grouped in some formal or informal way in their classrooms. Within-class pupil groupings showed little relationship to learning task assigned but were organisationally related to the sequence of a lesson (opening, applied work, close). Effective working within groupings may be hindered by lack of planning for interaction between pupils or within tasks, training for group support skills, teacher domination of cognitive (and other) tasks, and the omnipresence of stereotypical friendship as a basis for grouping. This social pedagogic exploration identifies many points of concern regarding current classroom practices in English secondary schools especially as group-based activity is likely to be a foundation for developing social and relational capital by pupils. Teachers could draw upon greater social pedagogic awareness in their promotion of within-class learning by giving greater consideration to the interpersonal activities (discussed by Daniels, 2001) that underlie the learning events associated with the enhancement of school achievement and performance. This consideration would necessarily include: the association of grouping size and composition to learning task; training of pupils for group support, communication and joint learning; transfer of some aspects of learning control to pupils (in cooperation and mutual learning); and a realisation of when to intervene in pupils' learning activities.

The issue of organising groups within the classroom as you are teaching is one you will be having to deal with on a daily basis in your classroom. This study unpicks some of the fine detail of this. It contains a number of points which could be relevant for your practice.

One of the findings from early in the extract is that the authors found *that classroom tasks were dominated by application and extension of pupils' existing knowledge. There was comparatively little evidence of the introduction and consideration of new cognitive knowledge and skills or practice tasks taking place in classrooms* (page 366). In other words, when pupils worked in groups there was little new knowledge generated. In the majority of cases, pupils were, in general, applying things they already knew.

Another finding from the research relates to the physical environment of the classroom and its affect on group-work activities. One of the things you will have a view on is the way in which your classroom is set out, and this, to some extent, does depend on the furniture you have in it. In classrooms with easily-movable tables, teachers often have different arrangements for different learning purposes. This study found that *secondary school pupils were seated in a range of grouping sizes but positioned mainly in rows; whereas previous primary school studies found children mainly seated around tables* (page 367).

REFLECTIVE EXERCISE

Does this accord with your experience of working within a secondary school?

How are the classrooms you teach in set out?

Have you tried setting them out differently?

What contribution does classroom layout make to learning, or to behaviour management?

What Kutnick et al., are saying is that they found groupings in operation, but doing so from within the confines of desks set out in rows. What they also noticed was that:

> ... while there were diverse learning tasks assigned in secondary school classrooms, there was little evidence of consistent planning for the grouping by size, composition, or ability. Planning for purposeful interaction within classroom groups did not appear to exist.

> (Kutnick et al., 2005, page 367)

This has ramifications for teaching, as it means that teachers had decided that group work was appropriate, but had not planned how to maximise the effects of it. This has significance, as becomes clearer later in the study, where it is observed that *there was some indication that pupils' within-class seating may not promote classroom learning, for example: (1) while 20% of classroom tasks concern new (cognitive) knowledge, 57% of these tasks took place in whole class settings where the teacher dominated proceedings...; and (2) practice and revision tasks (19% of assigned tasks) were least likely to take place in an individual setting as pupils were rarely seated as individuals* (page 367). What this means is that the classroom layout actually mitigated against effective learning in a number of instances. This clearly matters. There is little point setting up a learning situation which is doomed to be ineffective.

The way group work is organised can vary between school subjects. In science, for example, it could be that students are working together on an experiment; in geography they could be doing a map-reading task; in drama they could be creating a performance. Each of these requires a different application of the way in which the group will be working. What this article says is that *teachers in this study rarely provided support or training for group working skills* (page 368). This means that the groups are set in action without the pupils necessarily knowing the sorts of interaction, or, possibly, the sorts of learning, which are intended. What this means for you is that when you set a class to work in groups, it might be worth spending time working with the class on the best ways of working within groups to maximise learning. Some teachers have done this by modelling small sub-components of group work with groups of learners in front of the rest of the class.

One of the implications of this lack of training in group-work skills is that *it may be left to the power of friendship to provide the necessary circumstances for communication and support, allowing enhancement of cognitive activity* (page 368). Friendship groups are a common way of working, and of organising group work in secondary schools. This paper reports that friendship groups *were often stereotypical – legitimating gendered, ability and other preferences* (page 368). In other words, the groups were often same-sex, and more or less the same in ability. Does this matter? As the report goes on to observe, *activities within gendered friendships in secondary schools tend to include schools and learning issues among girls and exclude school/learning issues among boys* (page 368). In other words, the girls got on with the task while the boys did not. Dealing with this is a challenge for the teacher.

A further compounding of problems comes with the observation that *same ability groupings have been found to disadvantage certain pupils … low ability groupings rarely have the range of cognitive perspectives that will allow discussions to develop and that high ability groupings rarely share information* (page 368). This is another challenge. The issue of groupings in this section of the article shows that there are problems with friendship groupings, both in terms of cognitive response and in the ways in which teachers spend time with the learners. What is also uncomfortable is the notion that *polarisation and differentiation … may be shown to have its roots within the seating and working practices characteristic of classrooms* (pages 368–9). An ongoing debate in educational circles is that between mixed ability, and setting or streaming. However your classes are organised, there will still be differences between ability levels within them.

This study found that friendship groups were often the way in which teachers tended to organise students for group work.

REFLECTIVE EXERCISE

How do you organise groupings?

Apart from friendship groups, what other ways are there of organising groups within your teaching?

Despite the ubiquitous nature of friendship groups, there are other ways to organise pupils for group work. The National Strategies website provides some helpful examples, as Table 3.1 shows.

Table 3.1 *The benefits and limitations of different groupings*

Grouping	Benefits	Limitations	When to use
Friendship	Secure and unthreatening	Prone to consensus	When sharing and confidence building are priorities
Ability	Work can more easily be pitched at the optimum level	Visible in-class setting	When differentiation can only be achieved by task
Structured mix	Ensures a range of views	Reproduces the power relations in society	When diversity is required
Random selection	Builds up pupils' experiences of different partners and views; accepted by pupils as democratic	Can get awkward mixes and 'bad' group chemistry'	When pupils complain about who is allowed to sit with whom; when groups have become stale
Single sex	Socially more comfortable for some	Increases the gender divide	In contexts where one sex habitually loses out, e.g. competing to control the computer keyboard

(National Strategies, 2006, pages 12–13)

One of the comments you may get concerning your own classroom presence during your teaching practice relates to where you place yourself in the classroom. Ideally you will be able to see everything that is going on, and remain aware of all the pupils and what they are up to. Kutnick et al., also investigated this matter and found that many teachers tended to be near groups while they were working. They found that there was a high level of teacher presence during cognitive tasks. This could be due to the effects of Vygotsky's notion of the zone of proximal development (ZPD). This is one of Vygotsky's best known contributions to learning theory. The ZPD is the area between that which a learner is able to do with assistance now, and that which they will be able to do by themselves in future; in other words, *what the child is able to do in collaboration today he [sic] will be able to do independently tomorrow* (Vygotsky, 1987, page 211). Standing near to a group while they are working could well be a part of this, but as the authors observe, this will be problematic to maintain for all pupils in large classes. But, conversely, what also appears to happen is that *high levels of teacher presence during cognitive tasks appear to militate against pupils mutually developing new knowledge with their peers*. This means that the very presence of the teacher prevents the pupils from developing new knowledge between themselves. This, as the authors go on to observe, can also inhibit ownership of new knowledge, ensuring it rests with the teacher. Clearly, where you position yourself and what you do while pupils are working in groups is important. You will need to experiment with different approaches and reflect on the resulting impact on your pupils' learning.

In the final paragraph it is noted that *effective working within groupings may be hindered by lack of planning for interaction between pupils or within tasks, training for group support skills, teacher domination of cognitive (and other) tasks, and the omnipresence of stereotypical friendship as a basis for grouping* (page 369). This means that the teacher needs to not only plan for group work, but also to plan for what it is hoped will happen during the course of the group-work sessions. The authors explain what this could involve.

This consideration would necessarily include:

- the association of grouping size and composition to learning tasks;

- training of pupils for group support, communication and joint learning;

- transfer of some aspects of learning control to pupils (in co-operation and mutual learning);

- a realisation of when to intervene in pupils' learning activities.

This is quite a lot for you as a beginning teacher to deal with, but it certainly seems worthwhile to give some thought to grouping, and what you expect of your pupils.

REFLECTIVE EXERCISE

Next time you employ group work activities within your lessons, think about the following key points:

- *employing purposeful groupings, for example from the National Strategies grid;*

- *what sort of instructions for effective group work you want to give, or model, for the pupils prior to the group work commencing;*

- *what sorts of interaction you want from the group work;*

- *what the learning outcomes from the group work will be.*

Conclusion

This chapter has considered a number of aspects of your classroom practice. There are, we know, many things for you to be thinking about simultaneously as you learn to teach. We have tried not to spread this chapter too thinly. Rather, we have explored three key issues and applied them to your developing classroom practice. We have considered the nature of the professional knowledge of the teacher, and further discussed Shulman's notion of pedagogic content knowledge. We then linked this to thinking about behaviour management, and allied this to theoretical stances. Finally, we considered the important topic of pupil groupings. Clearly there will be a number of other aspects to consider within your own pedagogical stance on these issues. Throughout this book we emphasise the importance of critical reflection, and all of the readings in this chapter have, hopefully, given you both some food for thought and some ideas to try out in the classroom too.

C H A P T E R   S U M M A R Y

Starting from an exploration of what constitutes professional knowledge for the teacher, this chapter explores how particular aspects of a trainee teacher's classroom practice can be developed through reflecting on and applying ideas from the educational literature. Specifically, approaches to behaviour management and the grouping of pupils are explored in detail. As with all topics considered within this book, the practical and pedagogical implications of studying some of the theory of teaching and learning are encouraged through numerous practical and reflective tasks.

REFERENCES

Brooks, V, Abbott, I and Bills, L (2007) *Preparing to Teach in Secondary Schools: A student teacher's guide to professional issues in secondary education*, 2nd edn. Maidenhead: Open University Press.

Kutnick, P, Blatchford, P and Baines, E (2005) Grouping of pupils in secondary school classrooms: Possible links between pedagogy and learning. *Social Psychology of Education*, 8(4): 349–74.

Rogers, B (2007) *Behaviour Management: A whole-school approach*, 2nd edn. London: Paul Chapman.

Shulman, L (1986) Those who understand: Knowledge growth in teaching. *Educational Researcher*, 15(2): 4–14.

Vygotsky, L (1987) Thinking and Speech, in Rieber, RW and Carton, AS (eds) *The Collected Works of LS Vygotsky*. New York, London: Plenum.

Winch, C (2004) What do teachers need to know about teaching? A critical examination of the occupational knowledge of teachers. *British Journal of Educational Studies*, 52(2): 180–96.

WEBSITES

National Strategies Website: Introducing Tasks to Groups document, available from **http://nationalstrategies.standards.dcsf.gov.uk/node/84689** Accessed March 2010.

Chapter 4
Embedding assessment for learning

CHAPTER OBJECTIVES

By the end of this chapter you should have:
- considered a range of approaches to assessment, including formative and summative assessment and assessing pupil progress, and how these can be utilised to help develop your teaching;
- developed your understanding of formative assessment and how a more genuine approach to formative assessment can helpfully underpin your teaching in an integrated, sustained pedagogy;
- applied principles relating to formative assessment to other key areas of educational thought, including epistemological issues, considering how these inform your teaching practice and, in particular, relate to how pupils learn;
- looked at ways in which formative and summative approaches to assessment can be combined to help you understand the progress that your pupils are making.

Q Standards: Q26, Q27, Q28.

Introduction

Assessment will be a key part of your everyday work as a teacher. This chapter is designed to get you to think about the issues concerned with assessment, to challenge your assumptions, and to help you really connect teaching with learning.

REFLECTIVE EXERCISE

Think about what assessments you have used recently. What have you assessed, and why have you assessed it?

There are a lot of possible things you might have written here. Assessment is, or should be, at the heart of what teachers do, indeed, *to teach is to assess* (Swanwick, 1988 page 149). Your answers to this opening reflective task, based on your own experiences of assessment, are likely to include things like:

- to know what pupils can do;

- to know what pupils have learned;

- to help find out what pupils have understood;

- to give learners a grade;

- to improve learning.

All of these are aspects of assessment, and all are reflected in various aspects of published materials on assessment, of which there are many. Let us begin to untangle some of the issues concerned with assessment by thinking about some of the terminologies concerned, and how they are written about and reflected in the literature. You will probably be familiar with the terms 'formative' and 'summative' assessment, and so thinking about these will be a good place to begin this process.

Formative and summative assessment

REFLECTIVE EXERCISE

Give one example each of formative and summative assessment that you have employed in your teaching, or you have observed other teachers employing.

So, what is formative assessment, what is summative assessment, and how do they differ? The first extract we are going to consider is *Assessment and Learning: Differences and relationships between formative and summative assessments* (Harlen and James, 1997). Wynne Harlen and Mary James are both members of the influential Assessment Reform Group, and have researched and championed assessment, particularly formative assessment, as a key component of raising standards in teaching and learning.

As you read this article think about the following questions.

- What do the authors say formative assessment is for?

- What do they say summative assessment is for?

- What are the possible confusions?

- What are the relationships between teaching, learning and assessment?

EXTRACT ONE

Harlen, W and James, M (1997) Assessment and learning: differences and relationships between formative and summative assessments. Assessment in Education: Principles, Policy & Practice, 4(3): 365–370.

The aim of this paper is to share concerns that arise from the particular approaches to assessment adopted in the countries of the UK, but which will almost certainly have resonance in other countries, particularly in Europe, the USA, Australia and New Zealand. In outline the problems can be stated as follows:

- *that formative and summative assessment are both included in national assessment policies and in theory have different roles, but the way in which they have been related to each other in official documents means that the essential differences between them have been smothered;*

- *a consequence of the conflation of summative and formative purposes may be that either there is little genuine formative assessment (or what there is may not be recognised as such) or that teachers are struggling to meet both requirements and experiencing assessment overload;*

- *because formative assessment has to be carried out by teachers, there is an assumption that all assessment by teachers is formative, adding to the blurring of the distinction between formative and summative purposes and to teachers changing their own on-going assessment into a series of 'mini' assessments each of which is essentially summative in character;*

- *the equating of formative assessment with teachers' assessment coupled with the effective down-grading (in England, at least) of teachers' judgements in comparison with externally devised tests or tasks on account of the latter being used to create league tables, has led to the neglect of support for formative assessment;*

- *there is a need to recognise in theory and in practice the differences in function and characteristics between formative and summative assessment and to find a way of relating them together that preserves their different functions; in particular we want to argue that it is not necessary, and indeed it is not helpful, to be concerned with strict criterion-referencing in formative assessment.*

These problems have become more prominent in the UK since the introduction of the educational reforms of the late 1980s. The descriptions of attainment in the National Curriculum have provided criteria (at levels 1–10, recently revised to 1–8, in the National Curriculum and levels A–E in the Scottish Guidelines) for teachers to use in their assessment and have thus added rigour that was formerly missing. However, emphasis in the guidance to teachers has been on the application of the criteria to pupils' achievements, for the purpose of deciding what level they have reached, to the neglect of the genuinely formative use of assessment.

The framework of assessment and testing in the National Curriculum for England and Wales was set by the report of Task Group on Assessment and Testing, known as TGAT, published in 1988 by the Department of Education and Science (DES) and the Welsh Office (WO) (DES/WO, 1988). The recommendations in this report, which included the framework of levels of attainment, were accepted instantly and entirely by the government without consultation. However, during the course of the implementation of the report's recommendations there have been significant changes which have been well documented by Daugherty (1995) and Black (1997), and as a result not all present practice in assessment in England can be linked back to this report. Nevertheless, it was the TGAT report that put the terms formative, diagnostic, summative *and* evaluative *into common circulation and defined them. The distinction between formative and summative was made mainly in terms of purpose and timing:*

– formative, so that the positive achievements of a pupil may be recognised and discussed and the appropriate next steps may be planned
– summative, for the recording of the overall achievement of a pupil in a systematic way.
(DES/WO, 1988, para. 23)

The assumption that these were not different in kind is clear in the claim that some pur-poses could be served by combining assessment originally made for different purposes: 'It is possible to build up a comprehensive picture of the overall achievements of a pupil by aggregating, in a structured way, the separate results of a set of assessments designed to serve formative purposes' (DES/WO, 1988, para. 25).

The message that formative and summative are easily related in this way and are of the same kind was reinforced by concern for standardisation: 'in order to ensure compara-bility' (DES/WO, 1988, para. 44). This concern is rightly raised in relation to summative assessments which may be used to make comparisons between pupils or to provide results which can be aggregated to give whole-class or whole-school profiles. However, set beside the above view that summative assessments can be formed by simple aggrega-tion of formative ones, it leads to the inevitable conclusion that formative assessments must also be 'standardised'.

We believe that this relationship between formative and summative assessment is sim-plistic and has brought about a fundamental confusion in teachers' minds about these two kinds of assessment. The reliability of summative assessment has suffered from the confusion. For example, evidence from the evaluation of implementation of national assessment and testing in Scotland found that it was quite common for teachers to share this view of how a summative assessment of a child's work is reached: 'What would be a piece of C work for one child might not be for another, it depends on their background' (Harlen et al, 1995). Similar findings were reported by Gipps et al. (1995). However, the focus of this paper is on the detrimental effect of this confusion of purposes on formative assessment and on the role that assessment has to play in teaching for understanding. A central purpose of this paper is to propose a different relationship which will preserve the essential function of formative assessment in learning.

In the first part of the paper we consider the kind of learning we are concerned to bring about. This is followed by revisiting the nature of formative assessment and its role in learning, leading to a comparison of the characteristics of formative and summative assessment. In later sections we consider a different approach to linking formative and summative assessment and the consequences for developing this approach.

Learning with Understanding

We begin from the assumption that an important aim of education is to bring about learning with understanding. This has been called 'learning as an interpretative **process***' (Säljö, 1979; Broudy, 1988) or 'deep learning' (Entwistle & Ramsden, 1983; Marton et al, 1984; Entwistle & Entwistle, 1991). The term 'real' learning extends the notion of learning with understanding to suggest that it involves interaction with people, ideas, things and events in the real world. These are not the only kinds of learning. There are some things that are probably most efficiently learned by rote, such as number bonds, spellings, multi-plication tables; these are skills that are most useful to us when they have been practised sufficiently to become automatic. There are also bodies of knowledge (facts and informa-tion) that it is reasonable for society to expect teachers to teach and for pupils to learn,* *although there are still debates about* what *knowledge and* whose *knowledge is most important. However, the exponential increase in the amount of factual information in recent years and for the foreseeable future, coupled with the rapid changes in the nature of employment, indicate that there should be far greater emphasis on learning which can be transformed and applied to new circumstances than on learning facts and procedures applicable only in situations closely similar to those in which they were learned. Indeed, it is the need of the whole population to be able to translate and interpret what they learn that makes the case for universal schooling (Broudy, 1988). From his review of relevant research, Crooks concludes that 'there seems to be a strong ease for encouraging the development of deep strategies from the early years of the educational system' (Crooks, 1988, p.447).*

Crooks refers here to the simple but powerful way of identifying the approaches to learning which lead, on the one hand to understanding and on the other to rote memorisation, in terms of the distinction between deep *learning and* surface *learning, defined as follows (see, for example, Ausubel et al., 1978; Marton et al., 1984; Bntwistle & Entwistle, 1991):*

Deep Learning Approach	Surface Learning Approach
An intention to develop personal understanding	*An intention to be able to reproduce content as required*
Active interaction with the content, particularly in relating new ideas to previous knowledge and experience	*Passive acceptance of ideas and information*
Linking ideas together using integrating principles	*Lack of recognition of guiding principles or patterns*
Relating evidence to conclusions	*Focusing learning on assessment requirements*

Between surface learning and deep learning Marton et al. (1984) also proposed an intervening category which they called 'strategic learning'. This reminds us that efficient learning is often a combination of both surface and deep learning, for if we were to learn everything in depth we would have time to learn very little. Likewise, if everything was surface learning we could hardly describe ourselves as educated at all. Assessment has a role in all kinds of learning. In memorising facts and learning physical skills it is used to find out what facts or skills have been acquired and the feedback it provides to help further learning is in terms of what has not been learned. Assessment has quite a different role in learning with understanding and it is this that is the concern in this paper and which is now considered.

When something is learned with understanding (deep learning, 'real' learning) it is actively understood and internalised by the learner. It makes sense in terms of a learner's experience of the world and is not simply a collection of isolated facts which have been memorised. As noted above, it differs from rote learning essentially in that it is linked to previous experience and so can be used in situations different from that in which it was learned. Contemporary cognitive psychology supports the notion that understanding involves creating links in the mind and that 'making sense' of something depends on these links. Isolated pieces of information do not have links to existing mental frameworks and so are not easily retained in the mind. The identification and creation of links to exist-ing frameworks depends on the active participation of the learner and on the familiarity of the context of the material to be learned. Understanding, in this view, is the process of construction and reconstruction of knowledge by the learner. What is known and understood will, of course, change with new experience and as new ideas and skills are presented to help make sense of it. Thus the characteristics of this learning are that it:

- *is progressively developed in terms of big ideas, skills for living and learning, attitudes and values;*

- *is constructed on the basis of previous ideas and skills;*

- *can be applied in contexts other than those in which it was learned;*

- *is owned by the learner in the sense that it becomes a fundamental part of the way he or she understands the world; it is not simply ephemeral knowledge that may be mem-orised for recall in examinations but subsequently forgotten.*

It follows that to promote this kind of learning, what is needed are learning experiences that:

- *are well matched to the existing point of development of the ideas, skills, attitudes and values;*

- *have continuity with, and build on, previous experience;*

- *relate to current interests and experience;*

- *are perceived by learners as relevant, important, stimulating and valued for themselves, rather than simply for their usefulness in passing tests and examinations.*

The provision of learning experiences with these kinds of characteristics depends on the teacher:

- *having a thorough and deep understanding themselves of the subject matter to be taught, how pupils are likely to learn it and the difficulties and misunderstandings they are likely to encounter;*

- *having a clear idea of the progression in the ideas, skills, etc. which are the goals of learning and the course pupils are likely to take in this development;*

- *being able to recognise the point in this development reached by their pupils;*

- *knowing and being able to use various strategies to find out and to develop pupils' ideas, skills, etc.*

Our focus here is on the last two items in this list. Knowing about pupils' existing ideas and skills, and recognising the point reached in development and the necessary next steps to take, constitutes what we understand to be formative assessment. This is consistent with Sadler's (1989) definition. However, Sadler goes further to argue that, if improve-ment in learning is to take place, students need to come to hold a concept of quality roughly similar to that held by the teacher. They also need to be able to monitor the quality of what is being produced during the act of production, and to draw on a range of strategies to close any gap between their actual performance and the standard they are aiming for. This implies that part of the teacher's role in assessment for learning is to help students to come to these metacognitive understandings. Formative assessment, therefore, is essentially feedback (Ramaprasad, 1983), both to the teacher and to the pupil about present understanding and skill development in order to determine the way forward. Assessment for this purpose is part of teaching; learning with understanding depends on it. To use information about present achievements in this way means that the progression in ideas and skills must be in the teacher's mind – and as far as possible in the pupils' – so that the next appropriate steps can be considered.

Summative assessment has a quite different purpose, which is to describe learning achieved at a certain time for the purposes of reporting to parents, other teachers, the pupils themselves and, in summary form, to other interested parties such as school governors or school boards. It has an important role in the overall educational progress of pupils but not in day-to-day teaching as does formative assessment. As the next section of this paper attempts to show, it is the distinction between, and the articulation of assessment for these two purposes that is central to using assessment to improve educational standards.

For either purpose, if understanding is to be assessed, methods are required that involve learners in using their knowledge and linking it to real contexts. It cannot be assessed by asking for the recall of isolated, decontextualised pieces of information. The straightforward reproduction of knowledge rather than its application favours rote learning, and assessment which demands no more than this will inevitably shift teaching and learning away from understanding towards the memorisation of the information necessary to succeed in the assessment.

The key differences between formative and summative assessment are discussed with reference to the TGAT report (DES/WO, 1988), which first brought these terms into widespread use. Formative assessment is where *the positive achievements of a pupil may be recognised and discussed and the appropriate next steps may be planned*; and summative assessment involves *the recording of the overall achievement of a pupil in a systematic way*. A problem has occurred, Harlen and James observe, in that the fact that it was not made clear that these are different 'in kind' from each other. It is a discussion of these differences which forms the crux of this article. To understand why this is important we need to jump forwards a few paragraphs to where the differences between 'deep learning' and 'surface learning' are explored. It is likely that you want your pupils to understand what it is you are teaching them, and so deep learning is going to be a concern. Here, and in the next section, the authors really get to the heart of what formative assessment is, *knowing about pupils' existing ideas and skills, and recognising the point reached in development and the necessary next steps to take, constitutes what we understand to be formative assessment* (page 369). This means that formative assessment involves not only knowing what the pupils can do now but, importantly, what it is that they need to do next in order to progress their learning. To do this the learners need to understand what quality is in the subject they are studying, and what it is they need to do to be able to improve on their own current learning situation.

The implications for teaching and learning of this aspect of formative assessment take us back to the quotation from Swanwick above. Harlen and James express a similar view to Swanwick, *assessment for this purpose is part of teaching; learning with understanding depends on it.* In order to do this, you, the teacher, need to have a view as to what progression entails, both in the short and medium terms, and then be able to share this with the pupils.

This description of formative assessment is concerned with developing the potential of the pupils as learners, facilitating deep learning, and helping the pupils come to understand both where they are now, in terms of their learning, and what it is they need to do next. Notice that at no point have marks, grades, or National Curriculum levels been employed in these discussions. The authors observe this early on in the extract, with the observation that *emphasis in the guidance to teachers has been on the application of the criteria to pupils'* achievements, for the purpose of deciding what level they have reached, to the neglect of the genuinely formative use of assessment (page 366).

REFLECTIVE EXERCISE

How important are grading and providing a National Curriculum level in your everyday teaching?

Is this described by your school as formative or summative assessment?

If not, how is it described?

There have been a lot of confusions here. As the authors of this article have observed, a lot of guidance from the government via the DCSF and its predecessors has taken the form of 'helping' teachers to make judgements about their pupils' work using National Curriculum levels. Let us return now to the opening bullet points in this article, where a number of very significant points are made.

It is the contention of Harlen and James that approaches to genuine formative assessment have been downplayed in the UK (and other English-speaking countries) and have effectively been 'smothered'. As a result of this, teachers have changed *their own ongoing assessment into a series of 'mini' assessments each of which is essentially summative in character* (page 365), and that as a result of these confusions, many teachers are experiencing 'assessment overload'. These are important observations, and it will be useful for you to reflect on them in the light of your own experiences.

These are difficult questions. Many schools are struggling with assessment, and assessment overload is a common feature. Hopefully this article has made you think about some of the problems and difficulties associated with formative assessment.

Expanding formative assessment

To take this further, let is now consider a paper entitled *Assessment and Classroom Learning* (1998) by Paul Black and Dylan Wiliam, who, along with Harlen and James, are also members of the influential Assessment Reform Group (ARG). The work of Black and Wiliam has been particularly influential on governmental policy on assessment, and their research into formative assessment is internationally renowned.

As you read this extract, here are some questions for you to consider.

The extract begins with some discussions concerning the nature of formative assessment considered from a theoretical perspective. In an earlier section of the article, Black and Wiliam refer to the work of Sadler (1989) and Tittle (1994); aspects of those discussions are picked up in this next section, and it is these aspects which are of concern to us here.

diagnostic prescription of a teacher without understanding of its purpose or orientation will not learn. Thus self-assessment by the student is not an interesting option or luxury; it has to be seen as essential. Given this, the orientation by a student of his or her work can only be productive if that student comes to share the teacher's vision of the subject matter. Some (e.g. Klenowski, 1995) argue that this can be done by clarifying objectives, but others (e.g. Claxton, 1995; Wiliam, 1994) argue that these definitions must remain implicit if they are not to distort learning.

A development of this theory seems to call for links to compatible learning theories and to theories of the meta-cognition and locus of control of the learner. Tittle's (1994) frame-work emphasises three dimensions. The first, the epistemology and theories involved, can relate both to positions held in relation to learning in general, and to the particular epistemology relevant to the subject matter concerned. The nature of the epistemology, and so of the meta-cognition involved, in (say) aesthetic appreciation of poetry will be very different from that for (say) physics, and hence many features of formative assess-ment will differ between these two fields of learning. The second dimension is the more evident one of the assessment characteristics; it can be remarked here that in several of the studies reported here, little is said about the detail of these, or about the distinc-tive effects of the particular subject matter involved. Tittle's third dimension brings in the interpreter and user, and she particularly stresses the importance of these. In rela-tion to students, this emphasis is reinforced and developed by Sadler's arguments, but the teacher's beliefs, about the subject matter, about learning, and about the students and the class, must also be important components in any model, if only because it is on the basis of these that appraisals of Sadler's 'gap' must be formulated. Tittle also makes the important point that while modern conceptions of validity theory (e.g. Messick, 1989) stress the value-laden nature of assessment processes, the actual nature of those values is excluded, creating the impression that one (presumably reasonably coherent) set of values is as good as any other. Thus current conceptions of validity provide no guide as to what 'ought' to be going on, merely a theoretical framework for discussing what is going on. This emphasis on the ethical and moral aspects of assessment is a feature of the perspective outlined by Aikenhead (1997). He draws upon the work of Habermas (1971, p.308) and Ryan (1988) to propose that consideration of assessment can fail within three paradigms that are commonly encountered in the social sciences. One, the empirical-analytic, clearly links to the psychometric emphasis in standardised testing. The second, the interpretative paradigm, has to be adopted in formative assessment, and this link brings out the importance of understanding a learner's response in relation to that learn-er's expectations and assumptions about the classroom process, together with his or her interpretation of the task demand and of the criteria for success. In the third, the critical theoretic paradigm, one would seek a critique of the wider purposes being pursued, nota-bly the empowerment of the learner, and the choice between either selecting an elite or achieving excellence for all. This paradigm also calls into play the need for a critique of the learning goals (and of the assessment criteria through which they are operationalised) which should ask whose interests these goals are designed to serve.

Similar concerns motivate the theoretical framework proposed by Davis (1997) as a result of a detailed study of the changes (over a two-year period) of the practice of a single middle-school mathematics teacher in the way she reacted to students' responses to her questions. Initially, the teacher's reactions tended to focus on the extent to which the student responses accorded with the teacher's expectations (what Davis terms 'evaluative' listening). After sustained reflection and discussion with the researcher over a period of several months, the teacher's reaction placed increasing emphasis on 'information-seeking' as opposed to the 'response-seeking' which characterised the earlier lessons ('interpretive' listening). Towards the end of the two-year period, there was a further shift in the teacher's practice, with a marked move away from clear lesson structures and pre-specified learning outcomes, and towards the exploration of potentially rich mathematical situations, in which the teacher is a co-participant. Most notably, in this third phase, the teacher's own views of the subject matter being 'taught' developed and altered along with that of the students ('hermeneutic' listening). It is clear therefore that a commitment to the use of formative assessment necessarily entails a move away from unitary notions of intelligence (Wolf et al., 1991).

Expectations and the social setting

These last two analyses bring out a feature which in our view has been absent from a great deal of the research we have reviewed. This is that all the assessment processes are, at heart, social processes, taking place in social settings, conducted by, on and for social actors. Guy Brousseau (1984) has used the term 'didactical contract' to describe the network of (largely implicit) expectations and agreements that are evolved between students and teachers. A particular feature of such contracts is that they serve to delimit 'legitimate' activity by the teacher. For example, in a classroom where the teacher's questioning has always been restricted to 'lower order' skills, such as the production of correct procedures, students may well see questions about 'understanding' or 'application' as unfair, illegitimate or even meaningless (Schoenfeld, 1985).

As Tittle's (1994) approach emphasises, the 'opening moves' of teachers and students in the negotiation of such classroom contracts will be determined by their epistemological, psychological and pedagogical beliefs. For example, when a teacher questions a student, the teacher's beliefs will influence both the questions asked and the way that answers are interpreted. An important principle here is the distinction between 'fit' and 'match' (von Glasersfeld, 1987, page 13). For example, a teacher may set students problems in solving systems of simple equations. If students answer all the questions correctly, the teacher may well conclude that the students have 'understood' the topic, i.e. they assume that the students' understanding matches theirs. However, this is frequently not the case. For example, when asked to solve the following two equations

$3a = 24$
$a + b = 16$

many students believe that it is impossible, saying things like 'I keep getting b is 8, but it can't be because a is 8'. This is because in the examples encountered in most textbooks, each letter stands for a different number. The students' understanding is therefore not a match but only a 'fit' with the teacher's. The relationship between fit and match depends critically on the richness of the questions used by the teacher, and this, in turn will depend on the teacher's subject knowledge, their theories of learning, and their experience of learners.

EXTRACT TWO *continued*

A study of seven experienced elementary school teachers examined the implicit criteria that teachers used to determine whether students had 'understood' something (Reynolds et al, 1995). After studying and discussing video extracts and transcripts of lessons, seven 'indicators of understanding' emerged which were agreed by all seven teachers, although they were regarded not as a static check list, but rather as a series of potential clues to the level of the student's understanding:

1. *changes in demeanour: students who had understood were 'bright eyed' while those who had not appeared half-hearted;*

2. *extension of a concept: students who have understood something often take the idea further on their own initiative;*

3. *making modifications to a pattern: students who understand, spontaneously start making their own modifications, while those who don't understand imitate or follow rules;*

4. *using processes in a different context: students who have understood a particular idea often start seeing the same patterns elsewhere;*

5. *using shortcuts: only students who are sure of the 'big picture' can short-cut a procedure so that thinking up or using a short-cut is taken as evidence of understanding;*

6. *ability to explain: students who have understood something are usually able to explain it;*

7. *ability to focus attention: persistence on a task is taken as a sign of understanding. It may be that some teachers are content with 'fits' rather than 'matches' because they are unaware of the possibilities for students' conceptions that are different from their own. However, it seems likely that most teachers are aware of the benefits of richer questioning styles, but find that such approaches are difficult to implement in 'real classrooms' (Dassa, 1990). In this respect, computer software that enables teachers to provide formative and diagnostic feedback may have a role to play (Dassa et al, 1993; William, 1997), although there is little evidence so far about the actual benefits of such software.*

In turn, the student's responses to questioning will depend on a host of factors. Whether the student believes ability to be incremental or fixed will have a strong influence on how the student sees a question – as an opportunity to learn or as a threat to self-esteem (Dweck, 1986). Even where the student has a 'learning' as opposed to 'performance' orientation, the student's belief about what counts as 'academic work' (Doyle, 1988) will have a profound impact on the 'mindfulness' with which that student responds. The study of two middle-school teachers by Lorsbach et al (1992) cited in the earlier section on Current practice found that a major threat to the validity of test-result interpretation was the extent to which students could construct meanings for the tasks they were set, and the extent to which teachers could construct meanings for the students' responses. They also found that teachers used assessment results as if they gave information on what students knew, whereas, in fact, they were better indicators of motivation and task completion.

More specifically, the actual context of the assessment can also influence what students believe is required. My example is a study of a grade 5 geometry class (Hall et al.*, 1995) where performance was assessed in two ways – via a multiple choice test and with an assignment in which students had to design a HyperCard geometry tutorial. In the multiple choice test, the students focused on the grades awarded, while in the tutorial task, students engaged in much more presentation and qualitative discussion of their work. Perhaps most significantly, discussion amongst students of the different tutorials focused much more directly on the subject matter (i.e. geometry) than did the (intense) comparison of grades on the multiple choice test. The actions of teachers and students are also 'enframed' (Mitchell, 1991) by the structures of schools and society and typically knowledge is closely tied to the situation in which it is learnt (Boaler, 1997). Spaces in schools are designated for specified activities, and given the importance attached to 'orderliness' in most classrooms, teachers' actions are as often concerned with establishing routines, order and student satisfaction as they are with developing the student's capabilities (Torrance & Pryor, 1995; Pryor & Torrance, 1996). A review by Rismark (1996) shows that students are frequently marginalised and their work undervalued if they use frames of reference from their personal experiences outside school and Filer (1993) found that children learning handwriting and spelling in English primary school classrooms were constrained by the teacher to develop these skills in standard contexts, so that their own personal experiences were 'blocked out'. In this way, formal, purportedly 'objective' assessments made by teachers may be little more than the result of successive sedimentation of previous 'informal' assessments – in extreme cases the self-fulfilling prophecy of teachers' labelling of students (Filer, 1995).*

In trying to reconcile these effects of structure and agency, Bourdieu's notion of habitus (Bourdieu, 1985) may be particularly fruitful. Traditional approaches to sociological analysis have used coarse categories such as gender, race, and social class to 'explain' differences in, for example, outcomes, thus tending to treat all those within a category as being homogenous. Bourdieu uses the notion of habitus to describe the orientations, experiences and positions adopted by social actors, particularly in order to account for the differences between individuals in the same categories. Such a notion seems particularly appropriate for describing classrooms, in view of the fact that the experiences of students in the same classroom can be so different (Dart & Clarke, 1989).

Research – prospects and needs

The above discussion has clear implications for the design of research investigations. It draws attention to the range of important features which will combine to determine the effects of any classroom regime. In the light of such a specification, it is clear that most of the studies in the literature have not attended to some of the important aspects of the situations being researched. A full list of important and relevant aspects would include the following:

- *the assumptions about learning underlying the curriculum and pedagogy;*

- *the rationale underlying the composition and presentation of the learning work;*

- *the precise nature of the various types of assessment evidence revealed by the learner's responses;*

- *the interpretative framework used by both teachers and learners in responding to this evidence;*

- *the learning work used in acting on the interpretations so derived;*

- *the divisions of responsibility between learners and teachers in these processes;*

- *the perceptions and beliefs held by the learners about themselves as learners, about their own learning work, and about the aims and methods for their studies;*

- *the perceptions and beliefs of teachers about learning, about the 'abilities' and prospects of their students, and about their roles as assessors;*

- *the nature of the social setting in the classroom, as created by the learning and teaching members and by the constraints of the wider school system as they perceive and evaluate them;*

- *issues relating to race, class and gender, which appear to have received little attention in research studies of formative assessment;*

- *the extent to which the context of any study is artificial and the possible effects of this feature on the generalisability of the results.*

To make adequate report of all of these, let alone control them in any classical quantitative design, would seem very difficult. This is not to imply that reliable measures of outcomes, both of learning and of attitudes to the subjects learnt, are not to be sought – although one of the problems evident in many of the studies seems to be that although they are serving learning aims that the established methods ignore or play down, they have to justify themselves in relation to tests which are adapted to the established methods only. There is clearly a need for a combination of such measures with richer qualitative studies of processes and interactions within the classroom. If, as we believe, there is a need to evolve new approaches as quickly as possible, such studies might well focus on the problems of change and attendant disorientations. Particular attention ought to be paid to two specific problems. The first is the evidence in many studies that new emphasis on formative assessment is of particular benefit to the disadvantaged and low-attaining learners – evidence which is not supported in the results of other studies. The apparent contradictions here probably arise because there are some important features of the classrooms that have yet to be recorded and understood. If it is true that the ranges of school achievement might be narrowed by the enhancement of the achievement of those hitherto seen as slow learners, then there are very strong social and educational reasons for giving high priority to sensitive research and development work to see how to understand and tackle the issues involved.

The second problem, or clutch of problems, relates to the possible confusions and tensions, both for teachers and learners, between the formative and summative purposes which their work might have to serve. It is inevitable that all will be involved, one way or the other, in working to both purposes, and if an optimum balance is not sought, formative work will always be insecure because of the threat of renewed dominance by the summative.

We asked earlier what you understood by the term 'feedback'. This is an important aspect of formative assessment, and involves you, the teacher, discussing with the learners the aspects of formative assessment which we have discussed previously. In other words:

Feedback from teachers to children, in the process of formative assessment, is a prime requirement for progress in learning ... In everyday classroom terms this means teachers using their judgements of children's knowledge or understanding to feed back into the teaching process and to determine for individual children whether to re-explain the task/concept, to give further practice on it, or move on [to] the next stage.

(Tunstall and Gipps, 1996, page 389)

The way in which Black and Wiliam discuss feedback takes us into another important area of formative assessment, that of self-assessment. Again, we know that there is a wide variety of school-based assessment practices in operation. In this discussion self-assessment entails the student coming *to share the teacher's vision of the subject matter* (page 55). To move from this practical application of what you can do in the classroom to a discussion of learning theory may seem a little obscure, but it is important both in the context of gaining QTS, and of your future development, that you develop theoretical understandings of pedagogy, teaching, and learning. Your teaching style should be built upon firm foundations of knowing. The theoretical discussions which Black and Wiliam engage in build on the work already mentioned, of Tittle (1994). Essentially, Tittle refers to three dimensions of assessment. These are:

1. epistemology;

2. assessment characteristics, including assessment criteria for your subject;

3. the interpreter and the user of these; in other words you, the teacher, and the pupils.

Let us consider these with reference to your current and future stages of development. (Here there will be a marked gap between our theory and practice, as in true formative assessment we would want to personalise our discussions based upon our knowledge of you as learner, clearly impossible in a book!) Epistemology, that which is concerned with knowledge and knowing, will inform the way you teach. You will have views about what sorts of knowledge you value, and allied with this, views as to the knowledge types that your subject values, and what sorts of ways of knowing are important. Black and Wiliam use the example of the appreciation of poetry being different from knowledge in physics.

REFLECTIVE EXERCISE

Think about what knowledge is valued in your subject area. Refer back to earlier chapters which focused on issues associated with your identify as a teacher and your approaches to teaching and learning, and think about whether this informs your assessment practices, and if so, how?

What this means for formative assessment is that different types of valued knowledge require different formative assessment features. For example, kicking a ball better, improving skill at painting a picture, improving understandings of differential calculus, getting better at spelling, all require feedback, but each of them will involve different pupil–teacher interactions. This takes us into the second of Tittle's dimensions, the assessment characteristics for your subject. There will be very specific ways of knowing in, say, mathematics, which are different from, say, music. The ways in which you, the teacher, develop understandings in your subject will to some extent depend on the valued knowledge in your subject. This takes us back to Harlen and James, and you knowing what it is you want the pupils to improve at, and how and why. This in turn takes us to the third dimension, that of teacher and student. You will have your own beliefs about what is important, and it is likely that you will want your students to share those beliefs in order for them to improve their learning. This links to Black and Wiliam's next set of discussions, concerning paradigms of formative assessment.

The interpretative paradigm is likely to be of significant importance to you. It *brings out the importance of understanding a learner's response in relation to that learner's expectations and assumptions about the classroom process, together with his or her interpretation of the task demand and of the criteria for success* (page 55). This brings us to the issue of criteria. Assessment criteria are standard features of assessment, and are likely to feature in your work. Indeed, in our discussion of learning outcomes below we shall return to this theme. We do know that writing good assessment criteria is a difficult task:

> *Writing good criteria that do not trivialise what is being assessed is difficult. As written criteria look authoritative and then tend to be treated as the right criteria, if they have not been well-conceived, clearly this causes all kinds of problems.*

> (Freeman and Lewis, 1998, page 20)

In our current discussion, what matters here is sharing assessment criteria with the pupils. Black and Wiliam's brief discussion of critical theory is a useful case in point.

REFLECTIVE EXERCISE

Think back on a topic you have recently taught. Focus on the assessment criteria that you developed. These probably relate to the learning objectives that you planned. Consider the following questions.

Why do you have the assessment criteria you do?

How do they help the learners? Indeed, do they help the learners?

Who are the criteria for? Are they solely for you? Did you share them with the pupils?

How did you use them to generate assessment data?

We are emphasising formative assessment in this chapter as it holds the potential to significantly improve pupil learning. But there are challenges to the good use of formative assessment, and the construction and use of appropriate assessment criteria is one of them.

Black and Wiliam then move to a discussion of the social aspects of assessment. This discussion includes some useful material on questioning. We know that questioning is a key skill for teachers, and that it is a feature of most types of lessons. The notion of whether pupils' understanding 'fit' with yours or 'match' yours is quite difficult to establish in classroom settings. The effective use of questioning enables you to really probe the understandings of your learners. But these need to be carefully structured, and move to higher-order thinking; for example, as outlined in Bloom's taxonomy (Bloom, 1956). To do this as a beginning teacher you will need to plan carefully for questioning, and think about what you do with the answers that pupils give to these questions. Black and Wiliam list a series of clues as to how teachers can try to evaluate the potential level of understanding attained by the pupils. But you do need to be aware of the differences between understanding and motivation, and not confuse the two.

Caroline Gipps observed that, *assessment is not an exact science, and we must stop presenting it as such* (Gipps, 1994, page 167). Black and Wiliam make a similar observation when they say, *formal, purportedly 'objective' assessments made by teachers may be little more than the result of successive sedimentation of previous 'informal' assessments – in extreme cases the self-fulfilling prophecy of teachers' labelling of students* (page 58). The statement by Gipps and that of Black and Wiliam are something you need to be very aware of. Your assessments of pupils are your assessments; they may (or may not) be 'true' in some sense, but they are based on assumptions. This can be particularly problematic when it comes to labelling pupils, particularly with National Curriculum levels. Formative assessment takes as its premise the notion that every child can improve, and this might challenge *unitary notions of intelligence*.

Towards the end of the article is a series of bullet points which appertain to future research needs in formative assessment.

REFLECTIVE EXERCISE

Some of these bullet points are quite complex, but which could apply to the way you undertake formative assessment with your pupils in your classroom context?

The final point made by Black and Wiliam harks back to the work of Harlen and James, and is concerned with the potential dominance of summative assessment strategies. This if often apparent in schools, where there can be unhelpful mislabelling of approaches, with approaches being called formative assessment which are really mini-summative assessments. But summative assessment must and does have a place in the classroom, and it is to that which we now turn.

Assessing pupil progress

In the UK, any discussions of assessment rapidly turn to National Curriculum levels, and how they are, or can be employed. The next document we will consider is *Assessing Pupils' Progress – Assessment at the heart of learning*, which was produced by the QCDA (QCDA, 2008). As you read this document consider the following questions.

POINTS TO CONSIDER

Who is the intended audience for this document?

What advice does it give about assessment?

Is it informed by the Black and Wiliam, and Harlen and James documents we have considered previously?

What is its theoretical stance?

EXTRACT THREE

QCDA (2008) Assessing Pupils' Progress: Assessment at the Heart of Learning. *Qualifications and Curriculum Development Agency (QCDA), pp. 3–7.*

What is APP?

APP is the new structured approach to teacher assessment, developed by QCDA in partnership with the National Strategies, which equips teachers to make judgements on pupils' progress. It helps teachers to fine-tune their understanding of learners' needs and to tailor their planning and teaching accordingly, by enabling them to:

- *use diagnostic information about pupils' strengths and weaknesses to improve teaching, learning and pupils' progress*
- *make reliable judgements related to national standards drawing on a wide range of evidence*
- *track pupils' progress.*

The APP subject materials for teachers include:

- **the APP handbook** *to help teachers use the materials and implement the approach*
- **assessment guidelines** *for assessing pupils' work in relation to national curriculum levels, These provide a simple recording format providing assessment criteria for each of the assessment focuses in the subject*
- **standards files** *– annotated collections of pupils' day-to-day work that exemplify national standards at different levels. These help teachers reach consistent and reliable judgements about national curriculum levels.*

APP has been greeted enthusiastically by teachers piloting the approach. They say it provides them with a more well-rounded profile of their pupils' achievements. It has given them the confidence and ability to recognise how and when pupils are learning, in a variety of classroom contexts.

APP materials are currently available for key stage 2 and 3 reading, writing and mathematics. Materials are being developed for speaking and listening, science, ICT and foundation subjects at key stage 3.

How does APP work?

The APP approach is straightforward. In line with their school assessment policy and practice, teachers periodically review evidence of their pupils' work using the assessment guidelines and build a profile of their achievements.

Generating evidence from teaching

Through their day-to-day interactions, observations and ongoing assessment teachers see evidence of what learners understand and can do. APP is most effective when it draws on a broad range of evidence that shows what learners can do independently. Assessment evidence could include:

- *extended or shorter focused pieces of writing in a variety of different forms for a range of purposes*

- *information from different curriculum areas*

- *text annotation or visual organisers such as thought mapping, storyboards or timelines*

- *oral work such as pupil presentations to the class, contributions to class discussions, drama activities or discussions with teachers*

- *observations of learners' behaviour and interactions*

- *learners' self-assessment.*

Reviewing the evidence

When a teacher has enough evidence of what the learner is able to do independently in different contexts, they can apply the APP guidelines to make a periodic assessment.

The assessment guidelines cover two national curriculum levels with overlaps (levels 3 and 4, 4 and 5, 5 and 6, and so on). The teacher needs to select the appropriate sheet based on their judgement of roughly which level a pupil is working at.

Drawing on the evidence they have selected, the teacher then considers each of the subject assessment focuses carefully and highlights where the criteria have been met across the two levels.

Making a judgement

Once judgements have been made for each of the assessment focuses, the profile of highlighted criteria allows the teacher to make an informed decision about the overall national curriculum level at which the learner is working. The judgement is made in a holistic way, taking account of how independently, consistently, and in what range of contexts learners demonstrate their skills.

Using the assessment criteria inevitably involves a degree of interpretation and professional judgement. Standards files help ensure that judgements made by teachers are consistent and aligned with national standards. Regular collaborative assessment and discussion is another important way of ensuring that assessment standards are reliable and consistent.

Using information from APP

The assessment guidelines give detailed information that can be used to create relevant and measurable targets for improvement. They also support productive discussions between teachers, learners and parents.

EXTRACT THREE *continued*

What are the benefits of using APP?

APP puts the learner at the heart of assessment. It does this by providing a detailed and personalised profile that gives an overview of where learners are in the subject and what they need to do to improve.

The main benefits of APP are as follows.

- *It does not require special assessment activities but involves recognising evidence from the opportunities generated by planned teaching and learning.*

- *It reduces the need to use tests and specific assessment tasks to make assessment judgements by taking into account a far wider range of evidence. This gives a clearer and more accurate picture of learners' achievements and progress.*

- *It provides a valuable opportunity for professional development as it gives teachers effective tools to develop their assessment and teaching techniques.*

- *It provides a common language, enabling teachers to share and discuss the evidence they have of learners' progress, to build assessment expertise and develop confidence.*

- *It directly informs discussions with pupils and future planning, teaching and learning.*

- *It helps teachers identify gaps in their teaching. For example, when a periodic assessment showed little evidence of a particular assessment focus, teachers from the pilot found that APP influenced their planning and pedagogy.*

The table below shows some of the things teachers say they do differently as a result of using APP.

Practice before APP	Practice after APP
• define progress through tests and written exercises	• assess learning in relation to key assessment focuses
• use commercial tests and optional national curriculum tests	• develop a clearer idea of pupils' strengths and weaknesses and gaps in their experience
• set level for individual pieces of work twice per term	• observe pupils making choices about their learning
• focus on outcomes (for example exercises and end of unit tasks) rather than processes	• make use of spoken and written evidence
	• observe pupils trying different approaches to solving problems
	• collect evidence from a range of work in different subjects
	• assess across the range using assessment focuses
	• talk to pupils to find out more about how they tackle problems as well as whether they get the answer

Assessing pupils' progress (APP) is an initiative designed to improve teachers' practice with regard to assessment in the classroom. Depending on which subject you teach, you may be more or less familiar with APP, and what it means in your subject area.

There are some interesting terminologies employed in the document, which we need to critique. One of the key assumptions is contained in the first paragraph, namely that it *helps teachers to fine-tune their understanding of learners' needs and to tailor their planning and teaching accordingly* (page 3). In the extracts previously discussed in this chapter we have seen that formative assessment is very much concerned with doing this, with feedback, and with providing information about where pupils currently are in their learning, and what they need to do to improve. This is done by careful planning of reactive lessons, which are designed for where the learners are currently. What this means for you is that although you may be teaching the same topic to a range of classes in the same year, you will be adjusting your lesson plan according to the response from each class; 8Y may be racing ahead, whereas 8Z may need to spend longer in order to grasp the essentials of the topic in hand. From this assumption we can take it that formative assessment will be a part of the APP process. This is reinforced by the bullet point which foregrounds 'diagnostic assessment'. Diagnostic assessment was one of the four main uses of assessment originally proposed in the TGAT report (DES/WO, 1988) to which we have already referred. It was initially purposed with diagnosing learning difficulties in the individual pupil, whereas nowadays it is normally subsumed within formative assessment.

The issues of formative assessment so far discussed are then replaced in the second set of bullet points by phrases relating to summative assessment. The National Curriculum levels are themselves instances of summative assessments. There is a problem with the use of summative National Curriculum levels for individual pieces of work, which your mentors and other teachers may have discussed with you. The levels themselves were originally written solely for use at the end of a key stage, and the QCDA website used to say that *a single piece of work will not cover all the expectations set out in a level description*. The focus of APP on awarding National Curriculum levels shows that there has been a shift in thinking, because, as the next bullets show, APP will *help teachers reach consistent and reliable judgements about national curriculum levels*, and this is based on the *assessment guidelines for assessing pupils' work in relation to national curriculum levels* (page 3).

There is a move back, then to formative assessment, for in the next section, it is stated that *through their day-to-day interactions, observations and ongoing assessment teachers see evidence of what learners understand and can do* (page 4). This is an important point, and one which we need to consider the implications of in more detail than the QCDA supply. We have seen how formative assessment is designed to inform future progression, and we know that summative assessment is meant to certify pupil attainment at specific points. What has taken place in many schools is a conflation of the two, so that we have the formative use of summative assessment. Figure 4.1 gives a diagrammatic representation of this notion.

The formative use of summative assessment is recognised as an effective methodology for teachers to employ in order to develop the learning of their pupils (Harlen, 2005; Black et al., 2003). This may be helpful to you in applying some of the theoretical stances outlined in these and other writings on assessment into your day-to-day practice. What is also important is contained in the bullets related to *assessment evidence could include …* (page 4). Again the QCDA has not spelt out in detail what it means, but has included a useful range of sources of assessment evidence which teachers can employ. Critiquing this section, what it is saying is that the currently common practice of having an assessment lesson as a stand-alone session may not be the best way of operationalising good assessment strategies. You may meet examples of staffroom dialogue where a teacher says something like, 'We will be having an assessment lesson next Wednesday'. What the APP document is saying is that assessment opportunities occur in the course of normal teaching and learning encounters, and that using these will provide evidence for summative assessment.

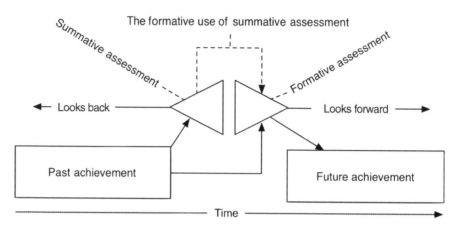

Figure 4.1 Assessment Modalities (Fautley and Savage, 2008, page 27)

In the short paragraph entitled *Using information from APP*, the notion of target-setting is introduced. Good target-setting is a key component of formative assessment, and having a secure evidence base on which to draw is helpful.

Target setting with stickers!
In a school recently, I noticed that pupils had stickers on the front of their book which said things like '4c' or '5a'. I asked the pupils what these were. 'Our target grades' was the reply. 'So', I asked 'what do you have to do to reach them?'. 'Work harder', they said.

The example described above is from a school where target-setting is employed, but not really focused in any meaningful way. The key information the pupil needs to know is 'What specifically do I have to do? Is it write my conclusions in a more extended way, measure the chemicals more precisely, try to keep my arm straight when bowling, hold the paintbrush a little looser?' or whatever. These are real targets, and pupils know when they have reached them. In other words, they can undertake self-assessment. Also, their peers can help them and you could imagine comments such as, 'You could extend that a bit', 'Use a smaller spatula', 'Keep your arm up', 'Don't hold it like a pencil'. These are peer assessments which focus on the learning. Knowing that you are a 4c, and need to 'work harder' to get to 4b is not very helpful.

This, of course, leads to a question about the place of sub-levels in the National Curriculum. It is likely that you will be asked to use them, yet at no point in the APP is their existence acknowledged. This is because they have no place in statute. But for good formative use of summative assessment you will want to know in as 'fine-tuned' detail as possible what the pupils have done, and what they can do.

Another of this document's coded messages comes in the form of the terminologies for the periodicity of assessment. Day-to-day assessment arises from classroom practice, whereas periodic assessment takes place less frequently, and is of a more formal, distinctly summative variety. So, how often is periodic?

> *Suitable timing for periodic assessment may be decided centrally as part of a whole school assessment policy or in consultation with colleagues. To carry out a periodic assessment a teacher needs to be confident that the learner has completed a wide enough range of work in different contexts to give a reliable picture of their overall performance. There also needs to be evidence that pupils can transfer the skills they have learnt. Periodic assessment should ideally be timed for when the information will be put to best use. This might be when the school requires teacher assessment judgements to be reported to parents, for example. Generally, periodic assessment is likely to be appropriate at two or three points in the year.*
>
> (QCDA website)

This statement helps considerably, and will be useful to you in your thinking about assessment too.

The final section of the document shows how the assessment burden can be reduced by thinking about APP. From the perspectives of the documents we have already considered, it is clear that good formative assessment strategies are welcomed as providing the best basis for developing learning.

The assessment details and arrangements outlined by the QCDA will need to be enacted by you in the classroom, and drawing on the materials from earlier in this chapter, ought to be evident in the way you plan for learning, and think about what takes place in your day-to-day work in the classroom, and so it is to this aspect which we now turn.

Applying assessment within your own teaching practice

In our work with trainee and beginning teachers, one of the most common concerns is that of having to write learning outcomes for each lesson. We know this is problematic, and so the next section, which has been adapted from our book on assessment (Fautley and Savage, 2008), will hopefully put some of this into focus for you.

As you read this next section, please think about the following questions.

From learning outcomes to assessment criteria

In Figure 4.2 the upper part of this diagram has been extracted and collapsed somewhat.

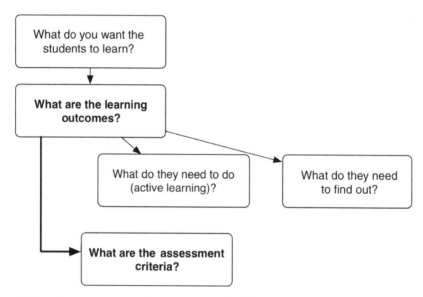

Figure 4.2 Learning outcomes and assessment criteria

In our original discussions we noted how good learning outcomes can be reapplied as assessment criteria. For many trainee teachers, and indeed for many practising teachers, we discussed how writing good learning outcomes can be problematic. We have also noted already that a common mistake made by beginning teachers is to confuse *doing* with learning. It is much easier to write task outcomes than it is to write learning outcomes. In a true learning outcome it is the learning which is the focus of your attention, whereas a task outcome is concerned more with action and activity, or simply with keeping the students busy.

You will sometimes hear teachers talking about 'good' activities to do with the students. You will also be able to find publications which are little more than collections of activities designed to occupy classes. You might think to yourself that something you have seen or experienced would make a good lesson. As we noted in our original discussions, what you need to do in these circumstances is to take a step backwards and ask yourself the question, 'What is it that the students will be learning in this?' If the answer is 'little or nothing', you need to consider why this activity should be done at all.

The role of differentiation

Another aspect of formative assessment is that of dividing up learning outcomes to allow for differentiation into all–most–some outcomes is a sensible way to begin this process. What assessment for learning should do is enable you and the students to know whether these distinctions have been met, and, if so, to what degree. In order to study this further, let us investigate some examples drawn from different curriculum areas as exemplar materials. It is important to note that although we are using specific subject areas and year groups to do this, the general principles concerned with lesson planning should be applicable across a range of ages, phases, and ability groups.

TEACHING EXAMPLE

Food technology

(In this and subsequent examples the numbers and letters in brackets refer to the National Curriculum identification system used at the time (for the subject in question).)

During Key Stage 3 students use a wide range of materials to design and make products. In this example the teacher is trying to ensure that knowledge and understanding are applied when making their product. Let us take the case of a Year 7 class preparing a salad.

The aims of this lesson are:

1. *To consider aesthetics and other issues that influence their planning (1e).*

2. *Select and use tools, equipment and processes to shape and form materials safely and accurately and finish them appropriately (2a).*

The learning outcomes are:

By the end of the lesson...

... all students will have learned:

- *to prepare and combine ingredients to make a salad that meets the design brief (1e, 4c, 7b);*

- *that a variety of ingredients can be used to prepare a salad that meets the design brief (1e, 4c, 7b);*

- *that ingredients can be prepared using different tools and methods of preparation (4c, 7b).*

TEACHING EXAMPLE *continued*

... most students will have learned:

- *to prepare and combine ingredients to make a salad that meets the design brief and be able to state how the design brief has been met (1e, 4c, 7b);*

- *that a variety of ingredients can be used to prepare a salad that meets the design brief, and be able to suggest alternative ingredients to those that have been allocated (1e, 4c, 7b);*

- *that ingredients can be prepared using different tools and methods of preparation and be able to justify the choices they have made (4c, 7b).*

... some students might have learned:

- *to prepare and combine ingredients to make a salad that meets the design brief and be able to state how the design brief has been met, covering all points (1e, 4c, 7b);*

- *that a variety of ingredients can be used to prepare a salad that meets the design brief, be able to suggest alternative ingredients to those they have been allocated and indicate where the alternatives fit onto the balanced plate (1e, 4c, 7b);*

- *that ingredients can be prepared using different tools and methods of preparation, be able to justify the choices they have made and suggest alternative methods of preparation (4c, 7b).*

Notice how the learning outcomes are sequential between the all–most–some divisions. In other words, the first learning outcome for all students becomes superseded by the first learning outcome for most students, and so on. These learning outcomes can clearly be seen to contain within them the seeds for assessment for learning to take place. It will be a straightforward matter for the teacher to decide which students have achieved what aspects of the learning required from them. Notice, too, that some aspects of learning can be uncovered only by undertaking discussions with the students. The learning is not solely contained in the work of the individual students in terms of the final plated outcome, important aspects of the learning are involved in the processes by which these outcomes were reached.

Let us dig a little deeper into these distinctions between learning and doing. There are times when learning may be contained *in* doing, and that physical activity supported by conceptual understanding is the aim of the lesson. In this case what you will need to do is formulate learning outcomes based on the fact that the students will be *learning to do*. As an example let us consider the case of a music lesson, where the students are learning how to play a 12-bar blues.

This lesson involves learning to do something, in this case perform, but simply saying that 'All students will perform a 12-bar blues chord sequence' does not adequately identify the learning. This is an example of lesson which can be undertaken at a number of different levels of complexity. So, as this lesson could be taught from Key Stage 2 through to postgraduate level, the learning outcomes need to indicate how previously-learned skills and knowledge will be developed, and that is why they are so specific. This might seem pedantic, but remember that by spending time crafting good learning outcomes, you will be making the assessment process transparent. In the case of this music lesson, the teacher will be able to know which students have achieved which learning outcome by observing the students practising, and listening to the final performances which result during the plenary stage of the lesson.

TEACHING EXAMPLE

Music

Learning outcomes (Performing):

By the end of the lesson...

... all students:

- *will have developed their understanding of chords and chord sequences by performing the chords (in root position or simple inversions) to a 12-bar blues.*

... most students:

- *will have developed their understanding by learning to play the 12-bar blues chords with stylistically appropriate rhythmic development.*

... some students:

- *will have further developed their understanding by learning to maintain the chord sequence while playing a stylistically appropriate bass line, riff or improvisation.*

What is happening in the music lesson is that understanding is evidenced in achievement. It is clear to see that this is another way of looking at learning. But what does this mean, 'understanding evidenced in achievement'? If someone tells you they can tap-dance, the proof is that they can. There are many complicated steps and routines involved in tap dancing, and the learner needs to develop an understanding of these, but the real proof will be in practical achievement. This is a case where *knowing how* is the form of knowledge which the lesson is addressing. What the music teacher has done in the example above is to clearly state which aspects of learning are important in that particular lesson. It is quite likely that this lesson will form one of a sequence based on the 12-bar blues, and although the students may well be playing the same piece of music next lesson, the learning is likely to be different, and will arise from the teacher's evaluation and formative assessments made during the course of this lesson. In other words, the *doing* might remain similar, but it is the *learning* which alters.

The notion of understanding evidenced in achievement is patently not unique to music. Here is an example drawn from a Key Stage 4 drama lesson.

Again we can clearly see how the teacher will be able to progress from the learning outcomes to an assessment of individual students' understanding as evidenced in achievement. A less thoughtful drama teacher might have produced a simpler version, along the lines of 'all students will create a character from the text'; although this satisfies the immediacy of a lesson, notice how it misses out the complexities of the learning experience, tells the students only what they will do, and ignores the quality or level of their learning; it is a task outcome, not a learning one. We discussed how important it was to share learning outcomes with students, and in this case using the full version of the learning outcomes will enable students to become attentive and responsible for their own learning. What this will also do is to enable peer and self-assessment to take place more readily, as the students will have a clearer view of what their own learning entails, how it fits in with the learning of their peers, and, importantly, what a successful learning outcome will look like.

TEACHING EXAMPLE

Drama

The aim of this lesson is developing character from text. The learning outcomes are divided into two areas, creating and performing.

Creating

By the end of the lesson... all students will have learned:

- *that contextual details from the text can form a basis for creating a character.*

... most students will have learned:

- *that contextual details from the text can suggest attitudinal features and can include these in their own created character.*

... some students may have learned:

- *that attitudinal features drawn from the text will affect their created character's relationships and interactions with other characters.*

Performing

By the end of the lesson... all students:

- *will have developed their understanding of the character in the text by including this understanding in their physical and vocal presentation of their own character.*

... most students:

- *will have developed their understanding of the character in the text by using a range of physical and vocal means to convey their attitude.*

... some students:

- *may have further developed their understanding of the textual character by showing, both physically and vocally, the way in which attitude has affected relationships with other characters.*

Learning evidenced in achievement need not be confined to academic or practical outcomes alone. In a Key Stage 3 art lesson on the topic of cutting a lino block, health and safety matters form an important component alongside the subject-specific learning that the teacher wants. In the next example, notice how the teacher skilfully develops these health and safety issues as part of her all–most–some learning outcomes.

TEACHING EXAMPLE

Art and design

The aims of the lesson are:

To provide opportunities for students to:

- *learn and experience the principles of cutting a lino block (2b, 2c, 5c);*

- *base lino cutting on the relief printmaking of the German Expressionist School (4c, 5d);*

- *understand the safety principles of lino cutting and exercise care with the use of tools (health and safety).*

The learning outcomes are:

By the end of the lesson...

... all students will have learned:

- *how to cut and gain experience of, cutting a lino block using appropriate tools (2b, 2c, 5c);*

- *to use lino cutting tools with safety.*

... most students will have learned:

- *the skilled application of mark-making achieved with the selection of appropriate tools, showing understanding of the media (2b, 2c, 5c);*

- *to achieve careful and skilful manipulation of lino cutting tools.*

... some students might have learned:

- *to apply appropriate tools to achieve skilled marks in lino cutting with an expressive outcome within the style of their studied artist (4c, 5d);*

- *a clear understanding demonstrated in their working practice of health and safety issues.*

Health and safety are not issues you can leave to chance, and this lesson shows how learning outcomes can be written to encompass this hand-in-hand with achievement.

Notice how the learning outcomes in all of these examples so far employ a sequential delineation. Sometimes, however, you may want to take a cumulative approach to differentiated learning outcomes, and ensure that all students are familiar with knowledge, skills and concepts required before you are able to move *most* or *some* students on to develop other aspects of learning. This is the approach adopted in this lesson plan by a maths teacher.

This notion of taking a cumulative approach to learning outcomes provides a different, but still linear, route towards assessment. In the case of the maths lesson the teacher will need to differentiate by learning procedure in order to facilitate and progress student learning. This will involve the teacher in making a series of formative assessments with regard to the attainment and understanding of individual students.

Maths

The aims of the lesson are:

To provide opportunities for students to:

* *use standard form display;*

* *know how to enter numbers in standard index form;*

* *convert between ordinary and standard index form representations.*

The learning outcomes for this lesson are:

By the end of the lesson...

... all students will have learned:

* *to write numbers in standard form;*

* *to convert numbers in standard form to ordinary numbers using a calculator;*

* *to make some simple calculations using standard form without a calculator.*

... most students will have learned:

* *to use a calculator to calculate using standard form.*

... some students will have learned:

* *to use standard form to make approximations and estimates.*

Making judgements

What we have said so far in this section is that by writing clear learning outcomes you will be able to use these as assessment criteria. But what does this mean in practice, and how will you carry this out? To examine this in a little more detail let us return to the example from the food technology lesson above. The 'base level' learning outcome, the one which all students will be expected to achieve was:

* All: that a variety of ingredients can be used to prepare a salad that meets the design brief.

This offers an opportunity for formative assessment in that the teacher will make a judgement concerning the way the students understand this task. We know, even if we are not food technology teachers, that the notion of a salad is a specific form of dish, and we are able to formulate a hypothesis as to the sorts of ingredients that we might reasonably expect to find contained in one. In order for the teacher to be reasonably certain that all the students in the class have grasped the concept of 'salad-ness', what she will have done is to have made a formative assessment that this is the case. This formative assessment need not be documented, it need not be a complex multi-part decision-making process, it is simply a judgement-call made by the teacher, that she can move a number of students, *most*, in the terminologies we are employing, onto the next stage in their learning. This is an important point for you to realise. Formative assessments of this nature are not big high-stakes ones; they are small, everyday decisions which you, the teacher, will make many times each lesson. The evidence required – remember we discussed having an evidence base upon which to make decisions – is that the students have evidenced their understandings either in achievement, or in discussion with you, and that as a result of these you can be reasonably confident that you can move on. There can be few things more disheartening to learners than being held back by the teacher.

From this formative assessment, that most of the students are ready to move on to the next level of learning outcome, the teacher will then move on to address the next level of learning outcome:

- Most: that a variety of ingredients can be used to prepare a salad that meets the design brief, and be able to suggest alternative ingredients to those that have been allocated.

Again, if you are a non-specialist food technology teacher you can still follow the logic of this learning outcome. Here the essential feature is that student achievement is evidenced in discussion. To be able to suggest alternatives does not mean they have to have the ingredients to hand. Neither does it close down learning, in that an element of creative or divergent thinking is appropriate here. The formative assessments made now will again be based on a judgement-call concerning student learning, and the final tier of learning outcome:

- Some: that a variety of ingredients can be used to prepare a salad that meets the design brief, be able to suggest alternative ingredients to those they have been allocated and indicate where the alternatives fit onto the balanced plate.

can now be considered, and again, this will be *evidenced* in discussion.

The section above is premised on the notion that a well-crafted learning outcome can become its own assessment criterion. It began with asking the reader to think about what it is that should be learned. This needs to be considered within the context of you as a beginning teacher. There are four normal scenarios which you are likely to encounter when in school with regard to planning and teaching. These are as follows.

1. You are given a school unit of work, and told to plan your lessons using it.

2. You are given a school unit of work, and told to plan our own units of work, and the lessons within it, for the time you are in the school.

3. You are told what the topic you should be teaching is, and are to plan your own units of work and lessons within this.

4. You are given free rein as to what to teach.

This means that you will be planning for learning on two levels, the macro and the micro. The macro level is the learning that will take place during a unit of work, which we are taking to mean medium-term planning, over a period of weeks. The micro level is the learning that will take place in individual lessons on a day-to-day basis (similar to the QCDA description considered earlier in this chapter). Learning, the extract observes, is difficult to legislate for, and it is much easier to plan for activities, for 'doing', than it is to plan for learning.

Differentiation in learning outcomes is a key part of your planning. Whether a class is mixed-ability, setted or streamed (these types of pupil groupings were discussed in Chapter 3), there is still going to be a range of abilities within every class that you teach, and you will need to cater for all the pupils you will be teaching. The next part of the reading discusses examples of differentiated learning outcomes for a range of National Curriculum subjects, and although these might not be the subjects in which you are involved, nonetheless they offer concrete examples of what differentiated learning outcomes can look like.

After the example drawn from music, the notion of understanding evidenced in achievement is presented. This relates back to the materials presented in Chapter 2, with its focus on teaching and learning, where we discussed different typologies of knowledge and knowing. Here, these are drawn together in the notion of understanding. This is relevant to our discussions concerning assessment because we will want to be teaching for understanding, and in many cases this will be evidenced in the ways pupils are able to demonstrate their achievements in our subjects. This presents problems for many beginning teachers in that there is a close link between skills, knowledge, doing and understanding. It is understanding which is the most important of these, as we do not want to produce pupils who simply regurgitate information without knowing what it means. This means that what is being sought is teaching for understanding. To help with this, Martha Stone Wiske (1999) posits four questions which will help the teacher.

1. What topics are worth understanding?

2. What about these topics needs to be understood?

3. How can we foster understanding?

4. How can we tell what the students understand?

(Wiske, 1999 page 230)

In your current stage of pedagogic development, as we saw in the four scenarios of unit of work planning above, you are most likely to be concerned with teaching topics which other teachers have chosen for you. This means that Wiske's item 1 has been done for you. We saw in Chapter 2 that you will be making decisions about what to include in your own curriculum later on in your career, and so what you will be needing to think about now are items 2, 3 and 4. You will need to plan for learning and, in the context of the current reading, what there is in the learning that, in Wiske's terms, can tell us what the learners have understood. This is where writing a good learning outcome helps. You can say 'all pupils will learn *x*', and then your evidence is in the achievements of the pupils. Let us consider what this means in more detail by considering all the readings from this chapter together.

Conclusion

We have seen in this chapter that Harlen and James, and Black and Wiliam, all stress the importance of formative assessment as being the method of assessment that is likely to make the most difference to pupil learning. While giving pupils tests in an endeavour to ascertain the extent of their knowledge can be tempting, remember the QCDA's guidance about using only summative assessments at a few key points each year. In a lesson-to-lesson, day-to-day way of working, formative assessment will tell you what you need to know, and it is this which will make a difference to your teaching, and, consequently, to pupil learning. Indeed, it is formative assessment that allows you to address Wiske's item 4, and to find out what the students have understood. This takes us back to one of the key aspects of your planning and enactment, that of knowing what the pupils have learned during the course of the lesson. This should be answerable by you in evidential terms. You know that the pupils have achieved the learning outcomes because you have evidence; and you can share this evidence with others.

Therefore, collecting assessment evidence becomes an iterative process in your teaching. There is no sense in pursuing a point if the class has already firmly grasped it; neither is there any point in so doing if they lack the necessary prior learning. Formative assessment makes a difference, but it needs to be worked at. As Dylan Wiliam observed.

> *If what you are doing under the heading of assessment for learning or formative assessment involves putting anything into a spreadsheet, if it involves using a pen other than for making comments in a student exercise book, then you are not doing the assessment for learning that makes a significant difference.*

> (SSAT Website)

What Dylan Wiliam is saying here is that formative assessment is not about giving National Curriculum levels or sub-levels, or entering data into spreadsheets. Formative assessment is for you and the pupils, not for systems.

C H A P T E R   S U M M A R Y

In this chapter we have looked at the role assessment has to play in your teaching. We have thought about ways in which you can use both formative and summative assessment in order to help the learning of your pupils, and we have seen how it is the proper, targeted use of formative assessment which is able to make a real difference in this area. Hopefully this has given you a range of things of things to think about, and some ideas to try out in your own developing practice within this important area.

REFERENCES

Black, P, Harrison, C, Lee, C, Marshall, B and Wiliam, D (2003) *Assessment for Learning: Putting it into practice*. Maidenhead: Open University Press.

Black, P and Wiliam, D (1998) Assessment and classroom learning. *Assessment in Education*, 5(1): 68.

Bloom, BS (1956) *Taxonomy of Educational Objectives, Handbook I: The Cognitive Domain*. New York: David McKay Co Inc.

DES/WO (1988) *Task Group on Assessment and Testing: A report*. London: DES.

Fautley, M and Savage, J (2008) *Assessment for Learning and Teaching in Secondary Schools*. Exeter: Learning Matters.

Freeman, R and Lewis, R (1998) *Planning and Implementing Assessment*. London: Kogan Page.

Gipps, C (1994) *Beyond Testing: Towards a theory of educational assessment*. London: Falmer Press.

Harlen, W (2005) Teachers' summative practices and assessment for learning – tensions and synergies. *The Curriculum Journal*, 16(2): 207–23.

Harlen, W and James, M (1997) Assessment and learning: Differences and relationships between formative and summative assessments. *Assessment in Education*, 4(3): 365–79.

QCDA (2008) Assessing Pupils' Progress – Assessment at the heart of learning. London: QCDA. **www.qcda.org.uk/assessment**

Sadler, D (1989) Formative assessment and the design of instructional systems. *Instructional Science*, 18: 119–44.

Swanwick, K (1988) *Music, Mind, and Education*. London: Routledge.

Tittle, C (1994) Toward an educational psychology of assessment for teaching and learning: Theories, contexts, and validation arguments. *Educational Psychologist*, 29(3): 149–62.

Tunstall, P and Gipps, C (1996) Teacher feedback to young children in formative assessment. *British Educational Research Journal*, **22**(4): 389–404.

Wiske, M (1999) What is Teaching for Understanding?', in Leach, J and Moon, B (eds), *Learners and Pedagogy*. London: Paul Chapman Educational Publishing.

WEBSITES

QCDA website: **http://curriculum.qcda.gov.uk/key-stages-3-and-4/assessment/assessment_and_curriculum/day-to-day-periodic-and-transitional-assessment/Periodic/index.aspx**

SSAT website **www.ssatrust.org.uk/pedagogy/PersonalisingLearning/Pages/embeddingcd.aspx**

Chapter 5
Choosing and using technology for teaching and learning

CHAPTER OBJECTIVES

By the end of this chapter you should have:
- considered the choice and use of pieces of ICT to design and develop opportunities for teaching and learning;
- used techniques drawn from sociocultural theory to help analyse and reflect on the use of ICT as a teaching and learning tool;
- developed basic strategies for finding out more about ICT and refining your own skills with it;
- planned how to make your future teaching with ICT more effective.

Q Standards: Q16, Q17, Q23, Q25a.

Introduction

Modern technologies mediate our lives in the early twenty-first century. They transform the ways in which we communicate, create and consume, whether that relates to our music, our photographs or writing. We will therefore take a moment to reflect on the considerable impact that technology has had on processes of teaching and learning in recent years. This chapter analyses some of these changes in light of three pieces of writing from a range of authors. It will challenge the way you think about technology and its use in education. It will encourage you to become a more critical and reflective user of technology, both as a tool in your own teaching and in the way that you design opportunities for your pupils to use technology to assist their learning.

The Q Standards talk about the use of ICT in a number of ways. Firstly, they emphasise the importance of your own ICT skills (Q16). This is why there is a specific skills test in ICT. They also discuss the importance of your teaching allowing pupils to develop their own ICT skills. This is not the preserve of the ICT teacher. All subject teachers are required to develop these through their subject. It is part of the 'functional skills' strand of the new secondary curriculum. But neither of these concerns is our main focus in this chapter. Here, we will be primarily focused on Q17, which states that you will 'know how to use skills in literacy, numeracy and ICT to support your teaching and wider professional activities'. This 'translation' of ICT skills and application of them in support of your teaching is an essential strand in the development of your teaching abilities.

ICT and mediated action

The first extract explores the notion of how we, as teachers, use technology as a 'tool' for teaching and learning. It is taken from a book by James Wertsch called *Mind as Action* (1998). In it, Wertsch, explores, through the use of sociocultural analysis, the relationship between human action and the cultural, institutional and historical contexts in which this action occurs. In our context, teachers are the 'agents' (to use Werstch's terminology); the 'cultural tools' are the technologies we are choosing to use; and the context would be, at least in a simple application of his work, your classroom. Wertsch calls the interplay between agents, tools and contexts 'mediated action'.

EXTRACT ONE

Wertsch, J (1998) Mind as Action. *New York: Oxford University Press, pp. 24–25.*

The specific notion of action I examine is mediated action. *In the pentadic terms outlined by Burke, this involves focusing on agents and their cultural tools – the mediators of action. Such a focus gives less emphasis to other elements in the pentad such as scene and purpose, but I would argue that it makes sense to gives the relationship between agent and instrument a privileged position, at least initially, in sociocultural research for several reasons. First, a focus on the agent-instrument dialectic is perhaps the most direct way to overcome the limitations of methodological individualism, the copyright age, the centralized mindset, and so forth. An appreciation of how mediational means or cultural tools are involved in action forces one to live in the middle. In particular, it forces us to go beyond the individual agent when trying to understand the forces that shape human action.*

Second, analyses of mediated action, or 'agent-acting-with-mediational-means'. (Wertsch, Tulviste, & Hagstrom, 1993), provide important insights into other dimensions of the pentad – scene, purpose, and act. This is because these other pentadic elements are often shaped, or even 'created' (Silverstein, 1985), by mediated action. To make this point is not to argue that one can reduce the analysis of these other elements to that of mediated action. Burke has demonstrated quite convincingly that such reductionism cannot work in the end. It is to say, however, that the perspective on human action provided by the agent-instrument relationship provides some important insights into the nature of other elements and relationships of pentadic analysis.

These first two points about mediated action point to a third – namely, that it is a natural candidate for a unit of analysis in sociocultural research. It provides a kind of natural link between action, including mental action, and the cultural, institutional, and historical contexts in which such action occurs. This is so because the mediational means, or cultural tools, are inherently situated culturally, institutionally, and historically. This is something I return to in more detail later in this chapter, but for now the point is that even when one focuses primarily on the individual agent's role in mediated action, the fact that cultural tools are involved means that the sociocultural embeddedness of the action is always built into one's analysis.

In the view outlined here, almost all human action is mediated action. Given this, one would expect that it is very difficult to provide an exhaustive list of action forms and mediational means, and this is indeed the case. My goal in this and the following sections is not to provide a rigid definition or system of categorization that would encompass every instance of mediated action or cultural tool. Any attempt to do so would be either so abstract or so expansive as to have little meaning. Instead, I outline a set of basic claims that characterize mediated action and cultural tools, and I illustrate each claim with some concrete examples. Specifically, I examine ten basic claims: (1) mediated action is characterised by an irreducible tension between agent and mediational means; (2) mediational means are material; (3) mediated action typically has multiple simultaneous goals; (4) mediated action is situated on one or more developmental paths; (5) mediational means constrain as well as enable action; (6) new mediational means transform mediated actions; (7) the relationship of agents toward mediational means can be characterized in terms of mastery; (8) the relationship of agents toward mediational means can be characterized in terms of appreciation; (9) mediational means are often produced for reasons other than to facilitate mediated action; and (10) mediational means are associated with power and authority.

Wertsch's key message here is that all human action is mediated action. Applying this to our discussion, all teaching involves mediated action. What does that mean? It means that our teaching is mediated by the tools we use. These tools could include our language, the curriculum framework, a chosen pedagogy or, as we will discuss below, pieces of ICT.

Wertsch goes on to list the ten key properties of mediated action. These are summarised in Table 2, together with a further sentence of explanation taken from later in the chapter that will aid your understanding of the concept.

1.	Mediated action is characterised by an irreducible tension between agent and mediational means	Cultural tools are powerless to do anything. They can have their impact only when an agent uses them
2.	Mediational means are material	The external, material properties of cultural tools have important implications for understanding how internal processes come into existence and operate
3.	Mediated action typically has multiple simultaneous goals	Mediated action is often organised around multiple, and often conflicting, goals due to the fact that the goals of the agent do not map neatly onto the goals with which the mediational means are typically associated
4.	Mediated action is situated on one or more developmental paths	Agents, cultural tools and the irreducible tension between them always have a particular past and are always in the process of undergoing further change
5.	Mediation means constrain as well as enable action	Mediated action can be empowering and enabling. But it can also constrain or limit the forms of action we undertake
6.	New mediational means transform mediated action	The dynamics of change caused by introducing new cultural tools in mediated action are often quite powerful and all too easily escape notice
7.	The relationship of agents toward mediational means can be characterised in terms of mastery	The emphasis is on how the use of particular cultural tools leads to the development of particular skills rather than on generalised abilities or aptitudes
8.	The relationship of agents toward mediational means can be characterised in terms of appropriation (i.e. taking something that belongs to others and making it one's own)	Appropriation always involves resistance of some sort. Cultural tools are often not easily and smoothly appropriated by agents. Some form of resistance or friction is the rule rather than the exception
9.	Mediational means are often produced for reasons other than to facilitate mediated action	Most of the cultural tools we employ were not designed for the purposes to which they are being put
10.	Mediational means are associated with power and authority	Where are power and authority situated? A focus on mediated action and the cultural tools employed in it makes it possible to 'live in the middle' and to address the sociocultural situatedness of action, power, and authority

Table 2 Properties of mediated action

Applying Wertsch's ideas to your classroom

Wertsch provides a very rich framework of ideas to consider in relation to the use of ICT in teaching and learning. In the following exercise, you are going to be asked to choose a particular piece of ICT that you use in your teaching and answer a range of questions about it (the tool) and your (the agent) use of it in the classroom (the context). In doing so, you will be considering how your action as a teacher is being mediated.

> ### REFLECTIVE EXERCISE
>
> *Choose a particular piece of technology that you are going to be using in your teaching in the near future. This could be a piece of hardware or software. Using the questions below which relate directly to Wertsch's ten characteristics of mediated action, construct a wider understanding of the impact that the piece of technology may have on the processes of teaching and/or learning. You are undertaking a sociocultural analysis of your use of a particular tool through mediated action. If possible, find another student or colleague who is using a similar piece of technology in their teaching and compare your approaches. You will find differences. Why?*

Wertsch's key point	Key questions
1.	How do you use a piece of ICT? How does your use of it give it 'power'? What type of power results and how is that power evidenced within the classroom?
2.	How does the external property of a piece of ICT affect the internal mental processes by which we use it? How are these mental processes informed and developed as we begin to use the particular piece of technology?
3.	Does the piece of technology, and its particular uses, fit neatly within the teaching context for which you are using it? Do you have to 'force' it to fit or does its design and function work naturally with the process of teaching and learning you are seeking to develop?
4.	What is the 'history' of the particular piece of technology that you are seeking to use? How might this affect your use of it today? Can you anticipate any problems? How might the technology develop further, particularly as you apply it within the teaching and learning context?
5.	How does the piece of ICT enhance the opportunities for teaching and learning in your subject? How does it constrain them?
6.	What evaluative or assessment processes can you build in to your use of the piece of ICT to ensure that you are fully aware of the impact that it is making in the classroom?
7.	What are the specific skills you are hoping that the piece of ICT will facilitate? What would 'mastery' of the technology look like, in terms of your teaching or your pupils' use of it?
8.	If appropriation always involves resistance of some sort, against what does the use of a piece of technology resist? What causes the friction? How could this be 'smoothed out'?
9.	Questions here relate to (3) and (8) above. How many of the technologies that you are using were specifically designed for the educational context? Even if they are, don't presume that they will naturally fit within your classroom context. What preparatory work can you do to ensure a 'best fit' in relation to the other cultural tools that are at work?
10.	What are the competing sources of 'power' and 'authority' at work within your classroom? How do the power and authority associated with a piece of technology play out with these other sources?

Table 3 Key questions

- *Sociocultural analysis is a powerful tool. It can be applied to any aspect of human action. How would a sociocultural analysis of the language you use in a classroom unfold? (For clues, read Chapter 3 of Wertsch's book).*

- *The design of a piece of technology is a key determining factor in its use. Many of the technologies that are used in education were not specifically designed for this context. This can be good and bad. On the positive side, it can result in a much richer range of potential tools (and imaginative use of these); more negatively, it can be quite a lot of work (on your part) to incorporate these tools.*

- *Pupils bring a range of knowledge and understanding about ICT to the classroom. Learn to appreciate this. If you do not, then your agenda may clash with theirs and problems can result.*

Developing your use of ICT

Having spent some time considering how to apply Wertsch's ideas to the choice and use of a specific piece of ICT, it will be helpful to consider how you can develop the use of ICT within your own teaching practice. Futurelab (2006) argues for a change in approach for teachers' professional development. It suggests that in respect of digital technologies, there is little research how teachers might learn to use them. Rather, there is a pervasive assumption that they will. The report highlights that the single biggest challenge to teachers learning how to use digital technologies in their teaching is the time required to develop their individual skills and confidence. If you are feeling under pressure during your course of initial teacher education, things will not get a lot easier when you are working full-time in a school either. You will need to be very good at time management in order to release the time that you will require in order to learn to use new technologies.

So, given that the research about how teachers learn to use digital technologies is somewhat lacking, how can you seek to develop your skills with new technologies prior to implementing them in your teaching? First of all, there is no substitute for working with the pieces of technology yourself. Make sure you spend time working through that new interactive whiteboard resource prior to doing so in front of Year 8 on a Wednesday afternoon. Secondly, you will need to be inventive in terms of finding practical support. Videos on YouTube may enable you to solve some of the practical 'how to' questions you might have with less trouble than you will encounter by trying to get permission from your head teacher to attend an in-service training event which would take you away from your classes for a day. Thirdly, try to find another member of staff who is slightly further ahead of you in terms of their knowledge and pedagogy with ICT. This can be a very powerful form of 'peer' professional development.

But this is challenging, especially given the huge range of other issues that you will be facing during the early part of your teaching career. One of the key things to try to do is to link up your wider teaching activities with technology. Try to resist the temptation to 'box off' technology to one part of your teaching role. Incorporate it within the whole of your teaching role – including the times you spend planning, marking, reporting, collaborating with others and developing new ideas. The Futurelab report into teachers' adoption of digital technologies puts it like this:

> *We face a considerable challenge. The processes of teacher learning are complex, even messy, and teachers' current working circumstances contain inherent constraints. Yet the possibilities for real change in the system do exist. If we can bring the technologies into situations that resonate strongly with teachers' sense of professional and moral purposes, we may yet see what might truly prove to be a renaissance, in which teachers would employ digital technologies for 'understanding, reflection, ingenuity and creativity', and, through these, support their own learning in new ways.*
>
> (Futurelab, 2006, page 41)

What do you think the phrase *resonate strongly with teachers' sense of professional and moral purposes* really means? For us, it implies a holistic approach to the use of technology as a key part of your emerging teacher identity (see Chapter 1). The Futurelab writers hope that teachers will employ technologies for *understanding, reflection, ingenuity and creativity*. By doing this, they suggest, teachers' own learning will be supported and they will become more adept at creating interesting opportunities for learning with and through digital technologies for their pupils. How can you achieve this? One very practical suggestion is to look beyond the boundaries of your own subject area and look at how ICT is being used in other contexts. This can give you clues about how to extend and develop the work within your own subject teaching. We will be exploring this further in Chapter 8. But as an example here, recent technological developments have transformed the way in which one can engage with the process of learning to play a musical instrument. How would the technologies of the Nintendo Wii, Sony Playstation or Xbox (Nintendo, 2009; Sony, 2009; UCan.tv, 2007) transform the approach to teaching about musical performance in a classroom? Can you think of similar situations in your own subject area?

POINTS TO CONSIDER

- *The extent to which technology can 'resonate' with your sense of purpose as a teacher is clearly related to several of Wertsch's properties of mediated action (especially numbers 2, 3, 8 and 9). The writers assert that certain purposes (e.g. understanding, reflection, ingenuity, creativity) may be more valuable than others. What do you think about this? As a simple exercise, consider the key concepts for your subject (part of the National Curriculum documentation at Key Stage 3). How can technology help promote each of the key concepts through skilful application and design?*

- *More practically, how can you build time into your working day to spend developing your skills with technology and assessing their educational potential? Although there are forums and sources of support online, there is no substitute for using the technology yourself and exploring its educational potential.*

Pedagogical applications with ICT: an example from the theory of online learning

As an example of the approaches to the selection, use and analysis of ICT in teaching and learning, we are going to consider a specific example of ICT use: the construction of an approach to online learning. Our second piece of writing comes from an online book published by Athabasca University (Anderson and Elloumi, 2004).

Following this extract, we will be considering some questions about how this example relates to our previous discussion.

EXTRACT TWO

Anderson, T and Elloumi, F (2004) The Theory and Practice of Online Learning, *Athabasca AB: Athabasca University, pp. 273–276.*

This chapter focuses on the role of the teacher or tutor in an online learning context. It uses the theoretical model developed by Garrison, Anderson, and Archer (2000) that views the creation of an effective online educational community as involving three critical components: cognitive presence, social presence, and teaching presence. This model was developed and verified through content analysis and by other qualitative and quantitative measures in recent research work at the University of Alberta (for papers resulting from this work see Anderson, Garrison, Archer & Rourke, N.d.) (http://www.atl.ualberta.ca/cmc).

Learning and teaching in an online environment are, in many ways, much like teaching and learning in any other formal educational context: learners' needs are assessed; content is negotiated or prescribed; learning activities are orchestrated; and learning is assessed. However, the pervasive effect of the online medium creates a unique environment for teaching and learning. The most compelling feature of this context is the capacity for shifting the time and place of the educational interaction. Next comes the ability to support content encapsulated in many formats, including multimedia, video, and text, which gives access to learning content that exploits all media attributes. Third, the capacity of the Net to access huge repositories of content on every conceivable subject – including content created by the teacher and fellow students – creates learning and study resources previously available only in the largest research libraries, but now accessible in every home and workplace. Finally, the capacity to support human and machine interaction in a variety of formats (text, speech, video, etc.) in both asynchronous and synchronous modalities creates a communications-rich learning context.

To provide a mental schema for thinking about learning and teaching in this context, Garrison, Anderson, and Archer (2000) developed a conceptual model of online learning that they referred to as a 'community of learning' model. This model (see Figure 5.1) postulates that deep and meaningful learning results when there are sufficient levels of three component 'presences.' The first is a sufficient degree of cognitive presence, such that serious learning can take place in an environment that supports the development and growth of critical thinking skills. Cognitive presence is grounded in and defined by study of a particular content; thus, it works within the epistemological, cultural, and social expression of the content in an approach that supports the development of critical thinking skills (McPeek, 1990; Garrison, 1991). The second, social presence, relates to the establishment of a supportive environment such that students feel the necessary degree of comfort and safety to express their ideas in a collaborative context. The absence of social presence leads to an inability to express disagreements, share viewpoints, explore differences, and accept support and confirmation from peers and teacher. Finally, in formal education, as opposed to informal learning opportunities, teaching presence is critical for a variety of reasons discussed in this chapter.

In a work on teaching presence, Anderson, Rourke, Archer, and Garrison (2001) delineated three critical roles that a teacher performs in the process of creating an effective teaching presence. The first of these roles is the design and organization of the learning experience that takes place both before the establishment of the learning community and during its operation. Second, teaching involves devising and implementing activities to encourage discourse between and among students, between the teacher and the student, and between individual students and groups of students and content resources (Anderson, 2002). Third, the teaching role goes beyond that of moderating the learning experiences when the teacher adds subject matter expertise through a variety of forms of direct instruction. The creation of teaching presence is not always the sole task of the formal teacher. In many contexts, especially when teaching at senior university level, teaching presence is delegated to or assumed by students as they contribute their own skills and knowledge to the developing learning community.

In addition to these tasks, in formal education, the institution and its teacher employees are usually fulfilling a critical credentialing role that involves the assessment and certification of student learning. This chapter focuses on these component parts of teaching presence, defining and illustrating techniques to enhance this presence, and providing suggestions for effective teacher practice in an online learning context.

Designing and organising the online learning context

The design and construction of the course content, learning activities, and assessment framework constitute the first opportunity for teachers to develop their 'teacher presence.' The role the teacher plays in creating and maintaining the course contents varies from that of a tutor working with materials and an instructional design created by others, to that of 'lone ranger,' in which the teacher creates all of the content. Regardless of the formal role of the teacher, online learning creates an opportunity for flexibility and revision of content in situ that was not provided by older forms of mediated teaching and learning. The vast educational and content resources of the Net, and its capacity to support many different forms of interaction, allow for negotiation of content and activity, and a corresponding increase in autonomy and control (Garrison & Baynton, 1987). Teachers are no longer confined to the construction of monolithic packages that are not easily modified in response to student need. Rather, the design and organization of activities within the learning community can proceed while the course is in progress. Of course, such flexibility is not without cost, as customization of any product is more expensive than mass production of a standardized product. Thus, the effective online learning teacher makes provision for negotiation of activities, or even content, to satisfy unique learning needs. However, within this flexibility, the need to stimulate, guide, and support learning remains. These tasks include the design of a series of learning activities that encourage independent study and community building, that deeply explore content knowledge, that provide frequent and diverse forms of formative assessment, and that respond to common and unique student needs and aspirations.

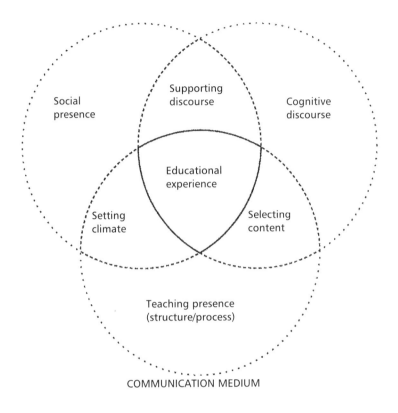

Figure 5.1 Community of inquiry

The article presents an interesting account of how teaching and learning in an online learning environment can be analysed. By now, it will be obvious that many of the defining characteristics of mediated action are apparent here. For example, learning in an online environment is not discrete or separate from learning in a traditional classroom. There are patterns of behaviour and communication that will have similarities. To that extent, the journey of teaching and learning from traditional classrooms into online spaces is one that needs to be recognised (Wertsch's fourth characteristic of mediated action) in order to appreciate fully the mental processes that teachers and learners will bring into that space (the second characteristic of mediated action). Anderson recognises that like in a traditional learning space, the teacher 'presence' is an integral part, not just related to the interactions that will occur within the online learning space, but also in terms of its design and the functionality that it affords.

Notions of power and authority come into play here (the first and tenth characteristics of mediated action). The visibility or invisibility of the teacher within the online space (in terms of its design and use) will be an important component in how pupils learn within that space. As you can appreciate, the tools of sociocultural analysis can give you powerful insights into how you choose, design and use particular pieces of technology in your work.

POINTS TO CONSIDER

Look back through the extract in light of the discussion about how Wertsch's principles of mediated action can be applied. Consider the following three questions.

1. *Anderson begins by making the point that learning and teaching in an online environment are, in some respects, similar to learning and teaching in any other educational context. But what are the key differences that he highlights?*

2. *The conceptual model of online learning outlined contains three 'presences' that are required for deep and meaningful learning. How are these 'presences' mediated or transformed through an online learning environment? How to they relate to similar concepts in a traditional classroom context? What are the critical roles that the teacher has to perform? How might these be different in an online learning environment compared with the traditional classroom?*

What about the future of ICT in education?

EXTRACT THREE

Somekh, B (2007) **Pedagogy and Learning with ICT: Researching the art of innovation.** *London: Routledge, pp. 119–121.*

New medium, new message: time for the end of school as we know it

In the UK, Stephen Heppell and his team at Ultralab (http://ww3.ultralab.net/projects/ notschool, accessed 7/8/2006) have successfully demonstrated a new approach to education through their NotSchool initiative. NotSchool works with school refusers, long-term truants and those excluded from school for bad behaviour, and has shown that by giving them access to a computer in their own home, removing all the structures and discourses of school (buildings, roles such as 'teacher' and 'student'), naming them as 'researchers' and working with them in non-coercive relationships where they are sometimes asked to take on the role of teaching adults, they are able to reconstruct their identities and respond positively to the respect they are being shown. NotSchool might be seen as a twenty-first century enactment of Illich's (1971) vision of Deschooling Society, made possible by the new digital media. In both the USA and the UK, Alan November (2001) has challenged schools and policy-makers to place the empowerment of students at the centre of their vision and practice. Cuban gives the reason for the failure of education policy-makers' visions for technology-induced radical change as originating from the fact that there has been no fundamental change in the system of schooling:

For such fundamental changes in teaching and learning to occur there would have to have been widespread and deep reform in schools' organisational, political, social, and technological contexts.

(Cuban, op. cit., p. 195)

Whereas, in the past, Cuban's accusations might have seemed unreasonable and Illich's vision unrealistic and unaffordable, NotSchool has actually demonstrated that, with the Internet and other ICTs, fundamental changes to teaching and learning and the whole institution of schooling are both achievable and desirable. The only pity is that it is seen by policy makers as a radical solution to the otherwise no-hope situation of school-refusers, rather than a model of fundamental change for the system as a whole.

Three bodies of theory enable the sociological imagination to reach a deeper analysis of the reasons why ICTs cannot be introduced into education as superficial additions to the existing system, but need to be located in radical institutional and systemic changes. All three focus upon the inter-relationship between ICTs and users which fundamentally changes the experience of being human and makes ICTs an indispensable past of that experience. The first is McLuhan's (1964, page 7) explanation that 'the medium is the message' at the heart of which is his theory that media are 'extensions' of ourselves. Writing at the time when the era of mechanisation was being replaced by the era of cybernation (or 'automation') McLuhan saw the telegraph as an example of 'the electric form, that ... ends the mechanical age of individual steps and specialist functions'. Telegraph technology – which I am taking here to be the forerunner of contemporary ICTs – is seen by McLuhan as a force which has brought about seismic change in the world of journalism and information management:

> *Any innovation threatens the equilibrium of existing organization. ... the outering or extension of our bodies and senses in a 'new invention' compels the whole of our bodies and senses to shift into new positions in order to maintain equilibrium. A new 'closure' is effected in all our organs and senses, both private and public by any new inventions. ... Naturally the effects on language and on literary style and subject matter were spectacular.*

> (McLuhan, op. cit., p. 273)

McLuhan's use of the language of the body and physical functions is not merely metaphorical, it expresses his understanding that a new medium in use becomes an extension of the body of the user and hence fundamentally changes the body's functions and means of expression. Rejecting any simplistic dichotomy of mind and body, he sees new media – of which for us ICTs are the contemporary example – as having fundamental personal and social consequences because they are extensions of ourselves.

The second body of theory is the work on the impact of ICTs on the self and identity formation carried out by Turkle (1984, 1995) over a period of more than 15 years. In her early work she probed the way that users of all ages – from young child-novice users of electronic games to post-doctoral students of computer systems and artificial intelligence – vested something of their own identity in the machine, seeing it as a 'second self' or responsive mirror. In her later work she focused on the relationship between users in the virtual world of 'cyberspace' and their playful construction of fantasy identities as a means of self-liberation and exploration of what it means to be human. Her descriptions of individuals constructing and reconstructing identity through 'living in the MUD' (Multi-User Domains) of online interactive simulation games provides fascinating insights into the ontology of human experience (Turkle, 1995, p. 11). She concludes that 'in the past decade, the computer culture has been the site of a series of battles over contested terrains' (op. cit., p. 267) and categorises the computer in three different ways: 'as tool, as mirror, and as gateway to a world through the looking glass of the screen'. The allusion to Lewis Carol's topsy-turvy world of an alternative psychological reality signals both creative power and loss of traditional certainties. Like McLuhan, she does not conceive of ICTs as separable from the identity of their human users.

The third body of work is activity theory, which embodies the Vygostskian concept of tools as mediators of human activity. The most powerful description of this fundamental inter-dependence of tools and human agents skilled in their use is Jim Wertsch's metaphor of pole vaulter and pole, neither of whom/which is capable of clearing the high bar without the other (Wertsch 1998). In a notable edited collection, Nardi (1997, pp. 17–44) refocuses activity theory specifically upon the analysis of human interaction with ICTs, presenting it as a 'potential framework for human–computer interaction research'. The chapter by Christiansen (1997) in Nardi's book draws upon the imaginative insights of sociology and cultural psychology to characterise the special nature of ICTs as lying in their capacity to be loved by their human users:

> Of course, an artefact cannot have feelings. It is the relationship between artefact and user that creates a feeling inside the user, which in turn is projected to the artefact. The tool relationship becomes a kind of filter through which the user experiences the artefact.
>
> (Op. cit., p. 176)

She goes on to explain that this relationship between tool and user lies at the heart of the conceptualisation of activity as defined by Leont'ev, following Vygotsky. Just as it was for McLuhan and Turkle, technology is seen as interdependent with human experience and action with the power to radically change the nature of human activities. But activity theory goes further to explain the way that institutional structures within national systems, with functions as diverse as education and the postal service (Engeström and Escalante 1997), construct and constrain the inter-relationship of humans and ICTs in mediated activity.

When the explanatory power of these three bodies of theory, which show that to be transforming ICTs need to become an integral part of human activity, is put alongside the practical example of NotSchool's success, the case for radical change of the school system becomes incontrovertible. The mutual constraints that render school leadership powerless to direct effective change from above and the informal networks of teachers powerless to produce creative change from below are clearly indicated in the evidence of (non-)impact of ICTs on education systems over a period of more than 20 years of high levels of investment by policy-makers. It is time for the end of school as we know it.

Our final extract, by a leading writer and researcher on ICT in education, presents a historical portrait of these ideas. Drawing on ideas from McLuhan, Turkle and, by now the familiar, Wertsch, Somekh discusses how ICT needs to become an integral part of teaching activity if meaningful change is to occur. Her citation of the case of NotSchool is an interesting one. Is there a danger of Somekh over-romanticising it here? Her thesis in this text is that 20 years of investment have rendered teachers *powerless to direct effective change* (Somekh 2007, page 121). NotSchool, by contrast, is a demonstration of how fundamental changes to teaching and learning and the *whole institution of schooling are both achievable and desirable* (ibid, page 119). This argument is part of a longer discussion within this chapter in which Somekh draws contrasts between the use of ICT in the home environment compared with that within the school. In her concluding paragraph in the chapter (ibid, page 122), Somekh states that:

> In the UK and the USA there are currently a number of significant initiatives aimed at radically changing aspects of schooling. These range from radical designs for new school buildings, to innovative deployment of mobile ICTs for use both at home and at school, and experimental formations of curriculum and pedagogy. They are all still considerably constrained by the technologies of national/state curricula, high-stakes testing and traditional pedagogies.

Educational researchers have a role to play in developing new scenarios for the use of ICT in education. But the group that Somekh fails to mention specifically are teachers themselves. Somekh's wider work has been to justify their place as key initiators and drivers of change through research methodologies such as action research (Somekh 1995, 2006; Somekh and Davis, 1997). You are in a powerful place to affect change in the educational system where it matters, at the interchange and interplay of thoughts and ideas between you and your pupils. A thoughtful and systematic approach to the choice and use of ICT for teaching and learning is what is required. The ideas and principles introduced in this chapter should help you along the way. But the key notion of this book is to become a reflective practitioner who makes imaginative links between theory and practice. Nowhere is this more needed than in the use of technological tools in education.

POINTS TO CONSIDER

What are the principles by which you are going to choose pieces of ICT to use in your forthcoming teaching?

How are you going to evaluate the effectiveness of these choices?

How has your consideration of ideas from the research literature helped or hindered your progress in this area?

Which ideas would it be beneficial to follow up through the further reading resources listed below?

C H A P T E R   S U M M A R Y

This chapter has explored the use of ICT with the processes of teaching and learning. It has considered how teachers choose and use pieces of ICT to design and develop teaching and learning opportunities. It has explored how mediated action, an approach drawn from the world of sociocultural theory, can help teachers analyse and reflect on their use of ICT in the classroom. Finally, it has considered some basic strategies for how teachers can find out more about ICT and plan to use it more effectively in their teaching.

REFERENCES

Anderson, T and Elloumi, F (2004) *Theory and Practice of Online Learning*. Athabasca: Athabasca University. Also available at **http://cde.athabascau.ca/online_book/** (accessed 15/10/09).

Futurelab (2006) Teachers Learning with Digital Technologies: A review of research and projects. Bristol: Futurelab. Also available at **http://www.futurelab.org.uk/resources** (accessed 20/10/09).

Nintendo (2009) Wii Music Coming to a Classroom Near You. **http://www.nintendoworldreport. com/newsArt.cfm?artid=17528** (accessed 12/10/09).

Somekh, B (1995) The contribution of action research to development in social endeavours: A position paper on action research methodology. *British Educational Research Journal*, 21(3): 339–355.

Somekh, B (2006) *Action Research: A methodology for change and development*. Maidenhead: OUP.

Somekh, B (2007) *Pedagogy and Learning with ICT: Researching the art of innovation*. London: Routledge.

Somekh, B and Davis, N (eds) (1997) *Using Information Technology Effectively in Teaching and Learning: Studies in pre-service and in-service teacher education*. London: Routledge.

Sony (2009) 'SingStar'. **http://www.singstargame.com/en-gb/** (accessed 24/3/09).

UCan.tv (2007) Hand2Hand. **http://www.hand2hand.co.uk** (accessed 11/3/09).

Wertsch, J (1998) *Mind as Action*. Oxford: OUP.

FURTHER READING

Jenkins, H, Purushotma, R, Clinton, K, Weigel, M and Robinson, AJ (2007) *Confronting the Challenges of Participatory Culture: Media education for the 21st century*. An occasional paper on digital media and learning. Chicago: The MacArthur Foundation.

Prensky, M (2001) Digital Natives, Digital Immigrants. *On the Horizon*, NCB University Press, 9(5): 1–6.

Chapter 6

Personalisation and personalised learning

CHAPTER OBJECTIVES

By the end of this chapter you should have:
- explored the concepts of personalisation and personalised learning;
- evaluated some of the psychological framework underpinning common pedagogical approaches within the personalised learning debate;
- considered how providing more opportunities for personalised learning can be conceived as part of a teacher's pedagogy;
- explored how ICT can help provide for more personalised approaches to learning within your subject;
- reaffirmed an approach to personalising learning within the pedagogy of the individual teacher.

Q Standards: Q10, Q19, Q25.

Introduction

'Every child matters.' This simple statement has transformed approaches to how we care for and educate our young people. The phrase was used as a title of a government Green Paper in 2003 and, eventually, the work within this paper underpinned the Children Act in 2004. The Every Child Matters programme has been the government's approach to the well-being of children and young people from birth to 19. It was built around the five key aims:

- be healthy;

- stay safe;

- enjoy and achieve;

- make a positive contribution;

- achieve economic well-being.

In 2007 the United Kingdom government published the Children's Plan. The aim of this ten-year strategy programme is to make England the best place in the world for children and young people to grow up. Whatever your thoughts are about the rhetoric and policy surrounding this simple phrase, we hope that there is one thing on which all teachers can agree – every child matters.

This chapter is about personalisation and personalised learning. As our first extract explores, personalisation should be at the heart of all public services, including education. Personalised learning is an extension of the concept of personalisation to the world of teaching and learning. This is where the majority of our attention will be. This extract, taken from a document entitled *A National Conversation about Personalised Learning*, was published in 2004, the same time as the Children Act. It was one of the most formative documents in the development of schools' responses to this new, emerging political agenda.

EXTRACT ONE

DfES (2004) **A National Conversation about Personalised Learning.** *Sudbury: DfES, pp. 4–7.*

What is personalisation and personalised learning?

Personalisation is a very simple concept. It is about putting citizens at the heart of public services and enabling them to have a say in the design and improvement of the organisations that serve them.

In education this can be understood as personalised learning – the drive to tailor education to individual need, interest and aptitude so as to fulfil every young person's potential. David Miliband, in his 2004 speech to the North of England Conference, described this as:

> *'High expectations of every child, given practical form by high quality teaching based on a sound knowledge and understanding of each child's needs. It is not individualised learning where pupils sit alone. Nor is it pupils left to their own devices which too often reinforces low aspirations. It means shaping teaching around the way different youngsters learn; it means taking the care to nurture the unique talents of every pupil.'*

Personalised learning is not a new DfES initiative. Many schools and teachers have tailored curriculum and teaching methods to meet the needs of children and young people with great success for many years. What is new is our drive to make the best practices universal. We want to help all schools and teachers establish their own approaches to personalised learning, so that across the education system the learning needs and talents of young people are used to guide decision making.

Principles at the heart of personalised learning

To build a successful system of personalised learning, we must begin by acknowledging that giving every single child the chance to be the best they can be, whatever their talent or background, is not the betrayal of excellence, it is the fulfilment of it. Personalised learning means high quality teaching that is responsive to the different ways students achieve their best. There is a clear moral and educational case for pursuing this approach. A system that responds to individual pupils, by creating an education path that takes account of their needs, interests and aspirations, will not only generate excellence, it will also make a strong contribution to equity and social justice.

This leads directly to the principles that can help guide our day to day practices:

- *for children and young people, it means clear learning pathways through the education system and the motivation to become independent, e-literate, fulfilled, lifelong learners;*

EXTRACT ONE *continued*

- *for schools, it means a professional ethos that accepts and assumes every child comes to the classroom with a different knowledge base and skill set, as well as varying aptitudes and aspirations; and that, as a result, there is a determination for every young person's needs to be assessed and their talents developed through diverse teaching strategies;*

- *for school governors, it means promoting high standards of educational achievement and well-being for every pupil, ensuring that all aspects of organising and running the school work together to get the best for all pupils;*

- *for the DfES and local authorities, it means a responsibility to create the conditions in which teachers and schools have the flexibility and capability to personalise the learning experience of all their pupils; combined with a system of intelligent accountability so that central intervention is in inverse proportion to success;*

- *and for the system as a whole, it means the shared goals of high quality and high equity.*

The rationale of these principles is clear – to raise standards by focusing teaching and learning on the aptitudes and interests of pupils and by removing any barriers to learning. The key question is how collectively we build this offer for every pupil and every parent.

This extract defines our key terms in a simple way. Personalisation is *about putting citizens at the heart of public services and enabling them to have a say in the design and improvement of the organisations that serve them* (page 4). In education, personalisation as a concept is extended to the concept of personalised learning, which is *the drive to tailor education to individual need, interest and aptitude so as to fulfil every young person's potential* (page 4). There is a clear resonance here with more recent and well known definitions of personalised learning contained with materials linked to the National Strategy for Inclusion. In one report (DfES, 2007), Christine Gilbert defined personalised learning as:

> *Taking a highly structured and responsive approach to each child's and young person's learning, in order that all are able to progress, achieve and participate. It means strengthening the link between learning and teaching by engaging pupils – and their parents – as partners in learning.*
>
> (DfES 2007, page 6)

Clearly, taking such a structured and responsive approach is going to require significant thought on the part of the individual teacher as well as the wider school community. We liked Gilbert's focus on this taking place through a partnership between teachers, pupils and parents. But at a basic level, in your work as a trainee teacher you will encounter pupils with many different educational needs and will need to make adjustments to your own pedagogy in response to them. The following reflective task asks you to begin thinking about how some of the rather grandiose claims for personalisation and personalised learning might actually impact on the processes of teaching and learning that you are wanting to develop and promote within your classroom.

Having read through the definitions and principles for personalised learning in this document, reflect on the following key questions.

- *How can you help every pupil to do better?*

- *What elements of your teaching need to be improved in order to do so?*

- *What would the key elements of an approach to personalised learning be?*

Exploring the research on personalised learning

In our introduction we presented the concepts of personalisation and personalised learning. The associated reflective task asked you to explore, in a basic way, how such approaches might impact on your work. Since the publication of that opening paper in 2004, there has been a plethora of guidance materials, approaches and strategies that have promoted personalised learning within education. But, contrary to popular belief, just because something is government policy does not necessarily mean that it will be beneficial for all. However, as we have discussed above, the mantra 'every child matters' is something that all teachers should agree on.

But the policy and strategy frameworks for personalised learning developed over the last ten years did not get produced out of thin air and it is worth taking a slightly longer view. There has been a long-standing investigation into personalisation and learning which has, in many cases, drawn on the psychological research literature for its roots. An exploration of the psychological frameworks or underpinnings of personalised learning would be a book in its own right. Here, we are going to discuss one author's contribution to the educational literature on personalised learning which helpfully draws on some of these psychological materials.

Working from an overarching construct which she calls 'psycho-pedagogy', our second extract written by Diana Burton, a Professor of Education at Liverpool John Moores University, explores some of the research literature associated with personalised learning. Personalised learning fits within what Burton describes as psycho-pedagogy because, as a pedagogy, it draws its roots from popular ideas within the field of psychological research. The bulk of her article explores some of the recent pedagogical trends in this field, represents their educational research basis (or lack of it) and the extent to which particular approaches towards personalised learning might or should be applied in teachers' work.

In the lead-up to our extract, Burton explores several, current psycho-pedagogical approaches to personalised learning (including learning styles, meta-cognitive approaches to learning, brain functioning and multiple intelligences). Burton's analysis is rigorous and often not favourable to recent developments in educational practices. It is worth dwelling for a moment on a few examples. For example, on the notion of 'learning styles' she says that:

A great deal of money has been made from the commercial application of learning style instruments in schools. Coffield et al (2004) reviewed 71, concluding that most including resources advocated by government education websites, were unreliable and of negligible pedagogical value. Effective teachers have always provided and will

*continue to provide rich and varied pedagogy that reflects the host of ways in which
learners interact with and process information. This is probably more appropriate than
attempting to match tasks to individuals.*

(Burton, 2007, page 10)

On brain functioning and the various claims about the impact of neuroscience on educational
practice, Burton urges us to be similarly cautious:

*Looking forward to 2020, Frith (2005) speculates that neuroscience will have
established the brain basis of our emotions, our sense of justice and our moral
sensitivity and that brain scans will be used to identify learning weaknesses. In-service
courses for teachers have propagated a host of labels to describe the application of
physiological knowledge about the brain to learning settings – mind-friendly learning,
mind-based learning, brain-based learning. Such tautologies are at least amusing and,
although research into how the brain functions has developed apace and offers helpful
insights to teachers, there remains a great deal we do not know.*

(Burton, 2007, page 11)

Finally, by way of introducing the main focus of Burton's work in our chosen extract and
as a way of raising alarms about the overzealous introduction and application of ideas
from the psychological literature to educational practice, the psychological concept of
'multiple intelligence' is commented upon. As many readers will know, this concept has
been developed through work done by Howard Gardner (Gardner, 1983, 1993) and others
(including, as Burton emphasises, Sternberg, 1985, 1999)). Burton's analysis here is that a
simplistic understanding and application of multiple intelligence is dangerous to educational
practice yet understandable given various contextual factors such as the way curricula are
organised around subject cultures and knowledge boundaries. She continues:

*It is easy to see how Gardner's model could gain currency at a common-sense
level since people often display particular talents or tendencies. Indeed, the school
curriculum and Hirst's (1975) forms of knowledge use similar categorisations. However,
if one sees cognition as the processing of information using fairly universal sets of
mental strategies it is difficult to conceive of separate, discrete intelligences. Sternberg
(1999) points out that although Gardner cites evidence to support his theory he has not
carried out research directly to test his model.*

(Burton, 2007, page 13)

Burton's view is that Gardner's model has become a popular educational 'device' in many
schools around the world because if offers an alternative to the common view of a single
intelligence that pupils have in particular quantities. Rather, Gardner's model encourages a
focus on multiple capabilities that an individual might exhibit and allows them to develop
them independently. However, the precise criteria by which this categorisation of intelligence
has been based has also come under criticism:

*White (1998) has critiqued Gardner's theory in detail, questioning the criteria on which
the designation of an intelligence is based and pointing out that much intelligent
behaviour can often rely on more than one of Gardner's intelligences at once. This
critique does not seem to have registered with educators as reliance on Gardner's
problematic explanation of intelligence persists in schools in many countries. Possibly*

this is a measure of the extent to which Gardner's theory resonates with long held common-sense views and reflects existing ways of organising knowledge through curricula.

(Burton, 2007, page 14)

Burton's work clearly exemplifies the difficulty of finding appropriate pedagogical responses to the rhetoric surrounding personalised learning. What seems like a simple statement ('every child matters' or 'personalised learning') can quickly become problematised as educators seek for pedagogical solutions. In light of this, while you are reading through this second extract make a list of some of the elements of personalised learning that are considered more favourably by Burton.

EXTRACT TWO

Burton, D (2007) *Psycho-pedagogy and personalised learning.* Journal of Education for Teaching, *33(1): pp. 14–15.*

Personalised learning

The areas of psycho-pedagogy considered above are embraced within the current trend for 'personalised learning' (Leadbeater, 2005) which, it can be argued, has its pedagogical and political roots in the 1990s vogue for differentiated learning. Weston (1996) described differentiation as a shorthand for the methods teachers use to enable each pupil to achieve their intended learning targets. The pedagogical discourse of the 1990s established 'differentiation' as a seminal term. Just as school inspectors will soon be looking for evidence of teachers personalising learning, no English inspection report was complete without a reference to differentiation and it was the key focus for teacher professional development. In 2001 the UK Labour Government sang the virtues of individualised learning, noting that 'it is becoming possible for each child to be educated in a way and at a pace which suits them, recognising that each is different, with different abilities, interests and needs' (DfES, 2001, p.20). This position clearly resonates both with definitions of differentiation and with the current preoccupation with personalised learning.

At that time the government (DfES, 2001) set out in a White Paper how diversity of provision would be achieved through different types of schools such as Specialist Schools, which demonstrated a particular subject competence, and Beacon Schools, chosen for their exhibition and dissemination of best practice. This has recently been extended through a commitment to creating 'trust schools' which will be independent of local authority control and will, it is claimed, create even greater choice for parents and pupils (DfES, 2005). The 2001 White Paper also described a range of ways in which pedagogical diversity was to be pursued. These included the use of different types of adults in classrooms, for example, classroom assistants and learning mentors, investment in ICT equipment, online curriculum 'catering for children of all abilities' (p. 5) and the facility for the most able pupils to progress at a faster pace. These initiatives have since been implemented via workforce remodelling in England (DfES, 2003) and there is now much more emphasis in schools and colleges worldwide on developing the learning technologies and software to support personalised learning. Sophisticated hypermedia systems can identify learners' interests, preferences and needs and adapt the content of pages and the links between them to the needs of that user (Triantafillou et al., 2004).

Social constructivist research (Vygotsky, 1978; Bruner, 1983) has repeatedly demonstrated the necessity, however, for group interaction and adult intervention in consolidating learning and extending thinking. Many teachers are familiar with these key ideas but Kutnick et al. (2002) caution that they may not think strategically about the size and composition of groups in relation to the tasks assigned, calling for educationalists to pay attention to the social pedagogy of pupil grouping. This is compounded in the UK by the requirement for whole class teaching within the national literacy and numeracy strategies. Myhill's (2006) extensive research has demonstrated that teacher discourse can sometimes impede pupil learning with cognitive or conceptual connections often ignored.

Personalised learning was further promoted in the subsequent White Paper (DfES, 2005) with an explicit call for the setting of pupils. Yet research provides no clear evidence that setting creates greater learning gains for pupils. In an extensive study that followed 6000 Year 9 pupils in 45 secondary comprehensive schools through to Year 11, Ireson et al. (2005) found no significant effects of setting on GCSE achievement in English, mathematics or science. In 1997 Boaler's review of research into setting revealed that, whilst there was a small advantage for the most able pupils if they were set, the losses for the less able when set were great. Boaler's own three-year study compared the GCSE mathematics results of 310 pupils in two schools, one of which set the pupils whilst the other taught pupils in mixed ability groups. She found that results were significantly better amongst the latter group even though test results from Year 7 indicated the pupils were of similar ability. A number of studies suggest that attempting to match tasks to learners' abilities may be less effective than providing differentiated, individualised teacher support to pupils working on the same task (see Burton, 2003, for a review). Until Frith's (2005) predictions about the implanting of microchips to enhance cognitive functioning or techniques to track an individual's learning within the developing brain in order to match teacher or teaching method to learner come to fruition, teachers will continue to need a detailed knowledge of each learner's progress, strengths and challenges in a particular learning context. Whether we call it personalised learning, differentiation or a learner-centred approach, the issue is not one that can be simply dealt with by governmental injunctions regarding setting, since in both set and mixed ability groups the individualised nature of pupil learning and teacher response is paramount.

In this extract Burton traces back recent developments in personalised learning to a number of factors. One of these, common in the 1990s, was the concept of differentiation. Differentiation is not the same as personalised learning. Differentiation was a strategy or pedagogy that teachers used to help ensure engagement and to monitor different responses to that engagement. For example, differentiation by task involved setting slightly, or significantly, different tasks to different 'types' of pupils; differentiation by outcome involved setting the same task to all pupils but planning for and expecting a different range of responses to that task. The elements of personalisation within differentiation as a strategy were variable and perhaps a little imprecise for the current educational climate and its focus on the individual learner. However, as the later part of the extract discusses, there has been a number of studies that show that approaches to differentiation by outcome in the classroom have demonstrated a greater impact on pupils' learning than setting individual tasks for individual pupils (what one might suppose could be the ultimate approach to personalised learning).

More recent developments, Burton notes, are in the field of information and communication technologies (ICT) and their application towards personalised learning. Several issues related to this were discussed in the previous chapter, but these will explored in more detail below through a practical task. Burton also highlights key lessons from the field of social constructivist research on learning and the importance of group work. We examined several of the ideas in Chapter 3. While this might seem something of an anathema to the theme of personalising learning, the composition or structure of groups, and the roles that pupils play within them, clearly allow for individualised learning approaches to develop. But this depends on careful planning and management by the teacher. Group work is not a recipe for you to take the back seat as a teacher. It requires skilful, deliberate and purposeful engagement to be done well. As we discussed in Chapters 2 and 3 through our consideration of the work of Vygotsky and Bruner, the situation of knowledge within groups and the dynamics that are generated for uncovering it can lead to the empowering of individual learners when set up skilfully by the teacher.

The conclusion of Burton's article suggests that an approach to personalised learning is likely to include a mixture of approaches and techniques. These might include differentiation strategies, applications of ICT, different approaches to the categorisation of pupils' learning styles or the setting of particular classes according to pupil ability. What Burton's work clearly shows is that whatever approach is taken, the role of the teacher and the development of their skilful pedagogy are central in ensuring that each pupil is given the opportunity to fulfil their learning potential.

REFLECTIVE EXERCISE

Differentiation by outcome and differentiation by task could be conceptualised as being at two ends of the differentiation spectrum. In the first, all pupils are set one task and you monitor the range of responses; in the second, and at its most extreme, all pupils are set their own individual task based on their perceived level of ability.

Which of these approaches is most common within your subject area? What would happen if you tried the opposite approach? In a forthcoming lesson, take up the challenge and reverse the standard way that you might set up a task and differentiate it for your pupils. If you want to be really brave, what would happen if you gave pupils the ultimate choice about the type of task they wanted to complete during the lesson? Would the pupils be able to identify an appropriate level of challenge and engagement more easily than you?

ICT and personalised learning

Up to this point in the chapter we have explored some of the policy surrounding personalisation and personalised learning, and considered the findings of one piece of research from this field. In the second half of the chapter things are going to get a bit more practical. Firstly, we are going to explore how one of the ingredients for personalised learning identified by Burton can be incorporated within your emerging pedagogy. Finally, through reading a third extract we are going to consider the wider elements of a pedagogy for personalised learning that you will need to develop.

As we considered in the previous chapter, the use of ICT in education has become something of behemoth. The powerful rhetoric about technology and the pervasive positivism that surrounds it can lead some to joyful, unadulterated enthusiasm for its every promise, and others to desperate cynicism about its impact or effect on education. Perhaps there is a middle road that represents the healthiest disposition? However, it is clear that technology is an important part of our education system in the twenty-first century. The constructive use of technological tools can have a positive effect on a pupil's education and there are many pieces of research that have documented this.

When it comes to the issue of personalisation and personalised learning with or through technology, there has been a considerable amount of work done by teachers and researchers showing these positive benefits. The Futurelab 'think tank' in Bristol has done some important work in this area. Their report (Futurelab, 2004) opens with some assumptions. Firstly, it makes clear that the focus for personalised learning with technology should not be driven by some kind of simplistic technological determinism (i.e. using technology for the sake of technology). Secondly, it states that for the majority of young people, technology is an important part of their daily lives. If, by the age of 21, young people will have spent 15,000 hours in formal education, they will also have spent 20,000 hours in front of a television and 50,000 hours in front of a computer screen (Futures Learning Practice, 2005). Young people are used to using technology to tailor their informal learning to their own interests. This gives us a tremendous opportunity within formal educational contexts. We need to make the link.

So, what should the relationship between personalisation and digital technologies be like? What can it achieve? Here, the report is clear:

> *We believe that the relationship between personalisation and digital technologies has the potential to reshape the education system around the learner and to enable the learner's voice to be heard more powerfully in shaping the curriculum, contexts and practices of their learning both in and out of schools.*

> (Futurelab, 2004, page 5)

Towards this end, the Futurelab team held a number of seminars on these themes with researchers, publishers, teachers, software developers and policy makers. The report establishes a Learner's Charter. You will need to access this online in order to complete the following task.

REFLECTIVE EXERCISE

Stage 1

Read the Learner's Charter (available from: **www.futurelab.org.uk/resources/ documents/opening_education/Personalisation_report.pdf)**

Stage 2

Consider each of the four elements of the Learner's Charter in turn (choices, skills and knowledge, appropriate learning environments and feedback). Think about how each area might begin to impact on your work as a teacher within a formal learning context (i.e. a school). How can your use of technology within your teaching assist you in designing opportunities for pupils to learn in this personalised way?

Stage 3

Choose one particular statement from one of the key four elements. For the purposes of this exercise, we are going to choose one bullet point from the 'Feedback' element, specifically:

> *To use diverse assessment tools to enable me to reflect upon and develop my own learning at times and in sites appropriate for me and in ways which inform decisions about my future learning.*

Identify a piece of technology, hardware or software, that you could implement within your teaching to assist a more personalised approach to pupils' learning. You could do this through discussion with a group of pupils. Why not try to build on the knowledge or technologies they have generated in their informal learning contexts? In our case, we are going to ask our pupils to use the cameras on their mobile phones to collect snapshots of their work in progress throughout a particular task. The pupils will upload these pictures to a specially designed part of the school network where they will write a short commentary about their work alongside their photographic evidence. This process will allow pupils to personalise their learning through the use of their camera as an assessment tool and facilitate their process of reflection in line with the 'feedback' element outlined above.

Stage 4

Implement your plan. Evaluate the impact through discussing with the pupils how they used the technology and whether or not the degree of personalisation that was achieved was helpful.

Establishing a wider pedagogy for personalised learning

ICT is one small part of your work with pupils. There are a large number of other aspects of your pedagogy that can be adapted and developed to help achieve a stronger approach to personalised learning. In this final part of the chapter, we will consider some of these issues through a helpful set of resources contained within a report published by the Department for Children, Schools and Families in 2008. Their resources identify a range of interrelated aspects for a pedagogy of personalised learning. There are nine of these in total, namely:

- high-quality teaching and learning;
- target-setting and tracking;
- focused assessment;
- intervention;
- pupil grouping;
- the learning environment;
- curriculum organisation;
- the extended curriculum;
- supporting children's wider needs.

Our discussion is going to focus around the first of these – the centrality of high-quality teaching and learning. This should be considered as the bedrock to any approach to develop personalised learning.

This section of the resource opens with a clear statement that all teaching is built around the interactions between teachers and pupils. With many different pupils, all with particular learning needs, in the classroom together, providing a personalised approach to each one is not going to be easy. However, there is a number of things that you will need to consider as you work on your pedagogy and try to achieve a truly personalised learning environment for each pupil. The most important element here is an effective approach to planning. This is not just about planning in terms of your subject, or the knowledge that you want to try and impart. It is about planning the learning that the pupils are going to engage in during the lesson. This is an important distinction to get hold of. Although with any group of pupils of a similar age there will be a certain amount they have in common, planning the learning and the types of engagement that you are hoping pupils will have within the classroom involves you considering their ability levels, the structure of tasks (open or closed), the types of presentational approaches you might adopt (e.g. explanations or modelling), the progression routes within the learning and much more besides. How can you begin to do this well? This is where our extract begins.

EXTRACT THREE

DCSF (2008) **Personalised Learning: A Practical Guide**. *London: DCSF, pp. 10–12.*

Most teachers have a natural instinct for supporting pupils with different needs. They differentiate. In discussion, teachers will often start with inclusive questions which establish a common understanding in the class, then ramp up the level of challenge to draw on able pupils who can help them to reach a higher level of challenge. In forward-looking schools, a novel variation on this is to reverse the process by pre-teaching children who might struggle with the key ideas so they arrive at the lesson more prepared and more able to contribute. Once a teacher is familiar with a class, it's easier to target questions sensitively to pupils to draw them in at the right level and help them to an answer.

An old practice in individualised help was to circulate during the 'heads down' period of the lesson to help pupils by exception when they were stuck. This emergency model still has applications, but it does spread the teacher very thinly and focuses efforts on a small number of children. Guided work (considered later in the 'Pupil grouping' chapter) offers an alternative approach and a fair distribution of time for all children. Working systematically with groups makes good use of teacher time, and those who have a teaching assistant to deploy can delegate the 'surveillance' of the other pupils. It is important that teacher time is distributed fairly and that groups of pupils are not disproportionately delegated to a teaching assistant. The pupils who most obviously call for individualised support are those who are furthest behind in their learning. In times gone past the preferred method was to give them separate, easier work. Unfortunately, this can have the effect of driving down expectations and outcomes. More recently, teachers are able to offer catch up classes and one to one tuition. But classroom teachers have other resources for supporting individuals: the help of teaching assistants, simplified resources and giving a head start on tasks. They can give personal advice as part of marking and feedback systems, or by introducing peer and self-assessment, or by inviting pupils to work on tasks together to show how they go about it. Many aspects of personalised learning are individualised, but many needs can be met in the classroom context without resorting to one-to-one remediation.

Effective planning and lesson design is the starting point for quality first teaching and learning. In schools that excel in this, it is viewed as a series of decisions which build a planned series of learning episodes. The choice of appropriate learning objectives is supported using the Primary or Secondary Frameworks or subject specifications.

1. *Locating the teaching sequence or lesson in the context of:*
   - *the scheme of work*
   - *the pupils' prior knowledge and understanding*

2. *Identifying the learning objectives for the pupils*

3. *Structuring the teaching sequence or lesson as a series of episodes by separating the learning into distinct stages or steps and selecting:*
   - *the best pedagogic approach to meet the learning objectives*
   - *the most appropriate teaching and learning strategies and techniques*
   - *the most effective organisation for each episode*

4. *Ensuring coherence by providing:*
   - *a stimulating start to the lesson that relates to the objectives*
   - *transitions between episodes which are clearly signposted for the pupils*
   - *a final plenary that reviews learning and identifies next steps*

In developing quality first teaching, schools often pay particular attention to the develop-ment of the strategies of questioning, modelling and explaining. These strategies are seen as being particularly important in advancing pupils' learning; all need to be adjusted to recognise the skills, interests and prior learning of individual pupils.

Strategy importance

Modelling *This is more than demonstrating. Through the teacher 'thinking aloud' it helps pupils to understand underlying structures, processes and conventions.*

Explaining *Explaining is crucial in helping pupils understand abstract concepts and events that are outside their own experiences.*

Questioning *When planned and correctly sequenced, questioning can promote higher order thinking skills and structure the development of knowledge and understanding.*

The key characteristics of quality first teaching can be summarised as:

- *Highly focused lesson design with sharp objectives:*

- *High demands of pupil involvement and engagement with their learning:*

- *High levels of interaction for all pupils:*

- *Appropriate use of teacher questioning, modelling and explaining;*

- *An emphasis on learning through dialogue, with regular opportunities for pupils to talk both individually and in groups:*

- *An expectation that pupils will accept responsibility for their own learning and work independently;*

- *Regular use of encouragement and authentic praise to engage and motivate pupils.*

There is much of value in this publication and we would urge you to explore it further. For now, we make the simple point that the most effective approach to personalised learning is located within the pedagogy of the individual classroom teacher. The extract mentions numerous pedagogical aspects which relate to every dimension of a teacher's work, including their planning, explanations, modelling, questioning, assessment and much more besides. Please do not read from this that developing a personalised learning approach within your pedagogy will happen automatically. It will not. However, it will build on more general teaching skills and techniques that you are doubtless beginning to obtain during your teacher training placements.

Conclusion

Over the coming years there will be a increasing range of top-down, business-led initiatives which claim to personalise learning and result in more effective learner engagement, cognitive acceleration, personalised learning styles, mental processing or whatever the latest educational catch-phrase might be. We would urge you to maintain a critical approach to what seem like quick-fix solutions to something as complex as teaching and learning. While there may be valuable components within some of these types of initiatives, as we have briefly shown, much of the psychology and neuroscience behind these innovations is at best only partially understood by some of those advocating these approaches and at worst deliberately manipulative. There may also be commercial agendas at play here which one should always be wary of.

For us, effective teaching and learning are centred on a strong relationship between the individual teacher, their emerging pedagogy and their pupils. All pupils deserve an education. Every child matters and their education is too important to be sold or manipulated by careless handling of complex ideas. Focus on your role in the classroom, hone and craft your pedagogy and listen carefully to your pupils. These are the keys to an effective, personal approach to teaching and learning.

C H A P T E R　　S U M M A R Y

This chapter has explored the concepts of personalisation and personalised learning. It has argued that the most effective approach to personalised learning is based in the skilful pedagogy of the classroom teacher. While grand schemes related to learning styles, multiple intelligences or other factors may contain helpful components, it is always wise to look beyond their public face and ensure that the psychological research underpinning them is strong. The benefits of focusing on the development of an individual teacher's skilful pedagogy are that approaches to personalised learning become contextualised within other pedagogical elements and approaches. They remain in the context and remit of the professional relationship between teacher and student which, we believe, underpins the most effective personalised model of teaching and learning.

REFERENCES

Burton, D (2007) Psycho-pedagogy and Personalised Learning. *Journal of Education for Teaching*, 33(1): 5–17.

DCSF (2008) *Personalised Learning: A practical guide.* London: DCSF. (Available at **http://publications. teachernet.gov.uk/**).

DfES (2004) *A National Conversation about Personalised Learning.* Sudbury: DfES (Available at **www.teachernet.gov.uk**).

DfES (2007) *2020 Vision: Report of the Teaching and Learning in 2020 Review Group.* London: DfES. (Available at **http://publications.teachernet.gov.uk/**).

Futurelab (2004) *Personalisation and Digital Technologies.* Bristol: Futurelab. (Available at **www.futurelab.org.uk/resources**).

Futures Learning Practice (2005) Glasgow 24–25 June. Seminar co-ordinated by the International Futures Forum and supported by the Scottish Executive and Scottish Enterprise Glasgow. For more information please see **www.internationalfuturesforum.com/fol**.

Gardner, H (1983) *Frames of Mind: The theory of multiple intelligences.* New York, Basic Books.

Gardner, H (1993) *Multiple Intelligences: The theory in practice.* New York: Basic Books.

Sternberg, R (1985) *Beyond IQ: A triarchic theory of human intelligence*. New York: Cambridge University Press.

Sternberg, R (1999) Intelligence, in Wilson RA and Keil FC (eds) *The MIT Encyclopedia of the Cognitive Sciences*. Cambridge, MA: MIT Press.

Coffield, F, Moseley, D, Hall, E and Ecclestone, K (2004) *Learning Styles: A systematic and critical review*. London: Learning and Skills Development Agency.

DCSF (2007) *Pedagogy and Personalisation*. London: DCSF. (Available at **www.standards.dcsf.gov.uk/ primary/publications/learning_and_teaching/pedagogy_ personalisation**).

Frith, U (2005) Teaching in 2020: The impact of neuroscience. *Journal of Education for Teaching: International research and pedagogy*, 31(4): 289–291.

Hirst, PH (1975) *Knowledge and the Curriculum*. London: Routledge.

White, J (1998) *Perspectives on education policy: do Howard Gardner's multiple intelligences add up?* London: Institute of Education.

National College for School Leadership: Leadership for Personalising Learning website
http://www.ncsl.org.uk/personalisinglearning.

Chapter 7
Creativity as a way of teaching and learning

CHAPTER OBJECTIVES

By the end of this chapter you should have:
- considered the nature of creativity and why it is relevant to all subjects and all teachers;
- examined the potential of creativity to develop approaches to teaching and learning in your own subject;
- applied three strands of creative practice within education to your work as a beginning teacher;
- considered the constraints to creativity in the classroom context and how these can be mitigated or removed.

Q Standards: Q10, Q14, Q25

Introduction

Creativity involves the use of imagination and intellect to generate ideas, insights and solutions to problems and challenges. Coupled with critical thinking, which involves evaluative reasoning, creative activity can produce outcomes that can be original, expressive and have value.

Creativity and critical thinking develop young people's capacity for original ideas and purposeful action. Experiencing the wonder and inspiration of human ingenuity and achievement, whether artistic, scientific or technological, can spark individual enthusiasms that contribute to personal fulfilment.

Creativity can be an individual or collaborative activity. By engaging in creative activities, young people can develop the capacity to influence and shape their own lives and wider society. Everyone has the potential for creative activity and it can have a positive impact on self-esteem, emotional wellbeing and overall achievement.

Creative activity is essential for the future wellbeing of society and the economy. It can unlock the potential of individuals and communities to solve personal, local and global problems. Creativity is possible in every area of human activity – from the cutting edge of human endeavour to ordinary aspects of our daily life.

(QCDA website)

Creativity, as described above in an extract from the National Curriculum, is a key component of learning in a wide range of subjects. There is a common misconception that creativity should be the province of arts subjects, and that it need not concern some aspects of the curriculum. This is far from being the case. Here are some extracts taken from the importance statements for various National Curriculum subjects, which show the range of applicability which creativity can have:

Mathematics:
Mathematics is a creative discipline.

Science:
The study of science fires pupils' curiosity about phenomena in the world around them and offers opportunities to find explanations. It engages learners at many levels, linking direct practical experience with scientific ideas. Experimentation and modelling are used to develop and evaluate explanations, encouraging critical and creative thought.

History:
History fires pupils' curiosity and imagination, moving and inspiring them with the dilemmas, choices and beliefs of people in the past.

Modern foreign languages:
Learning languages gives pupils opportunities to develop their listening, speaking, reading and writing skills and to express themselves with increasing confidence, independence and creativity.

None of these is a traditional arts subject, and yet they all feel that creativity is important enough to warrant inclusion.

This chapter looks at the place of, and role for, creativity in contemporary teaching and learning. Hopefully it will challenge you to be creative in your thinking about what is involved, and what could be involved, when considering pedagogy, teaching and learning in your subject area.

The first extract is a short one, and comes from a QCDA publication entitled *Creativity: Find It, Promote It!* (QCDA, 2004). We shall begin by considering just the opening of this document, and return to it later.

EXTRACT ONE

QCDA (2004) Creativity: Find it, Promote it! *Qualifications and Curriculum Development Agency (QCDA), pp. 7–8.*

What is creativity?
What comes to mind when you think of creativity? People being imaginative, inventive, taking risks and challenging convention? Do you think about originality and the value of what people produce? Perhaps you think you can only be creative if you are artistic.

A good starting point for defining creativity is 'All our futures: Creativity, culture and education', the National Advisory Committee for Creativity and Culture in Education's report (DfEE, 1999). This report states that we are all, or can be, creative to a lesser or greater degree if we are given the opportunity The definition of creativity in the report (page 29) is broken down into four characteristics.

First, they [the characteristics of creativity] always involve thinking or behaving **imaginatively**. Second, overall this imaginative activity is **purposeful**: that is, it is directed to achieving an objective. Third, these processes must generate something **original**. Fourth, the outcome must be of **value** in relation to the objective.

Debating the characteristics highlighted by this definition can be a helpful starting point for agreeing what your school actually means by creativity.

Imagination and purpose

Imagination is definitely a key part of creativity. But are all imaginative ideas creative?

Suppose someone imagined a blue and white striped unicorn. Would this be creative? It may be that no one has conjured up a unicorn like this before. But what is the point of the idea? If someone thinks of an imaginative idea like this and then does not take it any further, are they creative?

Creative people are purposeful as well as imaginative. Their imaginative activity is directed at achieving an objective (although this objective may change over time).

Originality

What do we mean by originality? What might we mean by originality when we are talking about pupils' learning? Original in relation to their previous work? Other pupils' work? Work that has gained public recognition?

When pupils are writing a poem, choreographing a dance or producing a painting, their work can be unique if it expresses their ideas and feelings. But what about work in subjects like science, history and maths? While it would be wonderful for a pupil to be the first person to discover a new scientific principle, this is highly unlikely. Does this mean that pupils can't be creative in these subjects?

In section 4 'How to promote pupils' creativity', there are suggestions about:

- ways that planning and teaching can be focused on promoting pupils' creativity within each teacher's existing curriculum plans

- how teams of teachers can develop a shared understanding of creativity and a consistent approach to promoting pupils' creativity across a subject team, a year group or a key stage

- how senior managers might develop an ethos that supports more creative learning and teaching throughout the school.

Sections 3 and 4, together with the examples that come with this booklet, could provide a focus for:

- analysing the evidence of pupils' creative thinking and behaviour and the learning and teaching strategies that promote this

- identifying and discussing the possibilities for applying these strategies to different subjects and contexts.

There are some interesting issues here. Obviously what you thought about these questions will depend on a number of factors, but let us try to uncover a little more about the nature of creativity, and why it is relevant across a wide range of subjects.

Creative approaches within education

The next extract is from the National Advisory Committee on Creative and Cultural Education report *All Our Futures* (NACCCE, 1999). The NACCCE was set up in 1998 to investigate the creative and cultural development of children and young people both in and out of school. It was chaired by the influential thinker and writer on creative processes, Ken Robinson.

EXTRACT TWO

NACCCE (1999) **All Our Futures: Creativity, Culture and Education**. *Sudbury: DfES, pp. 5–16.*

Introduction and summary

The purpose of this report

(i) *In 1997, the Government published its White Paper* Excellence in Schools. *It described education as a vital investment in 'human capital' for the twenty-first century. It argued that one of the problems in education is the low expectations of young people's abilities and that it is essential to raise morale, motivation and self esteem in schools. The main focus of the White Paper was on raising standards in literacy and numeracy. But this will not be enough to meet the challenges that face education, and the White Paper recognised this. It also said:*

> If we are to prepare successfully for the twenty-first century we will have to do more than just improve literacy and numeracy skills. We need a broad, flexible and motivating education that recognises the different talents of all children and delivers excellence for everyone.

EXTRACT TWO *continued*

It emphasised the urgent need to unlock the potential of every young person and argued that Britain's economic prosperity and social cohesion depend on this.

(ii) This report argues that a national strategy for creative and cultural education is essential to that process. We put the case for developing creative and cultural education; we consider what is involved; we look at current provision and assess the opportunities and obstacles; and we set out a national strategy. By creative education we mean forms of education that develop young people's capacities for original ideas and action: by cultural education we mean forms of education that enable them to engage positively with the growing complexity and diversity of social values and ways of life. We argue that there are important relationships between creative and cultural education, and significant implications for methods of teaching and assessment, the balance of the school curriculum and for partnerships between schools and the wider world.

What is this report about?

(iii) Our report develops five main themes:

The challenge for education

Education faces challenges that are without precedent. Meeting these challenges calls for new priorities in education, including a much stronger emphasis on creative and cultural education and a new balance in teaching and in the curriculum.

Creative potential

Creativity is possible in all areas of human activity, including the arts, sciences, at work, at play and in all other areas of daily life. All people have creative abilities and we all have them differently. When individuals find their creative strengths, it can have an enormous impact on self-esteem and on overall achievement.

Freedom and control

Creativity is not simply a matter of letting go. Serious creative achievement relies on knowledge, control of materials and command of ideas. Creative education involves a balance between teaching knowledge and skills, and encouraging innovation. In these ways, creative development is directly related to cultural education.

Cultural understanding

Young people are living in times of rapid cultural change and of increasing cultural diversity. Education must enable them to understand and respect different cultural values and traditions and the processes of cultural change and development. The engine of cultural change is the human capacity for creative thought and action.

A systemic approach

Creative and cultural education are not subjects in the curriculum, they are general functions of education. Promoting them effectively calls for a systemic strategy: one that addresses the balance of the school curriculum, teaching methods and assessment, how schools connect with other people and resources and the training and development of teachers and others.

Who is this report for?

(iv) Formally, our report is addressed to the Secretaries of State, and many of our recommendations do call for Government action at various levels. But education concerns everybody: children and young people, parents, employers, those in work, out of work or in retirement. Consequently, our report is also written for a wider audience:

- *for parents, who want education to offer the best opportunities for their children;*
- *for teachers and headteachers who see the potential range and vitality of young people's abilities;*
- *for school governors, who want their schools to be alive with energy and achievement;*
- *for other organisations who see themselves as partners in the education of young people and who want to find better ways of engaging with them;*
- *for business and union leaders who recognise the need for new approaches to preparing young people for the changing nature of work.*

Above all, our aim is to urge the need for a national strategy which engages the energies of all of these to provide the kind of education, in substance and in style, that all young people need now, and to enable them to face an uncertain and demanding future.

Why now?

(v) There are great opportunities now to promote young people's creative and cultural education:

- *The Government is committed to promoting the creative abilities and cultural under-standing of all young people through education. At the same time, it is introducing new patterns of funding to support extended curricula, specialist facilities and innovation.*
- *The business community wants education to give a much higher priority to promoting young people's creative abilities; to developing teamwork, social skills and powers of communication.*
- *Many professional and other organisations are keen to develop innovative partnerships with education, through visits, residencies and liaison schemes.*
- *New technologies are providing unprecedented access to ideas, information, people and organisations throughout the world, as well as to new modes of creativity, personal expression, cultural exchange and understanding.*

The opportunities are considerable: and so are the difficulties.

(vi) Issues of creativity and of cultural development concern the whole of education. They are influenced by much more than the shape and content of the formal school curricu-lum. These influences include methods of teaching; the ethos of schools, including the relationships between teachers and learners; and the national priorities that underpin the education service. Our consultations suggest some tensions in current provision.

- *Many of those who have contributed to our inquiry believe that current priorities and pressures in education inhibit the creative abilities of young people and of those who teach them. There is a particular concern about the place and status of the arts and humanities. There is also concern that science education is losing its vitality under current pressures.*

- *Many schools are doing exciting and demanding work but often they see themselves doing this in spite, not because, of the existing climate. This may be more a problem of perception than of fact. There is no comprehensive evidence available either way to us nor to the Government. Nevertheless, the fact of this perception, and how widespread it is, is evidence of a problem in itself.*

- *Outside organisations – museums, theatres, galleries, orchestras and others – have a great deal to offer the formal education sector. Many already have education and out-reach programmes. There is a compelling argument for closer working partnerships and we have found considerable enthusiasm for them. Many say they are poorly funded for educational programmes and that such work still has low priority.*

- *There are concerns about the supply of teachers and the extent to which current train-ing takes account of the importance of creative and cultural education.*

(vii) The key message of this report is the need for a new balance in education: in setting national priorities; in the structure and organisation of the school curriculum; in methods of teaching and assessment; in relationships between schools and other agencies. Over a number of years, the balance of education, in our view, has been lost. There has been a tendency for the national debate on education to be expressed as a series of exclusive alternatives, even dichotomies: for example, as a choice between the arts or the sciences; the core curriculum or the broad curriculum; between academic standards or creativity; freedom or authority in teaching methods. We argue that these dichotomies are unhelp-ful. Realising the potential of young people, and raising standards of achievement and motivation includes all of these elements. Creating the right synergy and achieving the right balance in education is an urgent and complex task, from national policy making to classroom teaching.

Structure of the report

(viii) The report is in four parts. In Part One, we set out our definitions and framework for creative and cultural education. In Part Two, we look at the implications for the school curriculum, for teaching and for assessment. In Part Three, we argue for a broad base of partnerships between schools and other agencies and consider issues of resources and training. In Part Four we present a series of detailed recommendations as a framework for a national strategy. The arguments of the report are as follows:

Part one: facing the future

1. The challenge for education

Education throughout the world faces unprecedented challenges: economic, technologi-cal, social, and personal. Policy-makers everywhere emphasise the urgent need to develop 'human resources', and in particular to promote creativity, adaptability and better powers of communication. We argue that this means reviewing some of the basic assumptions of our education system. New approaches are needed based on broader conceptions of young people's abilities, of how to promote their motivation and self-esteem, and of the skills and aptitudes they need. Creative and cultural education are fundamental to meet-ing these objectives.

2. Creative development

There are many misconceptions about creativity. Some people associate creative teach-ing with a lack of discipline in education. Others see creative ability as the preserve of a gifted few, rather than of the many; others associate it only with the arts. In our view, creativity is possible in all areas of human activity and all young people and adults have creative capacities. Developing these capacities involves a balance between teaching skills and understanding, and promoting the freedom to innovate, and take risks.

3. Cultural development

Culture too is often associated with the arts. However, we relate the arts to a broader definition of social culture which includes the impact of science and technology on ways of life and the increasing interaction between cultures. Young people need to be helped to engage positively with cultural change and diversity. The dangers of cultural intolerance make this task a particular priority. We argue that creative and cultural education are dynamically related and that there are practical implications for the curriculum and for the classroom.

4. Meeting the challenge

In this section, we draw together our arguments for creative and cultural education and show how in principle they contribute to meeting the challenges for education that we have identified. In Part Two we move from principles to practice.

Part two: a new balance

5. Developing the school curriculum

There have been many benefits in the introduction of the National Curriculum. There are also difficulties for creative and cultural education in the existing rationale, structure and levels of prescription. These issues need to be tackled to allow more initiative to schools within a clear framework of public accountability. All schools should review their provi-sion for creative and cultural education within and beyond the National Curriculum.

EXTRACT TWO *continued*

6. Teaching and learning

Creativity can be 'taught'. Teachers can be creative in their own teaching; they can also promote the creative abilities of their pupils. The roles of teachers are to recognise young people's creative capacities; and to provide the particular conditions in which they can be realised. Developing creativity involves, amongst other things, deepening young people's cultural knowledge and understanding. This is essential both in itself and to promote forms of education which are inclusive and sensitive to cultural diversity and change.

7. Raising standards

Assessment and inspection have vital roles in raising standards of achievement in schools. But they must support and not inhibit creative and cultural education. There is a need for a new balance between different types of attainment target in the National Curriculum, and between the different forms and criteria of assessment and inspection. Raising standards should not mean standardisation, or the objectives of creative and cultural education will be frustrated.

Part three: beyond the school

8. Developing partnerships

Schools are now able to work in partnership with a wide range of individuals and organisations to enrich provision for creative and cultural education. The benefits of successful partnerships, and the roles of various partners in creative and cultural education are different, but complementary. There is a great deal of good practice, but there is an urgent need to establish better systems of funding, training and quality assurance of the effectiveness of partnerships.

9. Funding and resources

Local management of schools has reduced many services and facilities that were once provided by local education authorities to support creative and cultural education. Co-ordinated action is needed to provide these services in new and imaginative ways in the short and longer term. There are also many new sources of funding available to schools and organisations through a wide range of schemes and initiatives. New patterns of partnership are needed between government departments and funding agencies to make more effective use of resources.

10. Training people

The new provisions in initial teacher training present serious difficulties to the future of creative and cultural education. Urgent action is needed to ensure a continuing supply of appropriately trained teachers. We also see new roles for continued professional development and the need to review the priorities for funding. New training strategies are needed for specialists other than teachers. Action is needed to improve the quality of training for youth workers to promote the creative and cultural development of young people.

Part four: a national strategy

We welcome the government's commitment to developing the creative capacities and cultural understanding of young people. We recommend that it should now co-ordinate a national strategy to promote higher standards of provision and achievement. This strategy should include action by the government itself and by the national agencies for the school curriculum, inspection and teacher training. It should also include action by local education authorities and schools and by other national and regional organisations. Throughout this report we make a wide range of specific recommendations that provide a framework for this strategy. In Part Four, we draw these recommendations together, indicate how they are related and the time scale over which some of them should be implemented and by whom. All of these recommendations are addressed to three principal objectives.

a. To ensure that the importance of creative and cultural education is explicitly recognised and provided for in schools' policies for the whole curriculum, and in government policy for the National Curriculum.

b. To ensure that teachers and other professionals are encouraged and trained to use methods and materials that facilitate the development of young people's creative abilities and cultural understanding.

c. To promote the development of partnerships between schools and outside agencies which are now essential to provide the kinds of creative and cultural education that young people need and deserve.

If these objectives were achieved the benefits would be felt by all young people, the education sector and by society as a whole.

How important is this?

(ix) There is intense concern with raising standards in education, and schools and the education sector in general are already deluged with reports. How important is this one? For some people, the very theme of this report may seem a distraction from the main business of raising standards. We do not think so. Our concerns are the same as everyone else's. How can education enable our children to make the most of themselves and take the best advantage of the opportunities and uncertainties that they face in a fast changing world? Let us anticipate some of the legitimate questions that might be asked of this report.

1. Isn't an emphasis on creativity and culture a distraction from the core concerns with literacy and numeracy?

We are not advocating creative and cultural education as alternatives to literacy and numeracy, but as equally relevant to the needs of this and of future generations. We support the need for high standards of literacy and numeracy. These are important in themselves. They can also enhance creative abilities: equally, creative teaching and learning can enhance literacy and numeracy. These are complementary abilities, not opposing objectives. The Government and the vast majority of people in education recognise this.

2. How are creative and cultural education relevant to raising academic standards?

Ability comes in many forms and should not be defined only by traditional academic criteria. Academic ability alone will no longer guarantee success or personal achievement. Every child has capabilities beyond the traditionally academic. Children with high academic ability may have other strengths that are often neglected. Children who struggle with academic work can have outstanding abilities in other areas. Equally, creative and cultural education of the sort we propose can also help to raise academic standards. The key is to find what children are good at. Self-confidence and self-esteem then tend to rise and overall performance improve. High standards in creative achievement require just as much rigour as traditional academic work.

3. What has this got to do with helping young people get jobs?

We live in a fast moving world. While employers continue to demand high academic standards, they also now want more. They want people who can adapt, see connections, innovate, communicate and work with others. This is true in many areas of work. The new knowledge-based economies in particular will increasingly depend on these abilities. Many businesses are paying for courses to promote creative abilities, to teach the skills and attitudes that are now essential for economic success but which our education system is not designed to promote.

4. Is this committee a lobby group for the arts?

This report does not represent a particular lobby. It expresses concerns across a wide range of public and professional interests about the balance and priorities of education as we move into the twenty-first century. Our members come from different professions and backgrounds: including science, the arts, education and business. Creative achievement is obvious in the arts but it is essential to achievement in all other fields including the sciences and business.

5. Is this a return to the progressive teaching ideas of the 1960s?

No. We are advocating a new balance between learning knowledge and skills and having the freedom to innovate and experiment – a system of education that fosters and channels the diverse abilities of young people and which gives everyone the opportunity to achieve on their own merits. This is why we link creative education with cultural education.

6. Teachers are already under enormous pressures. Are these recommendations going to add to the burden?

Good teachers and many high performing schools are already doing what we are recommending. We want to emphasise the importance of their work and to establish national priorities for creative and cultural education in all schools. The curriculum is already over-full and we think it should be thinned out. We want teachers to have more freedom to use their own creative and professional skills. Greater freedom for teachers in the classroom will help to promote creative teaching and this is essential to promote creative learning.

Looking forward

(x) The issues we are dealing with in this report are essential to the overall quality and standards of education. They are also difficult in terms of definition, policy and practice. We have found our own debates as a group exciting and enlightening. We have had an opportunity which is all too rare to meet across specialisms and to talk from a wide range of different backgrounds. We continually found that ideas and values that we thought particular to our own fields are common to us all. Too often, our own education had taught us otherwise. In what follows, we have tried to say as directly and clearly as we can what we are concerned with and what we are concerned about. We have tried to balance a discussion of definitions and principles with recommendations that are practical and feasible. We have not dealt in detail with all of the issues we raise: we have not done justice to every subtlety of argument on the way. Our task has been to balance depth with breadth, theory with practice and detail with brevity. In publishing this report we believe with even more strength than we did at the outset, that the tasks we identify are urgent and the arguments compelling; that the benefits of success are enormous and the costs of inaction profound.

(xi) In his introduction to Excellence in Schools *(DfEE 1997), the Secretary of State for Education and Employment relates the Government's aims for education to five priorities:*

- *the need to overcome economic and social disadvantages;*

- *the creation of greater fairness within the education system;*

- *the encouragement of aspiration;*

- *economic competitiveness;*

- *unlocking the potential of each individual.*

(xii) We believe that these are the right priorities for education; and that they are all related. Our aims are to show how these priorities can be realised through a systematic approach to creative and cultural education; to promote higher standards in creative and cultural education in all disciplines; to promote parity of provision between the arts, humanities, sciences and other major areas of education; and to stimulate a broad base of partnerships between schools and outside agencies. We see all of these as essential to realising the potential of young people; and to promoting the quality of national life and of individual achievement that are the ultimate purposes of education.

(xiii) The foundations of the present education system were laid at the end of the nineteenth century. They were designed to meet the needs of a world that was being transformed by industrialisation. We are publishing this report at the dawn of a new century. The challenges we face now are of the same magnitude, but they are of a different character. The task is not to do better now what we set out to do then: it is to rethink the purposes, methods and scale of education in our new circumstances. This report argues

that no education system can be world-class without valuing and integrating creativity in teaching and learning, in the curriculum, in management and leadership and without linking this to promoting knowledge and understanding of cultural change and diversity. The arguments and proposals that follow are to help set a course for the next century while addressing the urgent demands of the present.

There is quite a lot of substance here. Obviously this extract acts as an introduction to the much longer report which then follows it, but in many ways the extract can be considered to be a useful summation of what comes later. The paper begins with a discussion concerning the notion that education needs to be about more than just focusing on numeracy and literacy. Paragraph vii frames this, by observing that:

There has been a tendency for the national debate on education to be expressed as a series of exclusive alternatives, even dichotomies: for example, as a choice between the arts or the sciences; the core curriculum or the broad curriculum; between academic standards or creativity; freedom or authority in teaching methods.

(NACCCE, 1999, page 9)

This may be how you have experienced some aspects of your own teaching. Maybe you locate yourself with the core, or feel your subject is non-core; maybe you feel that your school prioritises some subjects, and as result, downgrades others. The NACCCE report tries to move away from over-simplistic dichotomies, and encourages its readers to engage with issues of raising standards throughout the education system. It endeavours to do this, as paragraph ii establishes, by encouraging a creative approach to education which *develops young people's capacities for original ideas and action* (page 5). This is surely something that many teachers would find it hard to argue with.

The report develops five main themes, and these are developed in paragraph viii. The first of these, 'the challenge for education', outlines some of the issues facing schools today. It may seem a big question to you at this early stage of your career, but there are some important challenges and changes that all teachers will have to grapple with. You are preparing learners for a future that does not yet exist. Knowledge has changed, as we have seen in earlier sections of this book. As an example, in Chapter 5 we saw how new technologies change the way people think about the world, and interact with each other. These have important implications for the work of educators.

Paragraph vii, section 2, deals with the issue of creative development, and talks of creative teaching, and allies this to perceptions of lack of discipline. Lack of discipline is not what is meant by creativity. Indeed, far from it. Being creative involves work, and active engagement on the part of both teacher and pupils. The phrase 'creative teaching' is employed here, and this, and related terminology, are an important contribution to the discourse of education which the NACCCE report has made. The terminologies used here, 'teaching for creativity' and 'creative teaching', are defined later in the document:

By teaching creatively we mean teachers using imaginative approaches to make learning more interesting, exciting and effective. Teachers can be highly creative in developing materials and approaches that fire children's interests and motivate their learning. This is a necessary part of all good teaching.

By teaching for creativity we mean forms of teaching that are intended to develop young people's own creative thinking or behaviour.

(NACCCE, 1999, pages 102–3)

Teaching for creativity is not a single method or technique. It can involve a wide range of methods and approaches. It is possible and we think desirable to teach for creativity in all areas of the curriculum.

(NACCCE, 1999, page 111)

These are useful distinctions, which should be of benefit to you in your planning for teaching and learning. Teaching for creativity involves you thinking about how you foster creativity in your pupils, whereas creative teaching concerns itself with ways in which you can deliver lessons in a creative way which makes the topic in question *interesting, exciting and effective*. This should be part of your normal planning anyhow, as part of your ongoing professional development; after all, would you want to plan for lessons which are boring, uninteresting and irrelevant?

Risk-taking is also mentioned in paragraph viii/2, and this should feature in your teaching too. Risk-taking is inherently risky! No one wants to fail, but in the early days of your professional development you should be taking risks. You need to find out how far you can 'push the boundaries'; what makes learning exciting is not plodding sedentary regurgitation lessons, but ones with drive and pace. You may want to introduce risk-taking gently, with selected classes, but introduce it you should.

Paragraph viii/3 widens the scope of the discussion to include all subjects. We hope it is fairly clear that what is being discussed here can apply across the curriculum, creative teaching can be found in all subjects.

REFLECTIVE EXERCISE

Ask your mentors to direct you to teachers who are known to employ creative techniques, whatever their subject specialism. Arrange to watch them in action. What can you take from their professional practice and pedagogy to apply in your own?

Paragraph viii/6 observes that *creativity can be taught*. This is a key message of this document, and links back to viii/2, where it is noted that *others see creativity as the preserve of a gifted few*. This is a point worth considering further. Writing about creativity, Margaret Boden makes a distinction with creative acts that take place which result in something new for the individual concerned. She terms these as being psychologically creative, in the sense of their having occurred to an individual. But these are not necessarily new to anyone else, i.e. they have not resulted in something which has never been seen before. She contrasts these with those ideas which, although coming into being in the same fashion, result in something which is new and original, and therefore of historical significance. The former, which we see every day in our classrooms, she designates as P-creative (from psychological) while the latter are rare occurrences, and H-creative (from historical):

> *If Mary Smith has an idea which she could not have had before, her idea is P-creative – no matter how many people have had the same idea already. The historical sense applies to ideas that are fundamentally novel with respect to the whole of human history. Mary Smith's surprising idea is H-creative if no one has ever had the idea before her.*

(Boden, 1990, page 32)

This distinction between two different types of creativity is important, as it allows for an individual pupil to produce something which is new for them, and which we as teachers can recognise and celebrate accordingly.

Paragraph viii/7 raises an interesting issue concerning assessment. We saw in Chapter 4 how formative assessment is efficacious in raising attainment levels. Here the NACCCE report is referring to summative assessment, and how this has a tendency, as some commentators have observed, for the tail of assessment to wag the curriculum dog. As we argued in Chapter 4, this need not be the case.

Paragraph ix contains some very telling observations. We know that creativity can be viewed by some as marginal, but creative approaches can raise attainment, as these comments from teachers who have been involved in creative interventions show:

> *I don't see a tension between [creativity and raising standards], I don't think they're mutually exclusive at all. I think that the creative … work in establishing a climate for change, a creative ethos, that to me helps raise achievement, helps raise performance. So I don't see a tension there whatsoever. If you go back to your traditional teaching in straight lines, it doesn't work to raise performance.*

> *The GCSE results were the best they've ever been in the school. Now, who knows, OK, it might have been, I think it certainly had a part to play in it. The most interesting comments were from the teachers themselves, when they said [creativity] fundamentally changed the way that they were now going to deliver, and that I think made a difference … we had some of our more challenging pupils, and believe me we have very challenging pupils here, telling others to be quiet because they wanted to listen, to get engaged, so you know that side of things, the attitudinal side was quite key, and certainly as a whole school one of the things that we continually battle with is work ethic.*

(Fautley and Hatcher, 2008, pages 46–7)

There is a number of other similar comments in these last few paragraphs.

REFLECTIVE EXERCISE

As you read these, how do they square with your own observations? Where is creative teaching and learning to be found in your subject, or in your school?

Constraints and limitations to creativity in educational practice

The next reading is from an article by Anna Craft. Anna Craft is a British author and academic, one of the leading commentators on creativity in education today. The article is entitled *Limits to Creativity in Education* (Craft, 2003).

POINTS TO CONSIDER

As you read through this extract, think about the following questions:

What do you think creativity is?

Thinking back to the NACCCE report, how is creativity fostered in your teaching?

Would you do things differently if some constraints were removed?

If so, what are those constraints?

EXTRACT THREE

Craft, A (2003) The limits to creativity in education: dilemmas for the educator. **British Journal of Educational Studies, *51(2): 118–125.***

Limits to creativity in education

I want to suggest, then, that there are four limits to creativity in education.

1. What does it mean? The limitations of terminology. *A challenge in any discussion of creativity, which could be thought of as a 'limitation' to the concept, is the difficulty of terminology. Creativity and imagination are distinct concepts (Craft, 2002; Elliott, 1971). Innovation, it could be argued, is distinct again, from both imagination and creativity. As far as creativity in the classroom is concerned, as the NACCCE report (1999) noted, there are distinctions between creative teaching and teaching for creativity. It could be argued that these are each distinct from creative learning (Jeffrey, 2001a, in press; Jeffrey and Woods, 1997). Yet, despite these distinctions in meaning, there is often slippage of the language in practice, so that we may refer, for example, to creative teaching as teaching for creativity when it is not necessarily having this effect. There are implications of such slippage in language, for what we value in practice. Valuing creative learning for example, is distinct from valuing creative teaching.*

2. Conflicts in policy and practice. *The tightening of control around both curriculum and pedagogy, as well as other aspects of the management and financing of schools in England, has formed, for some, a paradox (Craft, 1997; Woods et al., 1997). For, whilst creativity was being encouraged, the means by which this and other educational goals were being achieved were extremely constraining for teachers. In response to the tightening framework within which teachers were to work, creativity became, for some, a tool for personal and institutional survival (Craft, 1997; McCarthy, 2001; Safran, 2001; Woods, 1990; Woods and Jeffrey, 1996).*

Other limitations to creativity produced by the application of policy to practice are the discontinuities in the curriculum, as far as creativity is concerned. For example, the differences between creativity as conceived of in the early years curriculum, compared to the National Curriculum and the NACCCE report, are striking. The latter two are more concerned with the development of creativity as a cross-curricular – and transferable – skill. The NACCCE report acknowledges the role of playfulness in creative production, however its focus is boiling down an 'essence' of creativity. Creativity, or creative development, in the early years curriculum, is by contrast located in a specific set of domains – the creative and expressive arts including art, design and music, and it is linked strongly with early learning processes such as play in such a way that it is sometimes not clear what the distinction between play and creativity is. There is therefore, I would argue, some inevitable discontinuity in how the child's creativity may be supported in practice in the transition across the curricula. These difficulties are explored more fully elsewhere (Craft, 1999, 2000, 2002).

3. Limitations in curriculum organisation? We might ask, to what extent is the fostering of creativity limited by its subject context? Is it, for example, possible to foster creativity in physical education, mathematics, information and communications technology and English, equally? I would argue that creativity is most certainly relevant across the curriculum and is not subject-specific, although it is manifest distinctly in different subjects. Indeed, although creativity is often associated with the creative and performing arts, opportunities for developing learner creativity exist across the curriculum. Mathematics, and ICT, as I have argued elsewhere, for example, both provide distinct kinds of opportunities for learner creativity and each involves different pedagogical strategies to maximise this (Craft, 2001b). But this different manifestation does not necessarily imply any limitation in the fostering of creativity; rather, in principle, the opposite.

But it could be argued that the way in which the curriculum is presented and organised within the time available in a school day may offer greater or fewer opportunities for fostering learner and teacher creativity. For it might be argued that where the curriculum is taught as discrete subjects, this may constrain learner and teacher creativity, in discouraging thinking about themes which cross the subject boundaries. But are subjects of the curriculum, taught by themselves, necessarily a constraint to developing creativity?

4. Limitations stemming from centrally controlled pedagogy? Clearly, the fostering of creativity may be subject to the pedagogical limitations, as may any aspect of the curriculum. However, the challenges posed by holding creativity as a goal may be greater than those posed by other curriculum areas. For the establishment of an appropriate organisational climate for stimulating creativity, we are told, includes enabling pupils and teachers to feel:

- *that new ideas are met with encouragement and support;*
- *able to take initiative and to find relevant information;*
- *able to interact with others; and*
- *that uncertainty is tolerated and thus risk-taking encouraged. (Amabile, 1988; Ekvall, 1991, 1996; Isaksen, 1995)*

The establishment of these strategies in a policy climate which appears to treat teachers like technicians rather than artists (Jeffrey and Craft, 2001; Woods et al., 1997) and which attempts to centrally control both content and teaching strategies to an increasing degree, is challenging (Craft and Gabel-Dunk, 2002). Thus it may be that the fostering of teaching for creativity, creative learning and teaching creatively, are limited by a centrally controlled approach to pedagogy in some school years or contexts.

Social, environmental and ethical limits to creativity

Perhaps more fundamental than the challenges discussed so far are four questions which challenge the universality and very desirability of creativity.

1. Social limits – how culturally specific is creativity? *Creativity, whether 'extraordinary' or 'ordinary', is often presented as if it were a universally-applicable concept. But it may, by contrast, be quite culturally specific, in its strong emphasis on individuality, and the value it places on being able to think independently of social norms. For this may reflect values in cultures where the individual and the marketplace are held in high esteem. In a more repressive or conformist culture, creativity might be perceived to be less relevant and desirable. Clearly, cultural context may also affect a person's experiences of creativity and their ability to manifest it – although this may not be a totally predictable relationship. Thus, in a social context where choices and personal autonomy are severely restricted, the drive to find alternatives may be quite strong. On the other hand, it may be that avoidance of social or political sanctions and socialisation into submission, would, under such conditions, suffocate creativity.*

It is also possible that creativity may be imbued with social class based assumptions such as resilience, self-reliance, persistence and control over one's environment – also future-orientation, and greater individualism (Craft, 2002; Kluckhohn and Strodtbeck, 1961).

On the other hand, it could be argued that both extraordinary and ordinary creativity reflect the globalisation of significant aspects of Western culture. And although there may be a strong element of 'cultural saturation' in the concept of creativity, it could also be said that the increasing global influence of Western culture, including its markets, means that the relevance of creativity as a universal concept, may grow.

But we are not at that point yet. We still live in a world where there are distinct cultural identities both within and between nation states, as well as different traditions and value-sets. The universalisation of creativity in the current world is, it seems to me, premature and inappropriate. Creativity then, I would suggest, may well be limited by its cultural specificity.

2. Environmental limits. *The case for fostering creativity in education can be seen as a response to the conditions and pace of life and the global market economy, as discussed in the introduction. But, how desirable is the norm of innovation that the global economy demands? To what extent is it desirable to encourage and sustain the 'disposable' culture, where obsolescence is built in at the design stage of many consumer goods and where fashion dictates the need for constant change and updating? For there are clear environmental costs, to giving high value to the market, as if it were a divine force. To what*

extent do we, in the marketplace at any rate, encourage innovation for innovation's sake and without reference to genuine need? How desirable is it to encourage those values which present, via the market, 'wants' as if they were 'needs'? It could be said that a culture of 'make do and mend' might be something to be fostered, rather than looking to ways of changing what may be working perfectly well already, whether that be a system, or a relationship, or a service or a product.

3. *Ethical limits. How do we weigh up the use of creativity for destructive purposes? For creativity has, undoubtedly, a darker side. The human imagination is capable of immense destruction as well as of almost infinitely constructive possibilities. To what extent is it possible to generate systems which stimulate and celebrate creativity, within a profoundly humane framework, and to actively examine and encourage the critical examination of the values inherent in creative ideas and action? The role of educators is perhaps to encourage students to examine the possible wider effects of their own ideas and those of others, and to evaluate both choices and worth in the light of this. This inevitably means the balancing of conflicting perspectives and values – which themselves may be irreconcilable.*

4. *How do ordinary and extraordinary creativity connect? There have been numerous attempts to distinguish between ordinary and extraordinary creativity (this latter is sometimes known as 'high' creativity – Gardner, 1995). But what is their relationship to one another? Are they part of a continuum, as argued by Craft (2001a) and Worth (2001). Weisberg's (1993) model of creativity has been proposed as one of a number which may unify ordinary and extraordinary creativity (Fowles, 2002). However, these assertions need more investigation; for our understanding of what factors may trigger an act of extraordinary creativity is still imperfect. This has implications for education. For example, it may be that by stimulating the creativity of all children, we produce more creative behaviour at all points in the continuum, including extraordinary creativity. This assumption seems to underpin both policy and also some commentary on creativity in education. But is the assumption sound? We are currently limited by our understanding of creativity itself.*

Dilemmas for the educator

I have suggested, then, a number of challenges to the implementation of creativity in education, which include some fundamental limitations to the concept itself. I have proposed that creativity cannot necessarily be seen as a universal concept, equally applicable and relevant to diverse contexts. So, what dilemmas are raised for the educator, by the argument that creativity is not a universal concept? I want to propose three dilemmas of principle, and three of practice. Dilemmas of principle, then.

- *If creativity is culturally specific, how appropriate is it to encourage it within education? Stimulating creativity involves encouraging learners to adopt a way of life that not only presents itself as universal when it is not, but also the positive associations with creativity mask some possibly questionable values which are also associated with it. On the other hand, education in any cultural context will involve the teaching of some concepts as if they were universal; but like any other concept, creativity does not necessarily have to be taught in this way. Indeed, by its very nature, being about alternatives and possibilities, it offers the potential inherently for evaluating the worth of any creative outcome, by considering the implications of any new idea, product, service, etc. Thus, although creativity is always situated within a cultural context, by interrogating this, the assumption of cultural universalism may be challenged.*

- To what extent is the 'throw away society' a given? *How appropriate is the implication that creativity is a good thing for the economy, for the society and therefore for education? For implicit in this is the idea that innovation is of itself a good thing. That the old, or the borrowed, the inherited and the unchanging are not desirable, whereas the new is, by contrast, of paramount value, by virtue of its newness. For creativity, in the sense of the process which leads to constant change and innovation in products, contributes toward the economy, in that having a short shelf-life to any product means increased sales, and so on. How far is it appropriate for the fostering of creativity to occur without critical reflection on the environmental, social and other consequences there may be in treating the 'market as God' in this way?*

- To what extent does the fostering of creativity feed or challenge the status quo? *Fostering creativity in the classroom could feed the market as suggested. But fostering children's creativity could also lead to challenges to the status quo, and could lead to alternative modes of existence. How can classroom pedagogy reflect the schism between the assumption that creativity leads to increased wealth and the celebration of creativity as the 'other' or as the potential for the 'other'?*

As to challenges of practice, I want to raise three.

- The curriculum. *How can the curriculum be organised to stimulate creativity? A curriculum which is fixed, compulsory, which involves a great deal of propositional knowledge, and which takes up a great deal of learning time, may pose challenges to stimulating creativity – possibly more so than a curriculum which is more flexible.*

- Professional artistry within a centralised pedagogy. *The centralising not only of curriculum but also of pedagogy, in literacy and numeracy in any case, can be seen, as we know, as posing a challenge to professional artistry – and in this sense may be seen as restricting potential teacher creativity, at least in some parts of the curriculum and in some phases. So, how does a teacher balance professional creativity and judgement against the requirements to teach in certain ways?*

- The distinctions and potential tensions between teaching for creativity, creative teaching and creative learning. *The distinction between teaching for creativity and creative teaching was made by the NACCCE report (1999) which acknowledged that teaching for creativity may or may not involve creative teaching. The notion of creative learning is being theorised at present. There may be practical differences between each of these which need exploration and articulation.*

Summing up

Against the context of a political, social and economic discourse of creativity in education as a 'good thing', I have suggested in this paper that there are a number of potential limitations to the fostering of creativity in education, i.e. difficulties of terminology, conflicts between policy and practice, limitations in curriculum organisation, and limitations stemming from a centrally controlled pedagogy. More fundamentally I have acknowledged social, environmental and ethical limits to creativity, noting that creativity may not necessarily be seen as having universal relevance and value.

Finally, there are, as I have suggested, a number of professional dilemmas for the educator, which reflect the limitations discussed. It may not be popular to challenge creativity in today's discourse, but it is probably necessary if we are to move beyond two possible and perhaps common positions in education at present.

One of these is complacency which could be charicatured as follows: 'we have a curriculum and a framework which acknowledges creativity and which connects creativity, culture and the economy – so we need do nothing else than implement the curriculum as if it were unproblematic'. Clearly there are value positions and difficulties, not to mention real classroom dilemmas which such a complacent position effectively ignores.

Another position is that of 'resistance' to the technicising of education, where creativity is seen as a kind of resistance (Woods and Jeffrey, 1996), enabling the teacher to reclaim a degree of professional artistry against a backdrop of intensification and centralised control of pedagogy and curriculum. Framing creativity as a response to policy on pedagogy is thus polarising the positions of policy makers and 'the Other', the alternative response. It may also imply that creativity itself is unproblematic when framed as the opposite of a position which has been widely critiqued (Woods and Jeffrey, 1996; Woods et al., 1997).

So – challenging creativity is, I am proposing, necessary, if we are to provide learners with an education responsibly grounded in the context and demands of the twenty-first century. Addressing explicitly the limits to and dilemmas bound up in fostering creativity in education, as this paper has sought to do, is a start.

What Anna Craft is saying here is that there is a number of limiting factors which apply to the notion of creativity in education. She details these in this extract. Let us consider them from your perspective as a beginning teacher.

In discussing limitations of terminology, Craft uses the distinctions raised in the NACCCE report, which we discussed above, teaching for creativity, and creative teaching, and to these adds a third, creative learning. Creative learning has been defined as:

> *... simply any learning that develops our capacity to be creative. It equips young people with the knowledge and skills they need to succeed in today's world, nurturing ways of thinking and working that encourage imagination, independence, tolerance of ambiguity and risk, openness, the raising of aspirations.*
>
> (Creative Partnerships, 2005)

These three terminologies are not yet in common usage in schools, but they are clearly different from each other. You may find that generic discussions of 'creativity' do not use the exactitude which these distinctions allow. This is what Craft is referring to when she observes that *there are implications of such slippage in language, for what we value in practice. Valuing creative learning for example, is distinct from valuing creative teaching* (page 118). This will affect you in the way you consider and plan for creativity. Knowing that there are differences means you can think about what sorts of creativity you are employing in your lesson, and use the appropriate terminology at the right time.

In the section headed *Conflicts in policy and practice*, Craft notes that while creativity was being encouraged with one hand, obsessive targeting of educational goals with the other meant it was increasingly less likely to be happening. We also have the strange circumstance where creativity is viewed differently during the various phases of education.

REFLECTIVE EXERCISE

During your training you will probably be offered the chance to go into a primary school. How is creativity treated in the primary school (or schools) you visit? How do teachers feel about creativity? With the emphasis on literacy and numeracy, when do creative activities take place?

'Centrally controlled pedagogy' is another limiting factor with regard to creativity in schools. Your emerging pedagogy is likely to be formed to some extent with relation to perceived pedagogic norms. As standardisation of approach has taken hold, some would say that the opportunities for creative teaching have diminished. The National Curriculum is supposed to allow freedom for schools to develop appropriate local pedagogies; this should allow for divergent approaches.

The next section of the extract is concerned with social, environmental and ethical limits to creativity. This has some complex ideas within it. The cultural context of the schools in which you teach may be constraining factors in terms of how creativity is viewed. This will be a matter for you to consider, especially in cases where the 'western bias' of creative approaches may be a mitigating factor. Indeed, this links to ethical notions, should creativity always produce new, disposable ideas? Are creative responses to sustainability appropriate, and what would these look like?

We have considered the work of Margaret Boden, and her notion of p- and h- creativity. This links closely with Craft's descriptions of 'ordinary' and 'extraordinary' creativity. But how much creativity, she asks, is a good thing? Do you want creative disruption? And how does creativity begin? There are still lots of questions raised here that the academic and educational communities are working through.

The final part of the extract contains more by way of difficult ideas and food for thought. Some of these questions may seem to be very large ones for you as a beginning teacher to be grappling with, but there is a number of issues you will need to come to terms with as your career unfolds. But for now, let us return to where you are now, and ways in which you can foster creativity in your teaching at the moment. To this end, the next readings are from our book on creativity (Fautley and Savage, 2007). The first is about teaching creatively.

POINTS TO CONSIDER

As you read this, think about what the various subheadings mean for you in your current stage of pedagogic development.

EXTRACT FOUR

Savage, J and Fautley, M (2007) Creativity in Secondary Education. *Exeter: Learning Matters, pp. 25–28.*

Being an inspiration

Everyone remembers their good teachers, the ones that inspired them to love a particular subject or the ones that motivated and encouraged them when learning was difficult. What is it about these teachers that make them stick in your mind, even many years after you have left their classes?

Also, perhaps unfortunately, everyone remembers those teachers that didn't inspire, motivate or encourage them! For me, physics was one of those subjects I just didn't understand while at school. Imagine my surprise recently when, while working on an art and science project, I met an astrophysicist called Tim. He works at Jodrell Bank Radio Telescope (part of the University of Manchester) in Cheshire. He inspired me about space, in particular how planets and stars are born, how solar winds blow across the solar system and, of course, the sheer scale of the whole thing. On a recent visit, Tim informed me he had discovered a new star and that he was going to get the chance to name it! I enquired as to the whereabouts of this star.

If the earth were here*

and the sun were here*,

then whereabouts was his star? Approximately 3,000 kilometres away in that ↓ direction!

Now that got my attention! I wish that Tim had been my physics teacher at school. He has a way of presenting the complicated facts of astrophysics in a way that even I can understand and get excited about.

So, the first important point in this section is that we, as 'experts' in our curriculum fields, need to present the knowledge of that field in a way that inspires our students.

2. Knowing your subject inside out

In order to be an inspiration to your students, you must be completely familiar with your own subject area. This will allow you to concentrate fully on the delivery of that knowledge within the classroom. This is as true for teaching at Key Stage 3 as it is for teaching at Key Stage 5. Regardless of curriculum frameworks and modes of delivery that you will be required to work within, the students' initial source of inspiration and knowledge is you. If you are inspiring then your students will be inspired; if you are knowledgeable and can impart that knowledge in an inspirational way they will be encouraged to learn. But as we will go on to see in Chapter 3, while just knowing about your subject is vital, creating opportunities for pupils to be actively involved in the knowledge associated with your subject is equally important This will involve you in planning carefully and setting appropriate learning objectives that allow for and facilitate opportunities for pupils to be creative learners.

3. Carrying on being a learner

Of course, all of our subjects are in a constant state of change. We never know it all. To teach creatively, it will be important for you to maintain an active interest in your subject area and the current issues and concerns that are being raised within it.

As an example, the QCDA's recent consultation (Futures meeting the challenge) has many interesting points of departure and application for teachers. Not least, is the challenge to explore and utilise the potential of new technologies to link subject areas within the curriculum in new ways:

> *In a technology-rich world we need to review and modernise what and how we learn. Imagine how a graphic designer works today compared with 30 years ago. What should a modernised music, art or design curriculum be like? They may use technology as a tool for thinking, making or doing. Technology needs to be used more effectively to help develop learners' enquiry skills, logical reasoning, analytical thinking and creativity. It should support individualised and independent learning, while encouraging wider communication and collaborative learning.*
>
> *(QCDA, 2005)*

The QCDA promotes the use of technology as a force for change in developing a curriculum fit for the twenty-first century. It is clear from recent QCDA statements that such 'joined-up curriculum thinking' should be a priority as teachers not only seek to develop teaching skills but also the more general development of students' creativity, thinking skills, ability to communicate and ability to collaborate. We will return to this work in Chapter 5 when we consider how ICT can help us teach creatively and teach for creativity.

4. Making connections: how does your subject relate to other subjects?

While it is vital that you are able to make constructive links within your own subject area it is imperative that these also extend beyond to other related subjects. Creativity in one subject area does not exist in isolation from creativity in other subject areas. Perhaps this is a strength of much educational practice in the primary sector, where teachers have a little more flexibility to move around and between subject areas? Working within secondary education, the danger is to isolate your own subject from other related, or even non-related, disciplines in such a way that any potential creative spark that students bring with them to your lessons gets extinguished pretty quickly.

You may not feel as comfortable allowing students to develop their knowledge of other subjects within your own lessons. You may also be put under significant pressure to cover so much curriculum content the only practical consequence is that you will think that there is not any time within your lessons to allow for this kind of 'diversion'. Both of these concerns may be legitimate, but try and resist this kind of pressure. Teaching creativity must acknowledge that creativity itself is not limited to specific subject domains. In learning to teach creatively you will have to make connections across the curriculum in such a way that empowers you as a teacher to teach your subject in a new way, perhaps even in ways that you were not taught yourself! Incidentally, this will also create a more inclusive curriculum and educational environment for students, as we will consider in Chapter 6.

5. Developing high expectations

How often do you hear people moaning about today's young people? On occasions it is all too easy to disparage one's own students and put them down in front of other teachers. Try and avoid this at all costs. You have a tremendous opportunity and privilege. An important part of teaching creatively is having a high expectation of your pupils, both individual and collectively.

*Spend some time getting inspired about what your pupils might be able to achieve. As a first step, why don't you visit the Creative Partnerships website and read some of the stories of other teachers and students who have worked on a range of different projects (**www. creative-partnerships.com**) in all curriculum areas. These stories can be a constant source of encouragement and a real inspiration to us as teachers about what young people can achieve given creative teaching and opportunities for developing their own creativity.*

6. Stimulating curiosity

Stimulating curiosity is a vital part of teaching creatively. What is it that is particularly interesting about your subject? What might capture a Year 7 student's imagination? Are there any peculiarities or distinctive elements that you could use to engage them early on in their studies with you? Capturing and maintaining a student's interest is a prerequisite for effective teaching and learning. We believe that the majority of children are naturally curious about new things and you should seek to build on this in your teaching.

Additionally, do not fall into the trap of thinking that the only learning a student will do within your subject is within your classroom sessions. As teachers, we are constantly amazed at how students take ideas from our lessons and work through them in their own time, maybe individually or with groups of friends. The increasing availability of high-quality educational materials on the internet has revolutionised how children learn independently. Make links in your lessons to materials online that they will be able to follow up. Get away from issuing only written homework (that you will have to mark!), and encompass a broader range of resources to stimulate your students' curiosity for your subject.

7. Being an encourager

The best teachers are encouragers. There is a direct link here to teaching for creativity. Make sure that through teaching creatively you empower pupils by building them up rather than knocking them down. Communicate a 'can do' attitude in your subject rather than a 'this is difficult or complicated' one. As we will discuss in detail in Chapter 6, Crafts notion of little c creativity (Craft, Jeffrey and Leibling, 2001, p56) is built around the notion of possibility thinking as a way of life (note that this is not 'impossibility thinking'). We should apply this and state that teaching creatively is built around the notion of celebrating students' positive creative achievements.

8. Balancing lessons and allowing time for students to be creative

All teachers would like more time to teach their subject. Learning to make best use of the time that you have is an important element of teaching. Within your lessons you should seek to include a broad range of activities and opportunities for pupils to work together towards creative outcomes. Students will need the chance to work independently and learn the skills of working in a group with a range of roles. The creative processes that occur during your lessons will be facilitated by this process which we will explore in more detail in following chapters.

9. Finding your own teaching style

Finally, teaching in this way is a highly individual activity. There are many pressures on you as a trainee teacher and you may well feel that you are being told to teach in a particu-lar way. You may even disagree on the advice you are being given! Teacher training is a process of assimilating advice, experimenting with new approaches to teaching and then evaluating the outcomes. The point here is that there is a real danger of you teaching your subject in the way that you were taught. This could be good or bad (or somewhere in between), but either way it is not based on you! Teaching creatively requires you to teach your subject as you – not as some reconstructed memory figure.

There are significant pieces of educational research that explore this issue of teacher iden-tity (Coldron and Smith, 1999; Hargreaves, 1994; Maclure, 1993; Stronach et al., 2002). There is not the time or space to explore these in any detail here. Rather, we will leave this section with the following advice. You may well be the only geographer, artist, musi-cian, mathematician, etc. that your pupils will have direct access to week by week. What a tremendous privilege it is to have a group of young people looking to you for challenges, inspiration and motivation.

Learning to teach creatively is a process. We have identified nine features above that could form the starting point of a plan to initiate this process in your own teaching. Using Table 3.1, set some personal targets for your own teaching drawing on these ideas.

Table 3.1 Personal targets for teaching creatively

Teaching creatively	Target	Date	Review 1 (revise target if necessary)	Date	Date Review 2 (revise target if necessary)	Date
Being an inspiration						
Knowing your subject inside out						
Carrying on being a learner						
Making connections: how does your subject relate to other subjects?						
Developing high expectations						
Stimulating curiosity						
Being an encourager						
Balancing lessons and allowing time for pupils to be creative						
Finding your own teaching style						

Developing a creative pedagogy

Teaching creatively

We have already observed that you do not want to plan lessons which are boring and uninteresting. In this section there are some provocations for you to challenge your own teaching style.

> **REFLECTIVE EXERCISE**
>
> *Suppose you were influenced by a teacher you had. Do you want to be like them? Maybe they were influenced by a teacher they had, and so on. How far back does this tradition go? Is teaching in the twenty-first century the same as it was in, say, 1950? Should it be? What about 1920? Or 1890? Where should differences be made? Are twenty-first-century pupils exposed to the same cultural milieu as children from the above dates?*

This is a difficult reflective task. It's not about throwing the baby out with the bath-water, and having a creative free-for-all, but about thinking about the nature and purpose of skills and knowledge.

> **REFLECTIVE EXERCISE**
>
> *I spent hours at school in maths lessons learning to use a slide-rule. Many of you may not even know what a slide-rule is nowadays. Is there an equivalent knowledge 'chunk' in your subject that might be outdated in the future? Does it matter?*

You will want to be an inspiration to the young people you teach. You will be talked about at home, your exciting lessons will light the fuse for young minds. You have the most important job in the world!

We know that pupils expect teachers to know their subject inside-out, and this is important. But so is planning, and so is pedagogic content knowledge, and, as we saw in Chapter 2, one of the areas Shulman was concerned with was curricular knowledge. This is about making connections. Developing high expectations is important. It is often said that pupils will live down to your expectations if they are too low, so it right to be appropriately demanding.

Finding your own teaching style is something you will be working on. We want informed, reflective practitioners. This needs work from you, there is no short-cut.

Teaching for creativity

Turning now to teaching for creativity. One of the key components of this is questioning, and so the next reading is concerned with that aspect of your pedagogic practice.

EXTRACT FIVE

Savage, J and Fautley, M (2007) Creativity in Secondary Education. Exeter: Learning Matters, pp. 35–37.

Questioning

In thinking about teaching for creativity, each of the learning and task outcomes [listed earlier] describe specific types of knowledge and activity. What you want to do in your lessons is to direct the pupils towards creative processes, and in order to do this you need to think about how you will enable pupils to make progress in their learning and doing. A key component of this is questioning. Polanyi (1967, p4) wrote of how we can know more than we can tell, and with pupils this is especially likely to be the case. So, in order to try and access pupil knowledge you will need to develop questioning skills. A useful starting point for this is Bloom's taxonomy (Bloom, 1956). Bloom and his team developed a classification of levels of thinking according to cognitive complexity. They also found that at the time 95 per cent of teacher questions were at the lowest level! Bloom classified and labelled six categories of thought. Bloom's taxonomy was revised nearly 50 years later by Anderson and Krathwohl (2001). Figure 3.1 shows both the original Bloom taxonomy and the later version side by side. Both of these taxonomies are hierarchical: levels near the bottom represent lower orders of thinking, moving towards the apex which represents higher-order thinking.

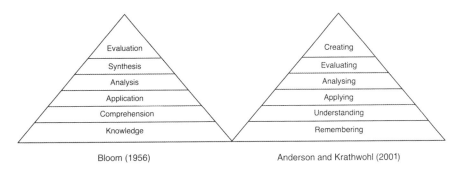

Figure 3.1 Bloom's taxonomy and revision

There are some significant alterations between the two versions. The Anderson and Krathwohl version changes the nouns to verbs, moves 'evaluating' down to take the place of 'synthesis' and adds a new top layer of 'creating'. For our purposes this is both helpful in that it places creating *into a framework of ways you can direct questioning, but is also seemingly problematic in that it appears that* creating *is the final stage in a sequence of cognitive processes. However, this raising of* creating *to higher-order thinking does not place it out of reach: what is does is to make it a logical part of the thought processes of your pupils.*

One of the tasks for you as a teacher is to develop the thinking skills of your pupils. Devise one question for each of the first three levels of the taxonomy (three questions in all) which helps check if the pupils are able to remember, understand *and* apply *a specific concept.*

Maybe you found this quite challenging? Asking questions is a skill, and, like all skills, needs practice to develop. Let us think about this and give you some starting points.

We have already noted how the each of the learning and task outcome statements listed [earlier] provide clues about the type of knowledge or skills involved. Let us now do the same for the various aspects of Bloom's taxonomy. Taking each of the levels of Bloom's taxonomy, let us ask what sort of cognitive involvement is happening in each and what questioning for this would look like. To do this we shall use both the original Bloom taxonomy and the more recent version, as some documentation you will meet in school (inter alia DfES, 2002) refers to the original, while others refer to the update. Table 3.2 shows the cognitive activity involved in each aspect of the taxonomy.

Table 3.2 Cognitive activity

Taxonomy descriptor	Cognitive activity
Creating	Come up with original ideas
Evaluating	Make judgements about effectiveness
Synthesis	Use multiple understandings
Analysing	Reflecting on understanding
Applying	Use understanding
Understanding	Demonstrate they know something
Remembering	Recalling information

The broad outlines of the right-hand column of Table 3.2 delineate cognitive activity, or what the pupils will be doing, in order to demonstrate achievement at each level. These are helpful in devising question areas as they help you think about what you and the pupils should be focusing on.

One way which many trainee and beginning teachers have found helpful in devising questions to develop knowledge is to start with a list of question 'stems' which form the first part of what you will ask. Table 3.3 provides some possible stems which you can use to devise questions for each level of the taxonomy.

Table 3.3 Question stems for Bloom's taxonomy

Knowledge/ remembering	Describe ... Describe what you are doing ... Show me what you are doing ... Can you remember how to ... Identify ... Can you recall ...
Comprehension/understanding	What is the idea behind this ... Can you show me an example where you ... What differences are there ... What is going on at this point ... Can you demonstrate ... Explain ... Illustrate ...
Application/applying	How will you go about ... What will you do to ... Can you think of (or show me) an instance where ... How will you carry out ...
Analysis/analysing	How might it have been different if ... What happens in the bit when you ... Can you explain what went on as you were doing that bit where ... Compare that with ... Can you distinguish between that and ... Are you able to describe how you ...

Table 3.3 continued

Synthesis	What would happen if you were to put your ideas together with hers …
	What would happen if you changed that bit where …
	How could you do this differently …
Evaluation/evaluating	What was successful …
	What changes might you make …
	Can you justify …
	How do you feel about …
	Why do you think that …
	Are you able to suggest …
Creating	Can you come up with a solution …
	Are you able to devise …
	Can you generate …
	How about a different response …
	What would that look like …
	What would that sound like …
	How would that be made up …
	Can you produce …

Using the stems in Table 3.3 you should be able to formulate questions that probe students' knowledge, concepts and skills. Yoiu should also find that you are able to use these stems to advance pupil thinking, by moving them from one level to another.

Questioning is a key skill for teachers. One way you can foster creativity is by the use of carefully constructed questions which lead learners through a sequence of thinking activities. This extract deals with some of these specifically with relation to Bloom's taxonomy (Bloom, 1956). What it suggests is thinking about planning for questioning using stems. This is useful advice for beginning teachers, and should allow you to think about ways you can plan for creative responses to be developed in your lessons.

This takes us to our final reading for this chapter, where we return to the QCDA publication *Creativity: Find it, promote it!* This extract links very closely to the previous readings in this section, and asks how teachers can promote creativity.

POINTS TO CONSIDER

How does this extract pull together many of the threads we have been discussing in this chapter?

EXTRACT SIX

QCDA (2004) Creativity: Find it, Promote it! *Qualifications and Curriculum Development Agency (QCDA), pp. 13–17.*

How can you promote creativity?

How can teachers promote creativity?

Teachers can promote pupils' creativity by:

- *planning tasks and activities that give pupils opportunities to be creative*

- *teaching in a way that makes the most of pupils' creativity.*

It is vital to get the pitch of an activity right from the outset. Unrealistically high expectations cause frustration and anxiety, inhibiting creativity. Unrealistically low expectations induce boredom and cause pupils to switch off.

So what should you do to **promote creativity when planning?**

Set a clear purpose for pupils' work

- *look for opportunities to promote creative responses in your existing schemes of work and lesson plans*

- *set clear learning objectives and build specific creativity objectives into planning; integrate these with subject-specific objectives*

- *structure a sequence of lessons, taking pupils through the creative process step by step; don't be too ambitious about what pupils can achieve in one lesson*

- *share objectives with pupils; this will help them to sustain their efforts over long periods*

- *plan for pupils to share their work with others; this tends to be very motivating.*

Be clear about freedoms and constraints

- *give pupils opportunities to choose ways of working and to shape the process, direction of work or outcome*

- *use a range of learning styles, for example practical experimentation and problem solving, role-play and dance, visual materials such as diagrams and cartoons, small group discussion and collaboration*

- *give pupils a clear brief*

- *limit time, scale or resources; constraints can stimulate new ways of working and improvisation.*

Fire pupils' imagination through other learning and experiences

- *give pupils first-hand experiences through visits and contact with creative people*

- *use stimulating starting points such as artefacts, problems, stories with human interest, topical events*

- *make activities relevant to pupils' lives*

- *build on what pupils find interesting and have already experienced both in and out of school*

- *look for opportunities to encourage pupils to apply their prior learning creatively*

- *give pupils opportunities to reflect on and share personal experiences and feelings.*

Give pupils opportunities to work together

- *give pupils opportunities to work with others from their class, year group and different age groups*

- *structure collaborative activities; if pupils have free choice, they often choose restrictive, gender-based groups*

- *monitor and manage the collaborative process carefully*

- *address the needs of individuals in each group.*

Once an activity is underway, teachers can actively foster pupils' creativity in a number of ways. You could try some of the approaches below, or some of the ideas in the examples of pupils' creativity on the website.
So what should you do to **promote creativity when teaching?**

Establish criteria for success

- *help pupils to develop criteria that they can use to judge their own success, in particular, the originality and value of their work (eg asking, 'What makes a good...?')*

- *help pupils to appreciate the different qualities in others' work and to value ways of working that are different from their own.*

Capitalise on unexpected learning opportunities

- *actively pursue pupils' ideas (where these are likely to be productive), without losing sight of your original teaching objective*

- *make the most of unexpected events; this can help pupils to overcome their fear of the unknown, develop problem-solving skills and think imaginatively*

- *be ready to put aside your lesson plan and 'go with the moment' if you judge this would be more effective for pupils' learning.*

Ask open-ended questions and encourage critical reflection

- *ask questions such as 'What if...?', 'Why is...?' and 'How might you...?' to help pupils see things from different perspectives and come up with new ideas*

- *encourage openness to ideas*

- *be willing to stand back and not give all the answers but provide helpful prompts, if necessary, modelling flexible and independent thinking and behaviour for pupils.*

Regularly review work in progress

- *regularly stop to review work in progress, discuss the problems pupils are facing and how they can solve them*

- *encourage pupils to share ideas with others and to talk about their progress*

- *help pupils to give and receive constructive feedback (confidence and communication skills are vital for this)*

- *reassure pupils that they can take forward someone else's idea if they think it is more successful than their own (while encouraging them to recognise that it is also acceptable to be different).*

You might find it helpful to collect evidence of how pupils respond in different lessons. Capture selected pupils' responses on paper, video or audiotape, or ask a colleague to observe pupils and note what happens during a lesson. What does this tell you about individuals? The class? Your teaching style? The classroom environment? What can you learn from pupils' responses to help you develop their creativity and your skills as a teacher?

How can teams of teachers promote creativity?

As a team, department, faculty or school, it is important that you share a common understanding of and expectations about creativity.

You could begin by talking about some of the examples of pupils' creativity that accompany this booklet or others that you will find on the website. Make this a starting point for reviewing your own teaching strategies (you could use the above checklists).

How could you work together to improve pupils' ability to ask questions? To explore ideas and alternatives? To evaluate ideas and actions?

What aspects of pupils' creative thinking and behaviour might best be promoted through your particular subject?

Ask each teacher in your team to identify an opportunity for promoting pupils' creativity in a planned lesson or activity and to build a creativity objective into the subject-specific objectives (for example to promote pupils' ability to ask questions or explore ideas).

As a team, talk about how you could achieve these creativity objectives. After the lessons, come back together as a team and compare and discuss outcomes.

How can senior managers and governors promote creativity?

Senior managers and governors play a vital role in establishing an environment in which creativity can flourish. The following checklist outlines some of the key steps they can take towards promoting pupils' creativity throughout the school.

Value creativity as a school

- *build an expectation of creativity into your school's learning and teaching policy*
- *make sure that you value the creative process as well as the final product or outcome*
- *show and share tangible changes that result from creativity*
- *consider involving all the school in an event to experience and celebrate creative learning.*

Encourage professional learning and development

- *develop a shared understanding of what your school means by creative learning*
- *lead a staff meeting on how teachers promote pupils' creativity*

- encourage the collaborative redesign of lessons

- make sure teachers have time to work together to plan learning in more creative ways.

Build partnerships to enrich learning
- work with higher education and other agencies to get new ideas and access to resources

- ask your LEA for support; it might be able to put you in contact with other schools focusing on creativity

- work with external professionals, such as a dance group, to help change the school's ethos.

Provide opportunities for pupils to work with creative people
- provide opportunities for pupils to work with artists, musicians, performers, designers and other creative professionals

- agree and provide key entitlements, such as the opportunity to work with artists, go to a theatre or learn a musical instrument

- tap into the creativity of staff, parents and the local community.

Provide a stimulating physical environment
- make sure that pupils have the space they need to be creative; for example, space for movement in dance and drama, to create on a large scale in art and design

- make sure that pupils have the resources they need to be creative; for example, high-quality materials, tools, apparatus, equipment

- give pupils access to film, video and the internet, which can help them to connect their learning to everyday experiences

- stimulate pupils' curiosity by ensuring they have first-hand experience of natural and made objects, and the natural and built environments

- involve pupils in creating a stimulating environment; for example, they could help redesign the playground, improve the school's built and natural spaces, develop murals

- celebrate creative learning in shared spaces, classrooms, outside areas and beyond school.

Manage time effectively
- give pupils opportunities to explore, concentrate for extended periods of time, reflect, discuss and review

- allow some flexibility in timetabling lessons, so that plans can be adjusted quickly

- give pupils sustained time for some work; for example a whole afternoon instead of two separate lessons in a week

- from time to time, set up a weekly project across the whole school, with a focus on creative learning

- allocate time to being more adventurous; for example a day or week every term when you encourage staff to try out different approaches.

EXTRACT SIX *continued*

Celebrate pupils' creativity

- *encourage, recognise and reward pupils' creativity with words of praise and certificates of achievement*

- *ask teachers to nominate quality examples of creative activities and responses and celebrate these at a school or year assembly for parents*

- *encourage pupils to value the creativity of their peers.*

There are many pieces of useful and helpful advice in this extract. Let us use it to consider answering the question posed in the task above, on how it pulls together the threads expounded in this chapter. The section begins with a theme we have explored before, that of careful planning. Planning for learning, and planning for tasks that support learning need to be done carefully and purposefully, at an appropriate level. This is something that you will improve at as you come to know your pupils. We have talked about expectations, what you should be aiming for with your pupils. Csikszentmihalyi (1992) writes of the state of flow, where challenges are not too great, nor too to slight. This is appropriate for the classroom, and, as the QCDA observes, is important to get right.

But planning for creativity is not an end in itself; you then need to bring the lesson alive, and off the paper. What this will involve is likely to be some creative thinking on your part. We have talked about risk-taking. One of the first steps towards risk-taking that beginning teachers have to take is to depart from the lesson plan. We have seen throughout that formative assessment is key to maximising learning. There will be times when you need to, and, indeed should, move away from your lesson plan to deal with issues that arise during the course of your lesson. This is a creative response, and it can be the beginning of creative teaching. The QCDA recommends asking open-ended questions, and especially 'what if...?' questions. These can really challenge pupil thinking. What if gravity was half as powerful? What if you were born 200 years previously? What if we turn it upside-down? What if he were born as a woman? And smaller, work-based 'what if' questions too. What if we play it backwards? What if we colour it in? What if you take that number away? What if you don't finish with that word?

REFLECTIVE EXERCISE

Construct some 'what if...?' questions to use with a class you will be teaching soon. Use them to stretch their thinking. Plan for some in advance, and try to formulate some as you are teaching.

Then reflect on this. How did it go? Will you do it differently next time? What did your mentor think? What if you were your mentor?

Conclusion

In this chapter we have seen that creativity is not only about the arts. All subjects have creative aspects to them. Using the three notions of:

- teaching creatively

- creative teaching

- creative learning

means that you are able to use the appropriate terminologies in your planning, and gives you a toolkit of language which helps you to think about ways in which creativity can be talked about, and gives you frames of reference to employ when thinking and planning. We know that thinking about teaching is problematic, and that discourse can be difficult. We know too that it is not always possible to put things into words. One of the key learning outcomes for you from this chapter will be to provide you with the linguistic terminologies whereby you can begin to think about the application of creativity, and of creative learning approaches with the classes you teach, and that you will have the appropriate words to use for this.

CHAPTER SUMMARY

This chapter explores the notion that creativity is not a special attribute of a gifted few, but a normal attribute for all our pupils. It is an important dimension of every curriculum subject. We have considered the nature of creativity in the classroom, and have discussed the ways in which planning for creativity can take place. Most importantly, we have argued that creativity is a vital part of an effective teacher's pedagogy. The best way to encourage our pupils' creativity is to be creative oneself. Lead by example.

EFERENCES

Bloom, BS (1956) *Taxonomy of Educational Objectives, Handbook I: The Cognitive Domain*. New York: David McKay Co Inc.

Boden, MA (1990) *The Creative Mind: Myths and Mechanisms*. London: Weidenfeld and Nicolson.

Craft, A (2003) Limits to creativity in education: dilemmas for the educator. *British Journal of Educational Studies*, 51(2): 113–27.

Creative Partnerships (2005) *CP and you/creatives*. **www.creative-partnerships.com:80/cpandyou/creatives/**

Csikszentmihalyi, M (1992) *Flow: The Psychology of Happiness*. London: Random House.

Fautley, M and Hatcher, R (2008) *Dissemination of Creative Partnerships Projects*. Birmingham: Birmingham City University.

Fautley, M and Savage, J (2007) *Creativity in Secondary Education*. Exeter: Learning Matters.

NACCCE (1999) (National Advisory Committee on Creative and Cultural Education) *All Our Futures: Creativity, Culture and Education*. Sudbury, Suffolk: DfEE.

QCDA (2004) *Creativity: Find it, Promote it!* London: QCDA.

WEBSITES

QCDA website: Source: **http://curriculum.qcda.gov.uk/key-stages-3-and-4/cross-curriculum-dimensions/creativitycriticalthinking/index.aspx**

Chapter 8
Enriching collaborations

CHAPTER OBJECTIVES

By the end of this chapter you should have:
- investigated the roles that subjects and their associated subject cultures play in forming and shaping secondary education;
- considered the findings from research into cross-curricular approaches to teaching and learning in secondary education and how these might relate to your own teaching practice;
- explored the production of a more collaborative, cross-curricular approach in your own teaching with another colleague;
- reflected on the notion of a cross-curricular disposition and pedagogy within your own subject teaching.

Q Standards: Q14, Q15, Q32.

Introduction

The second chapter in the final part of this book takes up the theme of collaboration. As you seek to move your teaching forwards, there will be plenty of opportunities to expand and connect the teaching that you are doing within your own subject area to various other things going on in your school and wider community. These will include extra-curricular activities, work being done within your local community by different groups and the informal learning that your own students are undertaking in different ways and places. Making connections between the work that goes on within your classroom and these wider learning contexts is an important thing to do. It contextualises the work that you are doing with your students in a helpful way and enables them to relate their learning in different contexts together in a meaningful way.

But perhaps the most explicit type of collaboration that you will be required to make early in your career will be demanded by various curriculum initiatives that include a cross-curricular aspect. As we will see, the term 'cross-curricular' has multiple meanings and considering which of these is most relevant or important to your work can be quite difficult. This chapter will explore what we mean by cross-curricular teaching and learning. It will give examples of approaches and help you apply ideas to your own teaching. This will assist you as you begin to make enriching links from your own subject area to the work of others.

Subject strongholds in the secondary curriculum

Courses and subjects that fail to reinvent themselves in the face of new circumstances are liable to decline or disappear.

(Kirk et al., 1997)

The concept of a 'subject' dominates the entirety of secondary education. As we have discussed in earlier chapters, our sense of security and identity often comes from being a subject specialist. Individual subjects play a powerful, organising function within the secondary school, shaping the nature of the physical spaces that we teach within as well as the practical issues such as the timetable. Individual subjects have particular pedagogical approaches that are cherished and valued by teachers. These are informed by a range of factors outside of the immediate school context. For example, spanning out from the school, numerous 'subject associations' exist that help to promote, strengthen and reinforce the position of subjects within education. Any attempts to break down the notion of the subject, or minimise its influence, can be fiercely resisted. The results of this subject focus within education are not always positive. Robin Alexander, a leading professor of education at the University of Cambridge, comments that *it is schooling that has reduced knowledge to 'subjects' and teaching to mere telling* (Alexander, 2008, page 141).

In light of all this, it is worth asking the question: where does this preoccupation with the subject come from? To answer this, we need to take a slightly longer, historical view surrounding the construction of the curriculum, the inclusion or exclusion of individual subjects and the subject communities which underpin these, and the effect that these groups have had on ongoing educational policy and curriculum development (such the National Curriculum at Key Stage 3) or new qualifications (such as the 14–19 diplomas).

The first extract explores these issues in a helpful way. It is drawn from a longer academic paper that explores the place of economics in the school curriculum. But, as with other extracts included in this book, do not be put off by this subject focus. It has much to teach all of us. In these two related passages from the opening of the paper, the nature of school subjects is explored in relation to a range of factors that have affected their development over recent years.

EXTRACT ONE

Jephcote, M and Davies, B (2007) School subjects, subject communities and curriculum change: the social construction of economics in the school curriculum. Cambridge Journal of Education, 37(2): 210–214.

School subjects and subject communities
School subject communities are neither harmonious nor homogeneous and members do not necessarily share particular values, subject definitions and interests. They are usefully conceived of as social movements comprising a shifting range of traditions represented by factions whose importance changes over time (Goodson & Marsh, 1996). Their diverse memberships create conditions conducive to contest, conflict and tension, both within a subject and between it and other subjects (Cooper, 1985), where we need to understand the 'effects of interaction across a series of boundaries between subject subcultures' (Cooper, 1983, p.208). Moreover, in the case of economics, whose members have

operated in a community of 'kindred' subjects, including business studies, it is apparent that both subjects and community members are in a state of transformation. As Goodson (1994) has suggested, in this process of transformation members of the subject community are not all powerful. Curriculum decisions are an outcome of micropolitical struggles that are located in the 'gendered power/knowledge networks' (Paechter, 2000, p. 31) and a product of the multiple power relations within and between subjects and within and between the fields of production.

Focusing on particular subjects, such as economics, in this way is to see them not only as intellectual systems but 'flesh and blood' social systems which confer senses of identity, authority and power. They are subcultural groupings within which there are competing ideological segments which represent both contested and consensual views about how the subject should be taught, what teachers' roles should be and what might be expected of students (Paechter, 1995). Subject community membership is not automatic but follows processes of selection and screening, both making it more difficult to change educational identities and tightening the boundaries between different subjects. The processes of socialization into a subject community underpin the tendency of loyalty to the subject, are self perpetuating and tend to create clear and bounded identity. This is especially evident at times of threat from other subjects for curriculum time and resources to which members tend to react not only by defending their ground but in order to protect careers.

Since the introduction of the National Curriculum and its associated mechanisms of enforcement it is often assumed that subject authority, power and control rests largely in the hands of Central Government. But as Ball (1994) reminded us, the state is not all powerful in shaping and bringing about change and there are ways in which those at recontextualizing and reproductive levels work either to support or subvert and reinterpret policies passed down from above. A study of the recent history of economics as a school subject (Jephcote & Davies, 2004) cast recontextualizers as mediators in processes of policy-making and implementation, seen to be motivated to use their power to protect their own interests. In Bernstein's (1996) terms, they operated in the field between that of production, where new knowledge is constructed and reproduction of pedagogic practice in schools. Some, including Government agencies, such as curriculum councils and school inspectors have been officially created by and are dominated by the state whereas others, including teacher trainers, examining bodies, researchers, independent curriculum projects and publishers operate in the pedagogic recontextualizing field. There is struggle among such recontextualizers for ownership of construction of the 'what' and how' of 'pedagogic discourse' (1996, p. 117) by ideological screening of 'new knowledge'.

Once the relative status of a subject as a singular is embedded in a curriculum structure it becomes fixed and difficult to alter and, at school level, the 'voice' of a department in relation to policy issues and resource decision-making, according to Ball (1987), tended to be linked to whether it was expanding, static or defensive. Newer subjects, such as economics have struggled to raise their status because they have often been perceived as a threat and because they have often been promoted by new or young teachers who have lacked institutional status. Potential for conflict arises either when the new encroaches on the subject matter of existing subjects or because of competition for time and resources and their impact on career development. Not only are teachers' identities in important ways constituted by their specialist subject and its status, from physics to physical education but their material interests, such as pay, promotion and conditions are interlinked with its fate. Their careers are pursued in departments whose status depends on the subject's status which, in turn, is derived, among other things, from the 'pecking orders' of universities and which subjects are the choice of able students (Goodson & Marsh, 1996). From the foregoing analysis, it is proposed that:

1. *The processes and outcomes of curriculum change are socially and politically constructed and are ongoing.*

2. *Subjects are made up of a loose community of factions which, in different ways, want to expand or defend particular versions of the subject.*

3. *The motives of those active in subject definition and control is not always clear and divisions between them tend to reflect allegiance to deep-rooted traditions and those who share them.*

4. *The overall thrust of a subject community (or segments within it) is to seek to establish the subject and insulate it from others so that, overall, there is loyalty to the subject.*

5. *Those who engage in subject definition and control adopt legitimizing rhetoric and strategies which are often a reflection of wider movements.*

6. *Subject specialists form coalitions with those across the subject community and, where possible, with agencies of change to share and/or appropriate resources and power – but:*

7. *Involvement in subject regions carries the danger of subservience to stronger disciplinary voices or the requirements of an 'integrating principle', while incorporation in generic curricular modes may carry all the taint of 'training'.*

8. *Whereas the overall impact of subject communities is to preserve the status quo, in any particular cycle of innovation and change, there is a fear of being left behind (Paechter, 1998).*

9. *Over time, the workings of different subject communities have led to the establishment of a hierarchy of school subjects.*

As Jephcote and Davies comment, once the status of a subject is embedded in a curriculum structure it becomes fixed and difficult to alter *(Jephcote and Davies, 2007, page 213).*

Analyse the position of your subject within the curriculum structures at different key stages. To what extent is it fixed? Can it be altered or adapted in any way? Read through the nine statements at the end of the extract again. Can you relate these to your own subject? What are the wider groupings, communities or factions that have a vested interest in your subject? Can you identify their involvement in recent years and the consequences of this on how the subject is perceived within curriculum structures? Finally, where does your subject fit within the hierarchy of school subjects *that Jephcote and Davies believe exists (Jephcote and Davies 2007, page 214)?*

Challenging the orthodox position

Recent educational initiatives have begun to chip away at the subject stronghold that dominates secondary education. As we will discuss below (in relation to our third extract), the most recent version of the National Curriculum (QCDA, 2007) contains a clear remit for developing cross-curricular approaches for teaching and learning. But these sentiments have a longer history too. The implementation of the first National Curriculum in 1992 was accompanied by an extensive range of discussion about the inclusion of cross-curricular elements. Some of the arguments will be familiar. Dufour, writing in 1990, stated that:

> *'Education' and 'curriculum' have not been defined in any previous Education Act, although the Education Reform Act, 1988, which is about both, does depart from this tradition by providing a definition of the curriculum along with a prescriptive list of subjects that must, subsequently, be taught.*

> (Dufour, 1990, page 1)

There was an obvious political influence at work here. This resulted in a 'prescriptive' list of subjects for inclusion in the first National Curriculum. There were winners and losers, (e.g. music and physical education were included, drama and dance were not). Political 'interference' was rife, with various education ministers asserting their own views and demanding numerous rewrites of curriculum documentation. This led Dufour to comment that:

> *While the status and context of different forms of knowledge will continue to be influenced by political and ideological considerations, political partiality should not be allowed to influence the final choice and status of particular subjects and cross-curricular themes for the school curriculum. The only question that should be asked is an educational one – how can all the subjects and themes fit together into the curriculum?*

> (Dufour, 1990, page 11)

Notice the reference to 'cross-curricular themes' in the above quote. Cross-curricular themes in the first version of the National Curriculum are directly comparable to the 'cross-curricular dimensions' within the current Key Stage 3 National Curriculum framework. Like their predecessors, the cross-curricular dimensions included in today's National Curriculum are in danger of being ignored given their non-statutory status and sense of 'policy overload'. Compare your own knowledge about the current National Curriculum and its implementation today against the following quote from Pumfrey back in 1993:

> *The sheer rate of change that is taking place in education is unprecedented. The volume of paper reaching schools and requiring responses is daunting, even to the most committed professional. The core and other foundation subjects are currently centre-stage. Unless teachers and schools are vigilant, the benefits of cross-curricular themes could be adversely affected. At present, the National Curriculum is far from fully in place in schools. The way in which various subjects as cross-curricular themes have been introduced into the secondary school syllabus has not been of the highest order. Too little preparation and consultation have led to controversial changes.*

> (Pumfrey, 1993, page 21)

This brief look backwards to the period of time surrounding the implementation of the first National Curriculum demonstrates many things. Firstly, the marriage of subjects and cross-curricular themes within the curriculum is not an easy one. Elsewhere, Savage (2011) has argued that separating cross-curricular elements within the curriculum requirements may lead to the greater marginalisation of cross-curricular approaches in teachers' work. Secondly, the imposition of large changes in curriculum design often means that teachers will focus on what they know (i.e. their subject), and not make the wider links that might have been envisaged by a 'whole' curriculum. Finally, although the benefits of a cross-curricular set of themes and skills were recognised by politicians and educators, the practical implementation of the curriculum itself meant that opportunities were missed and creative links were established between subjects or between subjects and cross-curricular themes.

These notions of the subject and cross-curricularity need to be untangled. They present opportunities for clear and focused research but, worryingly, very little research of this type been done. The next extract presents findings from one of the few large studies of cross-curricular approaches to teaching and learning in secondary education done by the Consortium of Institutions for Development and Research in Education in Europe (CIDREE). Their report for the European Union (CIDREE, 2005) surveyed 27 countries and identified a range of key problems in the implementation of cross-curricular approaches. The whole report is available online and, as with all extracts included within the book, is well worth reading in full. Here, we have selected a section towards the end of the report which identifies some of the problems they observed, as well as some of the solutions they anticipate developing.

EXTRACT TWO

Page, M, Schagen, S, Fallus, K, Bron, J, de Coninck, C, Maes, B, Sleurs, W and van Woensel, C (2005) **Cross Curricular Themes in Secondary Education.** *Sint-Katelijne-Waver (Belgium): CIDREE, pp. 67–70.*

Problems and solutions
Probably the most obvious observation is that problems relating to the implementation of cross-curricular themes are 'European' or maybe even universal. The project's literature survey (see part 1), drawing upon the limited sources available on this topic, identifies a number of problems relating to different factors. A number of them are situated at the level of the teacher; others are located at school or pupil level. Also elements like curriculum overload and a lack of time and resources complicate the implementation of cross-curricular themes. The analysis of the project's case studies confirms the existence of these problems. Moreover, the case studies offer a more differentiated and context-related view on these implementation problems. They make it possible to look at how these problems occur within the context of actual schools and how they influence the way these schools deal with specific cross-curricular themes. They also highlight problems additional to the ones identified in the literature survey. For instance, it seems that vertical and horizontal continuity in the different stages and sectors within the same school can be problematic (e.g. in the Flemish schools). Another example, found for example in the Hungarian and Dutch schools is the pressure of final exams and university entrance requirements on the implementation of cross-curricular themes. Some of the case studies also pay particular attention to the role of one or more co-ordinators of the cross-curricular work at schools and the problems related to that function.

A mere confirmation or extension of problems in the area of cross-curricular work is inter-esting but not sufficient. The project team was also interested in finding out how schools, with significant experience and due motivation in implementing cross-curricular themes, deal with the problems they encounter. In other words, what solutions did schools devise?

Teacher involvement

In the often problematic area of teachers' involvement and motivation, schools seem to combine two different strategies. The first strategy is to create, probably over a period of years, a general atmosphere or ethos among staff that delivering a particular cross-curric-ular theme is simply a necessity. The theme gradually becomes part of the school culture, of the staff's way of thinking and acting. An example is the Welsh school (4) dealing with work-related education in which staff are confident and convinced of the value of this approach and cooperate fully with the delivery, monitoring and evaluation of the pro-gramme. It is seen to be of crucial importance in an area of high unemployment, where the local culture often does not encourage acquisition of the necessary skills and where stereotypical attitudes to employment still exist, particularly in relation to gender issues. A similar example is prevalent in the Flemish school (1) dealing with social skills. The starting position there is that 'if you take the position that you would like to do for every child at school what you would do for your own children, then social skills are automatically dealt with'. The school is also convinced that 'pupils cannot function well in class groups which are not functioning well'.

The second and apparently also successful strategy to get the teachers involved is to have them working together or communicating in such a way that the cross-curricular theme involved is also better implemented. A Welsh school (4) has good procedures for coor-dinating cross-curricular work, and communication between the pastoral and academic elements of the curriculum is good. The Flemish school (1) made an inventory of what was already going on in the area of social skills, built upon that and worked its way up by means of meetings and individual discussions. Similarly, an English school (5) is aware of the fact that their mapping exercises 'need to be visited regularly' and that problems might otherwise occur, particularly as there was a wide range of views of the cross-curricular theme among both teachers and learners. In a Hungarian school (8) coopera-tion was never a problem since all agreed to develop changes, and 'rationally planned teamwork' soon produced spectacular results.

Another Welsh school (3) has a more far-reaching policy: 'Such problems as a teacher's reluctance to move away from a subject based approach are not accepted in the school and staff are appointed with the understanding that they will show commitment to the school's approaches'. The same school allocates time for regular planning, discussion and coordination and makes good use of expertise and resources from outside agencies and personnel.

Finally a Dutch school (9) used the introduction of a cross-curricular theme in order to enhance teacher development. Teachers were given ownership of the programme by involving them in the educational and didactical design of the cross-curricular theme.

Pressure on the curriculum

One of the Welsh schools (3) still considers pressure on the curriculum as a problem but this is alleviated to some extent by the choice of a two-week timetable which allows for a degree of flexibility and breadth. Additionally, this pressure is relieved by taking whole days off timetable for particular foci, and by spreading much of the factual content of the PSE-programme across subjects of the curriculum. In the Flemish school (1) dealing with learning to learn the head tries to solve curriculum overload by giving the teachers explicit autonomy to allocate time to issues other than pure subject content. The other Flemish school (2) organises a weekly course on social activities in the first year to release the curriculum pressure but fails to do so in the second year.

Pupils' involvement and motivation

In one Welsh school (3), the vast majority of the pupils respond positively to the school's approaches and is fully involved in the PSE programme. For a few, interest decreases as they move into years 10 and 11. The school is aware of this and works to address such lack of motivation by amending its programme and making it more interactive and relevant to pupils of this age and stage of development. A Hungarian school (8) also considers maintaining the students' interest as the greatest challenge as they quickly become bored if they always have to do the same kind of activities. This school aims at preventing this problem by more integrated planning and organisation. An English school (6) tries to involve more students by looking at mentoring between year groups. Another English school (5) is investing in a radical alteration of their management culture in seeking to support structural and ideological changes to 'embed student voice' into the heart of their practice. The implementation of the cross-curricular theme of 'citizenship' is a central part of these ongoing and proposed changes.

2 Assessment

Clearly, the least elaborated element of the cross-curricular process is pupil assessment. As the case study analysis illustrates, some of the schools involved developed techniques to monitor pupils' progress. For instance, an English school (5) has several monitoring and evaluation procedures common throughout the school. A Hungarian school (7) has a well-developed assessment and evaluation system, strongly focussed on the assessment of skills. Nevertheless, the project's schools generally think a lot of work remains to be done in this area. A few examples from the case studies to illustrate this point:

- *In the area of assessment, one school would like to develop a more effective methodology as well as to increase the level of professional assistance. (8)*

- *A Welsh school (4) sees the development of valid and reliable pupil assessment as problematic and wants to work to provide a system for accreditation for work experience for part-time work undertaken by students.*

- *The other Welsh school (3) says it needs to improve the quality and continuity of teaching and learning and is currently focussing on pupils' different learning styles and on effective formative pupil assessment for learning. The same school plans the* development of a detailed system to track pupils' progress as they move through the school and to find ways to gain accreditation for pupils' achievements in key skills.

- An English teacher (6) felt that there still was a 'desperate need to track students to compare outcomes with expectations'.

- There is no systematic pupil evaluation in the Flemish school (2) dealing with learning to learn. In this school, teachers feel that those pupils receiving extra individual care gain most in terms of learning competences.

Considering the fact that the schools which have taken part in this project are not the least developed in cross-curricular work and assessment in their respective countries, the main observation here is that if monitoring pupils' progress is considered important, more and better instruments and methods need to be developed. This particularly goes for the evaluation of qualitative objectives. It is easier to assess the knowledge of facts than to evaluate behaviour. Still, cross-curricular themes very often deal with behavioural aspects. If these are to be perceived as equally important compared to other objectives, some kind of evaluation or monitoring will be required. If not, in the prevalent European secondary education school cultures, they will, by a lot of the staff and learners, remain being perceived as having a lower status, as being of lesser importance, than the 'hard' quantifiable objectives in the curriculum. And for schools without any form of monitoring or evaluation, it is very hard to see whether their efforts have any effect at all on their pupils.

Educational policy and cross-curricular themes

Education ministers or education policy-makers seem to be sending out mixed messages to their schools when it comes to cross-curricular work. Six out of the ten case studies in this project are schools in which the work in progress on the cross-curricular theme was carried out in order to be in line with the national curriculum framework. In other words, implementing these cross-curricular themes is compulsory (table 1 in part I of this report gives an overview of which cross-curricular themes are statutory in 27 European countries).

Education policy expects schools to deliver. But at the same time, schools do not always seem to receive the necessary support or are not always able to create the necessary conditions to do so effectively and efficiently. There are a number of facts in these case studies to support this observation. First of all, schools complain about an overload of subject curricula and an inflexibility of timetables. Other schools experience a lack of infrastructure, space and especially time. There is also the pressure of final exams and university entrance requirements. Schools also refer to teacher training which is said to prepare new teachers insufficiently for working with cross-curricular themes.

The general message here seems to be that if schools are put under pressure to meet compulsory cross-curricular requirements, support has to be given in order for schools to do their work.

The problems and solutions identified by this piece of research are broadly categorised into issues located within the remit of the teacher, the school and the pupil. What did you make of the issues identified within the research? How do they relate to your understanding of how cross-curricular elements are being developed within schools today?

Cross-curricular approaches to teaching and learning today

The situation facing teachers today in respect of cross-curricularity is a challenging one. The recent introduction of a new National Curriculum at Key Stage 3 has, in one sense, learnt a lesson from history and is being implemented over a three-year period (2008–11). The 'big picture' of the curriculum (QCDA, 2009) illustrates the vast number of curriculum elements that need to be considered. Individual subjects are just one small part of this. However, unlike the cross-curricular dimensions which are non-statutory and fall outside the immediate remit of individual subjects, there is another way that you can begin to think about making links between subjects. Rather surprisingly, this springs from the subject materials contained within the Key Stage 3 curriculum framework itself.

A close analysis of every subject's programme of study reveals an important new emphasis on collaborative, cross-subject working. In each subject's 'Wider opportunities' section there are statements such as:

- develop speaking and listening skills through work that makes cross-curricular links with other subjects (English 4f);

- work on problems that arise in other subjects and in contexts beyond the school (Mathematics 4d);

- make links between science and other subjects and areas of the curriculum (Science 4k);

- make links between geography and other subjects, including citizenship and ICT, and areas of the curriculum including sustainability and global dimension (Geography 4i).

Alongside these calls for broader links to be made within subjects, there are major links that can be made within subjects through a consideration of the key concepts for each subject. Many of these are similar. As an example, the Key Concept of Creativity appears in numerous subjects, including English, music, art and design and technology. Key concepts should be at the forefront of the Key Stage 3 planning process in teachers' minds. If that is the case, they present an ideal opportunity to make links across subjects in imaginative ways.

These subject references require teachers to develop cross-curricular opportunities within their own work and are particularly helpful. They represent a significant shift in the curriculum orders and they are statutory.

But alongside these statutory demands, the inclusion of non-statutory cross-curriculum dimensions within the National Curriculum has received considerable attention. When teachers talk about cross-curricular approaches to teaching and learning, the cross-curricular dimensions are often the first thing discussed. In what has a striking resonance with the historical overview presented above, these dimensions cover the following areas:

- identity and cultural diversity;
- healthy lifestyles;
- community participation;
- enterprise;
- global dimensions and sustainable development;
- technology and the media;
- creativity and critical thinking.

The third extract we are going to consider is drawn from a guidance document produced by the QCDA. This document was written to provide help for teachers and schools who were wanting to incorporate these dimensions within their curriculum planning.

EXTRACT THREE

QCDA (2008) Cross-Curriculum Dimensions: A Planning Guide for Schools. *Qualifications and Curriculum Development Agency (QCDA), pp. 1, 5–7.*

What are the cross-curriculum dimensions?

The cross-curriculum dimensions reflect some of the major ideas and challenges that face individuals and society, and help make learning real and relevant.

The dimensions are unifying areas of learning that span the curriculum and help young people make sense of the world. They are not curriculum subjects, but are crucial aspects of learning that should permeate the curriculum and the life of a school.

The dimensions can add a richness and relevance to the curriculum experience of young people. Although dimensions are not a statutory part of the national curriculum, schools will find them useful in designing and planning their whole curriculum. They can provide a focus for work within and between subjects, in personal, learning and thinking skills (PLTS) and across the curriculum as a whole, including the routines, events and ethos of the school.

Individual dimensions should not be considered in isolation as they are often interdependent and mutually supportive.

Turning vision into reality

Once you are clear about what you want to achieve, you can make decisions about the best ways to successfully integrate the dimensions across your curriculum. Think about the entire planned learning experience. This includes lessons, events, routines, extended hours, out of school learning, locations and environment, as well as qualifications including new GCEs, GCSEs and Diplomas.

Build the dimensions into your curriculum in a way that reflects the specific needs, interests and context of your learners. Possible approaches that have been tried by schools include:

- *developing the dimensions through subjects, with links across subjects where there are common issues or areas of learning, such as a creative engineering project which links science, maths, geography and design and technology and focuses on the design of a sustainable product*

- *developing the ethos of the school around a dimension, for example a focus on cultural development where subject specialists develop cross-curriculum projects linking identity and cultural diversity*

- *creating compelling learning experiences that focus on a particular dimension or combination of dimensions, such as the use of media and technology to create a pupil-led internet radio station aimed at sharing views with the local community*

- *thematic days, activity weeks or events that focus on a particular dimension are combined wfth lessons*

- *activities that are integrated into the routines of the school, for example the promotion of physical activity and healthy eating at break and lunchtimes to enable learners to see the link between eating well, physical activity and feeling good about themselves*

- *educational visits or learning outside the classroom*

- *using experts from outside of the school to stimulate discussion and debate in assemblies or with specific groups of learners.*

Developing dimensions through subjects

The new curriculum balances subject knowledge with the key concepts and processes that underlie the discipline of each subject. Some subjects share key concepts and processes. Curriculum opportunities highlight the potential for links between subjects. Dimensions can be used to cut across the curriculum and make links to the major ideas and challenges that face society.

The dimensions can be developed through all subjects, with links between subjects where appropriate. They can provide a focus for work within and between subjects and help make learning relevant to young people's lives, experiences or aspirations.

*A good starting point for curriculum design linking subjects and dimensions is the national curriculum website (**www.qcda.org.uk/curriculum**). If you select a subject on the site and then go to the context tab, you can compare any section of the programme of study for that subject with other subjects. This useful tool can generate discussion between different teachers when designing compelling learning experiences, where subjects work together to develop a particular dimension to the curriculum.*

Schools are encouraged to build the dimensions into their curriculum in a way that reflects the specific needs, interests and context of their learners. Some powerful approaches devised by schools include linking history and cultural diversity, for example through the promotion of black and Asian British history, and developing pupils' understanding of science in real-life contexts, for example by investigating diet and health in schools across the world. The 'Curriculum in action' section of the national curriculum website provides many examples of subjects working towards different dimensions.

Building PTLS into dimensions

Personal, learning and thinking skills (PLTS), like cross-curriculum dimensions, can have a considerable impact on young people's ability to enter adult life as confident and capable individuals who can make a positive contribution to society. Systematically linking PLTS and dimensions when designing your curriculum will help learners see the relevance and interconnectedness of their learning.

The PTLS framework comprises six groups of skills:

- *independent enquirers*
- *creative thinkers*
- *reflective learners*
- *team workers*
- *self-managers*
- *effective particpants*

Each PTLS group is distinctive and coherent. The groups are also interconnected. Young people are likely to encounter skills from several groups in an one learning experience.

Making progress in creative thinking

St John's School and Community College wanted to develop a creative curriculum that placed 'learning to think' and 'learning to learn' at its heart, and enabled learners to make visible connections between different parts of their learning.

EXTRACT THREE *continued*

Creativity and critical thinking were developed as a key curriculum dimension, embedding PLTS into the learning experience. The learning journey is organised as a coherent, continuous experience. At every stage of the journey learners are encouraged to experiment with ideas, tackle problems together and find imaginative solutions. Far from being constrained by the idea of getting something 'wrong', they are given the freedom to work in a way that encourages independent enquiry, risk taking and collaboration. Critical reflection is an integral part of the learning experience, with pupils acting as 'critical friends', assessing each other's progress in each of the creative thinking skills.

*To read the full case study visit the national curriculum website 'Curriculum in action' section at **www.qcda.org.uk/curriculum**.*

The key reason that these cross-curricular dimensions have been developed is to make learning *real and relevant* (QCDA, 2009, page 1). They provide a unifying force to the curriculum and should permeate it throughout. For all these reasons, one might have thought that these cross-curricular dimensions should have been made statutory. Perhaps the QCDA is wary of some of the developments that recent history has taught them about overloading teachers with too much bureaucracy. But there seems little danger of that being true given the large number of policy documents being produced each month by various governmental agencies. Statutory or not, the cross-curricular dimensions do present an opportunity for teachers to develop collaborative, cross-curricular approaches to their teaching and learning. The following practical task will help you get started on this.

REFLECTIVE EXERCISE

This task will require you to work collaboratively with a colleague in a different subject area from your own. Why not work with another student who is undertaking a course of initial teacher education within the same school as you?

1. *Working with your colleague, select a cross-curricular dimension. Discuss how each of your subjects can contribute to the particular dimension you have chosen.*

2. *Identify a single lesson that you are going to teach within your subject in the near future. (If possible, choose a lesson when your colleague has non-contact time. This will allow them to visit your lesson and observe your teaching.) Work together on including a focus on the cross-curricular dimension you have chosen within the lesson. This need not be the lesson's main focus. Rather, try to use the dimension as a contextualising factor for the main learning objective(s) you have established. Use your colleague's alternative subject perspective to inform the way in which your chosen dimension might be introduced, the activities that you design for the students to undertake, or how you might assess their work.*

3. *Finally, teach the lesson. (If possible, visit each other's lessons and observe what goes on.) Afterwards, discuss how the shared approach to a cross-curricular dimension impacted on your work. How could its influence be expanded to include a whole scheme of work rather than an individual lesson? How could other subject areas contribute to this larger piece of curriculum development?*

At Key Stage 4, the situation in relation to cross-curricular approaches to teaching and learning is a little more complex. The revision of the National Curriculum here includes only the core subjects but, as in Key Stage 3, each contains references to cross-curricular ways of working.

English

- Analyse and evaluate the impact of combining words, images and sounds in media, moving-image and multimodal texts (2.2i).

- Develop speaking and listening/reading/writing skills through work that makes cross-curricular links with other subjects (4.1f, 4.2f, 4.3f).

Mathematics

- Work on problems that arise in other subjects and in contexts beyond the school (4d).

Science (in the explanatory notes)

- All pupils develop their ability to relate their understanding of science to their own and others' decisions about lifestyles, and to scientific and technological developments in society.

- Most pupils also develop their understanding and skills in ways that provide the basis for further studies in science and related areas.

(QCDA 2007, page 221)

Additionally, there are also references to cross-curricular working with Citizenship (4j), ICT (4h) and PE (4f) as well as the non-statutory Economic Wellbeing and Financial Capability (4k) and Religious Education (4i).

But perhaps the biggest innovation at Key Stage 4 has been the introduction of the 14–19 Diploma qualifications. These have resulted in a significant shift in the ways in which teachers from different subject specialisms are required to work together. As an example, the creative and media diploma contains elements from subjects such as music, visual arts, textiles, fashion, drama, dance, film and more; travel and tourism will involve subjects such as geography, history, economics and ICT. In addition, each diploma has functional skills and PLTS built into the assessment framework. Teachers working on these new diplomas will have to collaborate extensively on the design and delivery of new schemes of work that relate to the principal, specialist and additional learning strands. This is further complicated by the need to include elements of work-based learning and the need to support an independent student project with appropriate subject specialist input.

REFLECTIVE EXERCISE

Which of the new diplomas is most closely related to your own subject specialism? What potential challenges can you anticipate having to face as your subject is taught within a wider framework of subjects, ideas and learning approaches? Will it be important to maintain the identity of your subject within this mix? Or are you happy to see it being combined in new ways or contexts for learning that inspire young people?

Personalising cross-curricular approaches to teaching and learning

For many, cross-curricular approaches to teaching and learning are about collaboration (Ofsted, 2008). These collaborations may be informal, led by pairs or small groups of interested teachers. But in the majority of cases, cross-curricular work is initiated by a curriculum manager and is developed within a larger framework (e.g. a 'collapsed' timetable day, a special project of some sort, etc.). This emphasis is clearly identified towards the opening of our third extract (QCDA, 2008, page 1).

But there is another way that cross-curricularity can be approached. This relates to the development of your own, personal pedagogy that is infused with a cross-curricular disposition. Elsewhere, Savage has defined this as follows:

> A cross-curricular approach to teaching is characterised by a sensitivity towards, and a synthesis of, knowledge, skills and understandings from various subject areas. These inform an enriched pedagogy which promotes an approach to learning which embraces and explores this wider sensitivity through various methods.
>
> (Savage, 2011, pages 8–9)

In this definition, the emphasis is placed firmly on your subject-based pedagogy. It includes a number of key ideas. Firstly, note the sensitive approach that is required when approaching the knowledge, skills and understanding within another curriculum area. There is no room for a cavalier approach here. As we discussed above, individual subjects in the curriculum have a historical legacy that is underpinned in contemporary contexts in various ways, not least in others' conceptions about their subject and how it should be taught. Understanding and respecting this wider subject context is really important. In this respect, utilising a cross-curricular pedagogy within your own teaching should not be about weakening or watering down the subject dimensions elsewhere. Rather, the enriched pedagogy of cross-curricular teaching will embrace and explore your sensitivity towards, and synthesis of, the different knowledge, skills and understanding within curriculum subjects. In order for this to happen, there are at least two premises: firstly, you will need to understand your own subject to a high level; secondly, you will need to ensure that your subject knowledge is extended beyond your own subject area. When this occurs, you will be in a position to develop an authentic, personalised pedagogy of cross-curricular approaches for teaching and learning. Teaching in this way will be challenging, but the potential benefits for yourself and your pupils are considerable.

REFLECTIVE EXERCISE

- *Are there elements within your own subject pedagogy that make it difficult to work in a cross-curricular or collaborative way? If so, how could you begin to mitigate the effects of these?*

- *To what extent can you strengthen the cross-curricular or collaborative elements within your teaching? What strategies of professional or curriculum development could you employ to do this?*

- *How can you broaden your knowledge of other subject areas, including their subject pedagogies, to ensure that you treat them with the respect and dignity that they deserve?*

CHAPTER SUMMARY

This chapter has explored a range of ideas surrounding the concepts of cross-curricularity and collaborative approaches to teaching and learning. Starting from the premise that subject cultures play a significant role in shaping and forming the organisation of secondary education, it considered how research into cross-curricular approaches to teaching and learning relate to an individual teacher's pedagogy. Rather than seeing cross-curricularity as being dependent on collaboration, it argues for a cross-curricular disposition or mind-set than individual teachers develop within their own classrooms. From this, enriching subject-based and collaborative approaches to cross-curricular practice can emerge. The chapter has also considered the use of cross-curricular dimensions as a means of linking subjects, and also as a way of contextualising learning. However, their use should not stifle the larger shifts in practice that are required in order for cross-curricular approaches to teaching and learning to emerge through revitalised subject cultures.

REFERENCES

Alexander, RJ (2008) *Essays on Pedagogy.* London: Routledge.

CIDREE (2005) *Cross-curricular themes in secondary education.* Sint-Katelijne-Waver (Belgium): CIDREE. (Also available at **www.cidree.be**) [accessed 12/2/10].

Dufour, B (ed.) (1990) *The New Social Curriculum: A guide to cross-curricular themes.* Cambridge: CUP.

Jephcote, M and Davies, B (2007) 'School subjects, subject communities and curriculum change: The social construction of economics in the school curriculum. *Cambridge Journal of Education*, 37(2): 207–227.

Kirk, D, Macdonald, D and Tinning, R (1997) The social construction of pedagogic discourse in physical teacher education in Australia. *The Curriculum Journal*, 8(2): 271–298.

Ofsted (2008) *Curriculum Innovation in Schools.* London: Ofsted.

Pumfrey, P. (1993) Cross-curricular Elements and the National Curriculum, in Verma, G and Pumfrey, P (eds.) *Cross-curricular Contexts: Themes and dimensions in secondary schools.* London: The Falmer Press.

QCDA (2007) *The National Curriculum: Statutory requirements for key stages 3 and 4.* London: QCDA.

QCDA (2008) *Cross-curricular Dimensions: A planning guide for schools.* London: QCDA. Also available at **http://curriculum.qcda.gov.uk/key-stages-3and-4/cross-curriculum-dimensions/index.aspx** [accessed 12/2/10].

QCDA (2009) *A big picture of the curriculum.* **http://www.qcda.gov.uk/5856.aspx** [accessed 3/11/09].

Savage, J (2011) *Cross-curricular Teaching and Learning in the Secondary School.* London: Routledge.

Chapter 9
Moving onwards

CHAPTER OBJECTIVES

By the end of this chapter you should have:
- consolidated your understanding of the key themes considered throughout this book;
- applied the ABC of critical reflective reading to your future work;
- identified some technological solutions to support your further study;
- considered a rationale for teaching that merges theory and practice together in a symbiotic relationship.

Q Standards: Q7, Q8, Q29.

Consolidating the key themes

This book has been built around three key themes. These themes relate, broadly, to the opening stages of your teaching career. In the opening third of the book, we discussed issues relating to your teacher identity, approaches to teaching and learning and the nature of your chosen subject within these, and a number of basic, practical classroom issues that you will be facing as you start teaching. Chapters 4–6 explored areas such as assessment, technology and personalised learning in more detail. These areas, and others like them, help you to develop your teaching in new ways, building on the firm foundations established earlier in the book. Finally, we considered a couple of ways in which you could extend and enrich your teaching practice, namely through developing a more creative approach to your teaching, the learning that pupils will undertake, and through collaborative and cross-curricular ventures of various types.

> **REFLECTIVE EXERCISE**
>
> *Think back through the reading you have undertaken. Review your notes from any of the tasks that you have completed along the way. Which of the writers or ideas really stand out in your mind? Which have made the biggest impact on you and your teaching to this point? What was it about that writer, or that set of ideas, that caused this impact?*

As we discussed in our introduction, the choice of these themes and the various extracts that support them are, to a significant extent, highly personal to us as authors and teachers.

They relate to key ideas, writers and ways of thinking that we have both found helpful in our work. Other authors may have produced a different book. While some of these themes would probably have been similar, others may have been slightly or significantly different. Arguments about what should or should not be included could rage for some time.

But what is more important is that we have established some key principles for incorporating this type of critical and reflective study within a course of initial teacher education. It seems certain that in the years to come there will be many new ways developed through which students will be able to train to become teachers. There are, already, several different routes by which this can occur. Some of you will be studying on large postgraduate courses at a university, with or without a master's-level component; some readers will be working within graduate teacher placements and accessing academic content to support their studies through school mentors or via other school-centred networks; some readers may be studying remotely, through online provision, and seldom meet another student undertaking initial teacher education. Whatever the course, and its structure and systems of support, we believe it is vital that this academic process of reading, thinking and analysing ideas is central to your emerging teaching practice. As we argued in the Introduction, the 'ABC of critical reflective reading' provides a simple model. It has urged you to associate with ideas from the various extracts and apply them to your work. It relies on a broad and balanced range of materials which challenge your thinking, impacting on your own sense of criticality and reflection by taking you outside your comfort zone and requiring you to connect emerging ideas about teaching and learning with your own experiences.

There are probably some obvious holes in this model. But we believe it provides a simple starting framework for your work so far. We trust that you have found it a helpful mechanism that has underpinned your studies and resulted in positive improvements to your teaching.

Extending the ABC of critical reflective reading

> ### REFLECTIVE EXERCISE
>
> *Before you read ahead, think back over your course of initial teacher education. What big ideas or concepts have you studied or heard about that you have not read about here? Make a short list. You will need it for the next reflective exercise.*

As we have discussed, any book of this type has to be selective in terms of its content. In our Introduction, and above, we have given a justification of sorts for the themes and extracts we have chosen. Although other writers may have done it differently, what cannot be argued is that there is an extremely wide range of topics, issues and ideas that teachers face in their day-to-day experiences. Undoubtedly you will have identified some of these by completing the reflective exercise above. For those of you who need a few hints, we have identified a range of topics that might have been covered in your course of initial teacher education but that we have not been able to cover in much detail within this publication. These are presented in no particular order of importance.

- Identification of, and provision for, gifted and talented pupils.

- Models of curriculum development.

- Educational evaluation (as distinct from educational assessment).

- Performative approaches to teaching.

- Social class and its impact on learning.

- Equal opportunities.

- Health and well-being.

- The 'enterprise' agenda.

- Thinking skills.

- Functional skills across the curriculum.

- Alternative qualifications and their impact on the way that knowledge is structured within the wider curriculum.

We could go on, but we are sure you are getting the picture by now. At certain points in your teaching career, you may be required to consider any of the above issues. We will imagine a couple of scenarios to help ground this idea in your thinking.

Scenario 1

As an NQT, you have been appointed to a new post in a small high school. The previous head of department left the school in less than ideal circumstances. You are given the responsibility of writing the new Key Stage 3 schemes of work for the department. Your only previous experience of planning was for a six-week scheme of work for Year 8 at your second teaching practice school. You will need to learn how to create a long-term plan across the key stage. You have heard about how it might be done but have no practical experience. You need some help with models of curriculum development. What do you do? Where do you turn?

Scenario 2

Your head of department approaches you in the corridor. She has just come from a meeting with the head teacher. The school is considering making an application for an 'enterprise' specialism. The head teacher wants each department to feed back a list of possible approaches to embed enterprise within each curriculum area. You are given the job of scoping this out within your subject. Again, what do you do? Where do you turn?

Both these scenarios help us get a grip on a whole range of practical applications for 'knowledge' that teachers will face in their professional lives. While most of this book has focused at the level of your individual pedagogy (and this is where your primary concern will have been in your initial teacher education course), the scenarios presented above both come from recent examples that newly qualified teachers have faced. They take the need for new knowledge outside your own pedagogy and begin to impact on the work of an individual department (Scenario 1) and the wider school (Scenario 2).

As with any aspect of improvement that you want to make to your own pedagogy, these scenarios demand that you have a strategy for obtaining and analysing information quickly. But, as we are sure you have begun to appreciate by now, one thing that most teachers do not have much of is time. However, as we have seen throughout the book, and argued for in both in the Introduction and the opening of this chapter, it is essential that we use the literature (by which we mean research findings, policy documents, books, blogs and other sources of information) to inform and challenge our thinking. This allows us to become critical and reflective. It empowers us to move beyond the confines of our own thinking, prejudice and limitations and move our teaching practice into new, fertile directions.

So, what are the practical approaches or methods that we can adopt to help this process of information-gathering and analysis? To answer this, we would like to draw on a number of technological 'tips and tricks' to help. Over time these will change (as with any technology). However, the broad principles behind them will remain.

1. Use existing collections of knowledge to minimise the time spent searching for new knowledge

The internet contains a number of fantastic resources that will help you access the knowledge that you need to find quickly and easily. One of these, the Teacher Training and Resource Bank (TTRB: **www.ttrb.ac.uk**), is world-leading and should be your first port of call. The TTRB is a large collection of educational resources for all those working in education, including teacher trainers, teachers, mentors and students. The diverse range of resources is organised in helpful ways to assist searching in relation to general and specific themes. The TTRB also allows a greater degree of personalisation of its content through features such as 'My TTRB' and the provision of RSS feeds (see below). A particular strength of the TTRB is the way that it encourages users to look across and between subject boundaries to the common elements of teaching and learning that affect us all.

The TTRB aims to:

- make the teacher education professional knowledge base more easily accessible;
- reference effective practices in all subject areas and across phases;
- increase the quality and range of resources available;
- raise the status of educational research and knowledge;
- promote and effect change by supporting tested knowledge transfer and adoption strategies;
- provide a personalised support service for teacher educators and those training to teach.

In line with our criteria for broad and balanced sources of literature, the TTRB contains numerous types of resources, including:

- conference papers;
- LA reports;
- government reports;
- a range of journal articles;
- book reviews;
- research reports;
- statistical data;
- examples of students' and trainees' work;
- links to video resources from teachers' TV;
- links to other web resources.

But the TTRB is much more than a collection of links (otherwise it might as well just be a search engine). Rather, each resource is accompanied by a review, written by an experienced team of reviewers from the teaching community. The reviews are structured under a series of useful headings including:

- what the resource is;
- the aims of the resource;
- key findings or focus;
- the quality, authority and credibility of the resource;
- the implications for teachers or students.

These reports range in length, but they all provide useful insights that should allow a user of the TTRB to make a judgement about a particular resource's usefulness and importance. In other words, part of the 'associating' process within our ABC for critical reflective reading has been done for you. The reviews also contain links to related articles or resources and further links where the user can find out more if needed. There is, of course, also a link to the actual resource reviewed. All the resources reviewed on the TTRB are available online and for no fee. This has had an implication on what is included on the TTRB; for example, articles published in subscription journals appear only if they have been released by the publisher for open access via the TTRB. Again, this is vitally important for busy teachers who seldom have access to university libraries or individual subscriptions to educational journals. It avoids that frustrating moment when you have found an interesting article but realise that you will need to pay for it in order to get beyond the abstract.

Searching for resources within the TTRB is similar to any search engine. Each resource is 'tagged' with a number of headings. This allows a user on the TTRB site to search through the resources quickly and easily. There is one additional function that is worthy of note. Users can append search terms from the British Education Index Thesaurus. This provides a useful way of clarifying a search term if one is struggling to identify the precise focus for a particular search. Resources can also be searched by 'type', 'author' and alphabetically.

A second organisational feature of the TTRB is based on the Professional Standards for Teachers. Users can search resources that relate to any of the individual or groups of standards (professional attributes, professional knowledge and understanding, professional skills). This will be particularly helpful for you when you are seeking to develop your work in response to a process of performance management or appraisal.

Again, in line with the third dimension of our ABC for critical reflective reading, the resources contained within the TTRB will help challenge your thinking. They will also help you to connect with new ideas and apply them to your work. Apart from the resources and reviews themselves, one of the most helpful functions is a glossary that provides definitions of commonly-used terms in education. Do you need to know about analytic phonics, details of the national statistics socioeconomic classification methodologies, what an 'unaccompanied child' is, or how you could adopt a psychodynamic approach to understanding a particular feeling or experience? All these, and many other items, are exemplified, discussed and clarified there.

There are also regularly updated news and events sections that contain details about recent policy announcements, education-related stories from the media, conferences, etc. Both these pages can be subscribed to via RSS feeds (along with RSS feeds on features, latest resources and articles with podcasts). Not sure what an RSS feed is? Don't worry! There is a page about that too.

REFLECTIVE EXERCISE

Using the list that you identified in the second reflective exercise of this chapter, or the range of ideas suggested by us, choose one area to focus on. Visit the TTRB site at www. ttrb.ac.uk and conduct some quick searches. Use the glossary or the British Education Index Thesaurus to refine your research terms if needed. Scan the reviews of the resources that you find. Try to make some quick decisions about which, if any, of the referenced resources will be worth accessing and reading in more detail. Try to get your choice of resources down to three or four in total. The key thing in this task is speed. While it might be pleasant to take a leisurely stroll through 20–30 resources, as a full-time teacher you will often not have time for this. Be decisive and use the tools within the TTRB to gain access to key ideas quickly.

---

2. Make the new knowledge come to you

One of the great Web 2.0 innovations has been to empower individual internet users with a range of tools to collect, create and publish content. The benefits of these tools can be seen all over the internet. The use of social networking sites, blogs and Twitter all help users to present themselves and their ideas to the whole world. But finding your way through all this content can be difficult. With so much to choose from, where do you start?

Making use of existing collections of knowledge is helpful. We have discussed, at length, how one set of resources provides a vital starting point for the busy teacher. But there are technological solutions that teachers can utilise to help make the content come to them. One of the simplest and most commonly used devices is the RSS feed. RSS stands for Really

Simple Syndication or Rich Site Summary (depending on who you believe invented the term). Either way, it provides a way for new content from multiple websites to be delivered to your internet browser window quickly without you having to visit numerous sites. There are numerous online guides which help you set up RSS feeds so we will not be going into a lot of technical detail here. However, the principle of using a RSS reader (like Google Reader) and subscribing to feeds from your favourite websites (including the TTRB, the *Guardian* and BBC education sites and the majority of other educational internet portals) will allow you to revolutionise the way that you work. New content will come to you rather than you having to go out and look for it. Once the subscribed content has been delivered, you can perform keyword searches or more complex searches in the standard ways.

3. Return the favour: why not share your content with the world?

While it is easy to benefit from the numerous technological innovations that allow us to retrieve and analyse information quickly and easily, how many of us spend time putting our own thoughts, ideas and materials back into cyberspace? Within the world of teaching, it is apparent that teachers all over the United Kingdom are reinventing the education wheels within their own schools due to a lack of concern or priority given to sharing their work with the wider world. When we talk to teachers, there is one response to this observation – 'We are just too busy doing what we do'. This vicious circle needs to be broken. Introspection of the type we have warned against in this book is a very real possibility for teachers who do not make a conscious effort to lift their heads above the 'busyness' parapet and engage with ideas (whether those ideas come from academic sources or from other teachers).

As an aside, we are often amused by comments from teachers who attend training events being run by universities or other bodies. While most of them enjoy the training sessions, they often comment that the lunch or the break was the most beneficial part of the day. Why? Because it allowed them time to talk with other teachers.

So, at the beginning of your teaching career why not make the conscious decision to connect with other teachers using some of the technologies available today. For some, the creation of a blog where you can discuss ideas and share your teaching materials may be a way forward. You can see one example of this approach by one of the authors of this book at **www.jsavage.org.uk**. For others, social networking sites may be a way forward. Many of you use these tools within your personal lives; why not create a new and separate portal for your professional life? More recently, innovations such as Twitter allow us to share ideas quickly and, helpfully, in less than 140 characters. (For some of us, this is quite a challenge.) For a busy teacher, scanning a page of tweets from carefully selected sources is easy. You can find lists of educators doing this already at **http://listorious.com/**. But put something back. Why not become a proactive twitterer of interesting educational content and ideas and get others to follow you?

Finally, there is a range of time-saving technological devices out there to help you link together your digital content in a helpful way. Many of these centre on a good RSS reader such as Google Reader. Having set that up, you can facilitate a stream of content to other places (e.g. your blog or Twitter) using devices such as Twitterfeed. URLs for these devices can be found at the end of the chapter.

4. A word of warning: look for depersonalised content too

Developing approaches to the collection and analysis of personalised content like this is all well and good. But sometimes it is helpful to take a wider view and consider information from sources outside your RSS feeds. By doing this regularly, you can look outside the box of one's own interest (and prejudices?) and begin to find things of interest. As an example, let's return to what is probably the largest collection of educational resources, the TTRB. While you can search through resources on the TTRB under subject headings, we would encourage any user of the TTRB to take a more generic view as often as possible. Thinking outside the box of your own subject can be unsettling and challenging. It will force you to make new connections and view things differently. But we have found that the most useful and interesting work can be done when specific subject-related issues begin to collide with more general educational issues. The TTRB is great at encouraging this kind of inter-subject educational discourse. Towards this end, do not discount the 'happy accidents' that can occur through the general sifting through of resources outside the field of your own particular subject.

Taking care of your career

In this final section of our book, we want to spend some time considering your future teaching career. While your initial teacher education course will have been, in various combinations, challenging, frustrating, rewarding and tiring, there are some key differences to working as a teacher within a school full-time.

Firstly, the pupils will view you differently. You will be a formal part of the establishment and this normally aids the development of respect for your position from the majority of pupils. Secondly, the pupils know that you are going to be there for the long haul. This aids the development of individual relationships with pupils. Teaching in this context will feel quite different. But, thirdly, you will be teaching a lot more. Moving up from a 50–60 per cent timetable to an 85–90 per cent timetable is a considerable shift. Suddenly, that free time you had to spend planning and evaluating your work disappears. You have to work quickly and make decisions about your teaching with confidence and decisiveness. Finally, you will work with a significant degree of autonomy. While you will have a mentor within the school to guide you through the induction process, for large portions of time you will be left to get on with the job of teaching. Most young teachers find this an exhilarating time. In your training you will have got used to frequent visits to your classroom from various mentors and tutors, all with an interest in your work. The freedom of teaching 'for real' is wonderful. But with this autonomy comes a great responsibility. The requirement for you to become self-critical and reflective is suddenly more urgent. After all, if a tutor or mentor is not going to point out areas for your development as a teacher, who will? Performance management and appraisal systems can help here. But the week-to-week monitoring of your teaching and the diagnosing of areas for your own pedagogical development will largely be down to you.

This makes the key message of this book particularly important. The habits of critical reflective practice that you have established during your training will be essential as you face the challenges associated with your new role. Therefore, it will come as no surprise that the Core Standards for Newly Qualified Teachers (TDA, 2010a) contain the following advice:

C7: Evaluate their performance and be committed to improving their practice through appropriate professional development.

C8: Have a creative and constructively critical approach towards innovation; being prepared to adapt their practice where benefits and improvements are identified.

In the guidance material that accompanies these standards, there are some clues as to what this might mean. Primarily, these standards are about how you will be required to review the effectiveness of your teaching and the impact that this will have on learners. This can be done in a number of ways.

- *Using your induction entitlement to a 10 per cent reduced teaching time-table to engage in professional development opportunities and activities.*

- *Taking opportunities to engage with coaching and mentoring, reflecting with others about your own progress against your identified development needs and the needs of learners.*

- *Seeking evidence about improvements to learning, teaching and children and young people's development and well-being from a variety of sources such as recent and relevant research and the practice of other colleagues, in school and beyond.*

- *Applying constructive criticism to new ideas, research and approaches and contributing to change and innovation by taking informed risks to promote and adopt them.*

- *Discussing with learners themselves, parents, carers and colleagues issues concerning their well-being, progress and attainment.*

- *Using assessment to monitor learners' work and progress and taking appropriate steps to refine your teaching approach and/or modify planning as required.*

(TDA, 2010b)

Several of the key words within this advice resound with the messages of this book. It mentions 'reflecting' on your own progress, 'seeking evidence' from a 'variety of sources', applying 'constructive criticism' and taking 'informed risks' (i.e. not uninformed ones). All of these points, and many others that we have made throughout this book, depend on you developing and sustaining an approach to critical reflective practice, of which reading will be a central component. Our hope is that we have shown you the way. Try not to leave the teaching profession in the way you found it. Make a positive change for the better. It will make teaching a more enjoyable career. But, more importantly, you will make a positive impact on the lives of those you teach. There can be no stronger or better motive.

POINTS TO CONSIDER

- *What practical steps can you take to ensure that you remain critical and reflective of your own teaching during your NQT year and beyond?*

- *What opportunities can you develop to apply the ABC of critical reflective reading to your work over the next year?*

- *How can you utilise the opportunities for masters-level study (perhaps the MTL) within your new teaching role?*

C H A P T E R   S U M M A R Y

This final chapter is slightly different from those that have preceded it. It aims to do a number of things. Firstly, it consolidates the range of themes considered during this book. Secondly, it considers a number of issues that you will face in the next stage of your teaching career. It urges you to adopt an informed critical and reflective stance towards your own teaching; informed, that is, by a broader range of reading, thinking and analysis. It considers a number of technological solutions to help you adopt and maintain this stance throughout your career. Finally, it revisits some of the standard educational theories regarding the interrelationship of theory and practice, arguing that balancing these two components is an essential part of becoming an effective teacher.

TDA (2010a) *Core Standards for Newly Qualified Teachers.* **www.tda.gov.uk/teachers/ professionalstandards/standards/attributes/ppd/core.aspx** [accessed 15/3/10].

TDA (2010b) *Core Standards: Newly qualified teacher guidance.* **www.tda.gov.uk/teachers/ professionalstandards/standards/guidance/theme5.aspx** [accessed 15/3/10].

Blogging software: There is loads of software out there. Why not try Wordpress? Free wordpress blogs can be created at **www.wordpress.com**.

Google Books: **www.google.com/books**

Google Reader: **www.google.com/reader**

Google Scholar: **www.google.com/scholar**

Listorious: **http://listorious.com/** (lists of people using Twitter for various purposes. Search for 'education' and you will find many teachers sharing their work in this way.)

Twitter: **www.twitter.com**

Twitterfeed: **www.twitterfeed.com**

Index